STUDY GUIDE
TO ACCOMPANY

BASIC
ECONOMICS
DOLAN/VOGT

Second Canadian Edition

STUDY GUIDE TO ACCOMPANY

BASIC ECONOMICS

DOLAN/VOGT

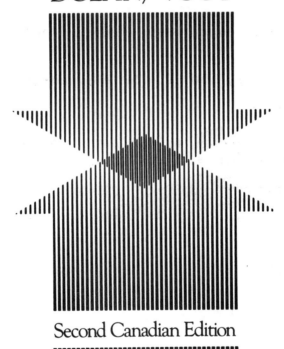

Second Canadian Edition

BEVERLY J. CAMERON   EDWIN G. DOLAN

HOLT, RINEHART AND WINSTON OF CANADA, LIMITED

Canadian Cataloguing in Publication Data

Dolan, Edwin G.
  Study guide to accompany Basic economics, 2nd
Canadian edition

Supplement to: Dolan, Edwin G. Basic economics. 2nd
Canadian ed.
ISBN 0-03-921674-8

1. Economics. I. Cameron, Beverly J. II. Dolan,
Edwin G. Basic economics. III. Title.

HB171.5.D582 1983   330   C83-098445-3

Acquisitions Editor: Michael Roche
Developmental Editor: Vivien Young
Managing Editor: Dennis Bockus
Copy Editor: Ruth Peckover
Production Manager: Anna Kress

Printed in the United States of America

3 4 5 88 87

ACKNOWLEDGMENTS

The author is grateful to the following people who have made valuable suggestions for the second edition of this study guide:

    J.E. Peters (Cariboo College)

    Barry Sharpe (Niagara College)

    Baker Siddiquee (University of Manitoba)

    I would also like to thank the Canadian Association of Business Economists for the use of their 1981 Salary Survey data and all the newspapers, wire services, agencies, and authors who kindly let me use their articles in the application sections of this study guide.

    In addition, I would like to thank Norman E. Cameron, St. John's College, University of Manitoba, for numerous comments and suggestions that he made during the preparation of this manuscript. Any errors or omissions, however, remain my responsibility.

    Last, but not least, I would like to thank Michael Roche, my editor; Vivien Young, my developmental editor; Ruth Peckover, my copy editor; and all the others at Holt, Rinehart and Winston of Canada, Ltd., who worked on this study guide.

Beverly J. Cameron
Winnipeg, Manitoba
September 1983

Contents

Careers in Economics / 1
How to Use This Study Guide / 14

Chapter 1	What Economics Is All About: The Canadian Setting
Chapter 2	The Basis of Trade, the Price System, and the Market Economy
Chapter 3	Supply and Demand - The Basics
Chapter 4	The Role of Business and Government in the Canadian Economy
Chapter 5	The Circular Flow of Income and Product
Chapter 6	National Income and National Product
Chapter 7	The Goals of Stabilization Policy and the Performance of the Canadian Economy
Chapter 8	The Determinants of Planned Expenditure
Chapter 9	The Multiplier Theory of National Income Determination
Chapter 10	Fiscal Policy and the Multiplier Theory
Chapter 11	Chartered Banks and Other Financial Intermediaries
Chapter 12	The Supply of Money
Chapter 13	The Demand for Money and the Money Market
Chapter 14	The Interaction of Money and the Multiplier
Chapter 15	International Trade and the Balance of Payments
Chapter 16	The Interaction of the Foreign Sector and the Multiplier
Chapter 17	Unemployment and Inflation: The Modern Dilemma
Chapter 18	The Dynamics of Inflation and Unemployment
Chapter 19	Combating Inflation and Unemployment
Chapter 20	Supply and Demand: Building on the Basics
Chapter 21	The Logic of Consumer Choice
Chapter 22	The Theory of Cost
Chapter 23	Supply Under Perfect Competition
Chapter 24	The Theory of Monopoly
Chapter 25	Oligopoly: Competition Among the Few
Chapter 26	Advertising and Monopolistic Competition
Chapter 27	Market Failure and Government Regulation
Chapter 28	The Economics of Energy
Chapter 29	Foreign Ownership and Control of Canadian Business
Chapter 30	Factor Markets and Marginal Productivity Theory
Chapter 31	Labor Unions and Collective Bargaining
Chapter 32	The Problem of Poverty
Chapter 33	The Economics of Population and Development
Chapter 34	Capitalism Versus Socialism

Chapters 1-19 are included in Basic Macroeconomics.
Chapters 1, 2, 3 (revised to include part of Chapter 20), 4, and
21-34 are included in Basic Microeconomics.

CAREERS
IN ECONOMICS

Keith D. Evans
California State University, Northridge

and

Beverly J. Cameron
University of Manitoba

THE GENERAL VALUE OF
AN ECONOMICS DEGREE

In describing the qualities essential to a good economist, John Maynard Keynes, himself a leading member of the profession, remarked:

> He must study the present in the light
> of the past for the purpose of the
> future. No part of man's nature or his
> institutions must lie entirely outside
> his regard.[1]

As you begin the study of economics, you will quickly become aware of the breadth to which Keynes refers. There seem to be no limits to the reaches of economic inquiry; it encompasses both the far-reaching and the everyday. Your first exam may well include a question relevant to today's newspaper headlines. At the same time, economics is very much a part of everyday life. Indeed, a discussion with a local merchant concerning the price of an item for sale may lead you to the conclusion that many people think an understanding of economics comes intuitively; however, it is not a subject to be left to common sense alone.

The trained economist is a valuable and respected member of many organizations - be they private businesses, public utilities, governments, or universities - and the career opportunities for an economist are limited only by the resourcefulness of employers and employees. The following sections will show you how an economics major can prepare you for a wide variety of careers as an economist, or how training in economics can help prepare you for a professional career in a related field such as law. Even if your career interests lie in other directions, the analytical training that is emphasized in economics courses can generally make you more adaptable to changing employment opportunities after graduation.

Further, there are definite benefits to you in having a better understanding of how our private enterprise economy works and in

---

[1]John Maynard Keynes, Essays in Biography, ed. Geoffrey Keynes (New York: W. W. Norton & Company, 1963).

having a basis for comparing it with centrally planned economies. Often, people have indicated that in their first career jobs they felt lost in a maze - they had no perspective on what relationship their jobs had with the larger goals of the firms that employed them. A background in economics can ease that shock. The analytical training, with specific applications to real-life situations, makes it easier to come to grips with events in the world around us.

One respondent to the Dryden questionnaire, which was sent to currently employed United States economists, put it this way: "My work in economics prepared me well for career advancement and flexibility because of the emphasis my economics study placed on cause and effect relationships, on the link between incentives and resultant actions, all of which have helped me develop a rational and productive way of generating results-oriented thinking." Another replied that the most useful part of his training in economics was the "flexibility, perspective, and ability to deal with intangibles and uncertainty." Still another successful career economist reflected on the importance of an economics degree this way: "It taught me the ability to think and to reason."

You cannot possibly learn all you will need to know in three or four years of university, but in pursuing a degree in economics you can learn how to think well. With that ability your opportunities will be immensely varied and exciting.

WHAT KINDS OF CAREER OPPORTUNITIES ARE AVAILABLE TO AN ECONOMICS MAJOR?

What type of work might you actually do as an economist? In general, and depending upon the amount of education you ultimately receive, your future lies in three areas: working in one of a wide variety of positions in private business; serving in a local, provincial, or federal government agency; or teaching economics at the college and university level. In fact, many economists combine their primary work in one of these fields with part-time work in another. It is not at all unusual for a business economist to teach part-time or for a professor to be a consultant to business or government.

Economics as an academic subject goes back more than a century and a half. In practical terms, economists found their theories influencing federal government decisions more and more as the Depression of the 1930s occupied world-wide attention. It was not until after World War II, however, that private businesses began to realize the extent to which economic theory might be applied to solving business problems and to formulating business policies. Economists are employed by manufacturing firms, transportation companies, utilities, banks, institutions with financial interests, communications organizations, insurance firms, investment brokerages, retailing companies, and more.

Large business organizations employ economists directly. Smaller firms hire the services of economic consultants as needed. Regardless of their size, businesses are aware that government policies and subsequent actions will have an economic effect. One function of the business economist is to analyze and interpret government policies in the light of their effect on the economy in general and the specific firm in particular.

In its booklet Business Economics Careers, the National Association of Business Economists, an American organization, (A similar Canadian organization, the Canadian Association of Business Economists, is based in Toronto.), states that "the business economist's primary function is to apply economics to business problems." To do this requires the ability to understand the economic implications of events taking place in the world, to project how those events might affect the functioning of the business in question, to prepare guidelines for the decision makers in the organization, and to be able to communicate concepts, principles, and conclusions clearly, effectively, and concisely. Possessing these qualities prepares a business economist for work in many fields.

The NABE stresses that business economists follow no set patterns. The most successful, established economists have high job mobility because their ability to interpret the economic effects of national and international events on a particular sector of business makes them especially adaptable to changing business requirements. For example, while a bank economist might specialize in short-term and long-term forecasts of the markets for money and credit, and an industrial economist might devote more attention to economic methods of forecasting company sales, each is essentially using economic knowledge to predict how events occurring outside of the organization will affect the organization itself and how best to plan for the future of the business. A consulting economist, while often providing general economic forecasts to a number of companies, finds the greatest success in becoming a specialist in some field. His or her particular expertise is then recognized and sought out.

The main function of an investment economist might be to help relate the economic outlook to investment analysis and portfolio decisions, while an insurance company economist might provide special guidance related to investing the company's funds and marketing its insurance policies. Again, each economist uses the knowledge he or she has acquired to forecast how external events will act upon the particular business involved and how economic and business principles apply to the internal operation of the firm.

A trade association economist might provide analysis of current national economic problems affecting business; prepare testimony and testify before parliamentary committees; write articles for trade and professional journals; forecast economic trends; serve as a spokesperson for industry and business in public speeches, or as an advisor to government and industry groups; and do consulting within the trade association.

A government economist may perform essentially the same tasks as the economist who works in business, as far as forecasting the outcome of economic conditions is concerned. The emphasis, however, may well be on formulating policy rather than reacting to policy changes, since the governmental agency can be in a position to initiate economic changes. The government economist may be called upon to do research on major policy issues, and to draft speeches for government officials.

An _academic economist_ concentrates upon the understanding and improvement of economic theory. In teaching theory, the academic economist stresses how economies function and how a knowledge of economics applies to business and government decision making and to decisions people have to make as individuals. In addition, such a person may devote some time to research, writing, and consulting with business firms, government agencies, or private individuals.

The Dryden questionnaire asked members of the National Association of Business Economists and the Society of Government Economists in the United States to reflect on the value of their college educations and on what advice they might have for people just beginning the study of economics. Of those whose major was economics, more than two-thirds of each group reported that their college studies had been very useful to them in their first full-time job; and from the vantage point of their ultimate careers, more than half still felt their college educations were useful in carrying out the duties of their present occupations. What courses did they feel were of such lasting value? Both business and government economists most frequently mentioned courses in microeconomic and macroeconomic theory, econometrics (the application of statistical techniques to obtain quantitative estimates of relationships suggested by economic analysis), money and banking, forecasting, international economics, and those courses which provided specific applications of economic theory to the decision-making process or which had applications to public policy.

Respondents also emphasized the importance of courses involving the economic and business applications of statistics and accounting, as well as the study of related business institutions, especially financial ones. Important, too, were courses on how to use computers and how to program them. Mathematics courses were emphasized as having been helpful. Along with the reference to applied statistics, there was frequent mention of such courses as analytical geometry, calculus, and linear algebra.

One necessary skill for an economist, whether academic, business, or government, that cannot be overemphasized, is the ability to make the results of his or her work understandable to a wide range of people. To be useful, economic analyses and forecasts must be understood by those who make the decisions for a business or government agency. An economist must, therefore, be able to write and speak clearly and be able to present sophisticated economic ideas in a way that can be understood, even by people with less economic knowledge. Recognizing this necessity to make their work clear and usable to other people, both the government and business economists placed high value on courses that improved their written and oral communication skills.

The NABE advises potential business economists to strive to be generalists rather than specialists, and to have some familiarity with as many of the major fields of economics and business administration as possible. In addition to those areas mentioned by the respondents to the Dryden questionnaire, economics and business administration courses also examine economic and business history, national income and public finance, business cycles and government stabilization policies, corporate finance and industrial organization, marketing and consumer behavior, labor and collective bargaining, purchasing and personnel policies, and economic development and comparative economic systems.

Some of those who answered the Dryden questionnaire had not majored in economics at the undergraduate level. Many of them said they had benefited from the broad-based arts education they acquired before pursuing economics and business study while earning advanced degrees.

It should, perhaps, be added that the course of study guidelines presented here must be taken in the spirit in which they have been given - as suggestions from practicing professional economists. When you are planning your particular course of study to fulfill the requirements of your college or university and to satisfy your interests, these guidelines cannot, and should not be expected to, replace the need for personal faculty advisement.

How important is an advanced degree? For an academic economist it is a necessity. The master's degree is the minimum qualification for teaching at the community college level, and the Ph.D. is required for most university teaching.

According to the Dryden questionnaire, 80 percent of the government economists who responded indicated that they considered an advanced degree very important, and 11 percent considered one moderately important. Of that number, 56 percent specified a Ph.D. as the required degree, while an additional 25 percent specified a master's degree.

Business economists surveyed by the Dryden questionnaire placed less importance on an advanced degree. Only 57 percent rated it as very important, and 25 percent as moderately important. Those responses were much more evenly distributed regarding which advanced degree is of the most importance. Almost 30 percent favored the M.B.A. (Master of Business Administration), while another group of equal size suggested pursuing either an M.A. or an M.S. degree in economics or business administration. Only 35 percent considered a doctorate essential. Again, these opinions are presented here as guidelines that can be one source of help to you as you make your own career decisions.

The Dryden questionnaire was not circulated in Canada, but since the job market for economists is similar in the United States and Canada, the results of this survey are valuable to Canadian economics students.

WHERE ARE ECONOMISTS WORKING AND
WHAT ARE THEIR AVERAGE SALARIES?

A good source of information regarding the current employment of economists is the latest survey conducted by the Canadian Association of Business Economists. C.A.B.E. mailed questionnaires to its members in 1981 and received almost 300 responses.

Since the sample size is small, some of the results are insignificant in a statistical sense. Further, C.A.B.E. is a relatively small association whose members are not evenly spread across the nation or throughout the profession. Even so, the survey results provide a useful guide to the type of jobs Canadian economists perform and the salaries they receive.

General Results

More than sixty percent of the economists who responded earned between $25,000 and $50,000, with women generally earning less than men. A large number of the women were grouped in the middle salary ranges, as Table 1 shows.

Table 1
Distribution of Base Salary
1981

Base Salary	Total		Men		Women	
	Number	Percent of Total	Number	Percent of Total	Number	Percent of Total
Under $15,000	2	0.7	2	0.8	0	0
$15,000-19,999	4	1.4	2	0.8	2	4.8
$20,000-24,999	25	8.7	18	7.7	7	16.7
$25,000-29,999	35	12.2	25	10.2	10	23.8
$30,000-34,999	42	14.7	34	13.9	8	19.0
$35,000-39,999	36	12.6	32	13.2	4	9.5
$40,000-49,999	64	22.4	56	23.0	8	19.1
$50,000 and over	78	27.3	75	30.7	3	7.1
Total	286	100.0	244	100.0	42	100.0
Mean	$41,993		$43,255		$33,309	

"Salary Survey: 1981 Canadian Association of Business Economists," tables reprinted by permission of Duncan Smeaton.

WHAT IS THE EMPLOYMENT OUTLOOK
FOR ECONOMISTS IN THE 1980s?

Before launching into some "fearless forecasts" about the employment outlook for economists in the 1980s, it might be well to include a bit of caveat emptor. Let the buyer, whether of tangible goods or intangible ideas, beware. Any predictions made today about future employment prospects assume continued economic and political stability in North America. All forecasts about the future are fallible, but general predictions for economists can be made.

As the Canadian Association of Business Economists Survey shows, Canadian economists work in a large variety of jobs and industries.

Job prospects for different types of economists may not be the same. In particular the outlook for those who seek careers as academic economists is not as bright as it was in the 1960s and early 1970s. Most colleges and universities face declining enrollments and tight budgets, which means that few new positions will be created. An article by Charles E. Scott in the May 1979 American Economic Review concludes that academic employment for economists will be lower than during the boom period of the 1960s.[2]

Because of the relative difficulty of obtaining satisfactory employment in an academic setting, many people who might otherwise have directed themselves toward a career in higher education are now accepting nonacademic jobs. Many of the economists who had prepared themselves for academic jobs but who could not find openings hold Ph.D. degrees. With many of these Ph.D.s accepting nonacademic jobs, graduates with bachelor's degrees may find it difficult to compete for some jobs.

The federal and provincial governments also provide a number of employment opportunities for economists. If the size of governments continues to increase, and assuming that hiring freezes are not frequent or long, economists should continue to find government positions.

The largest employer of economists will probably continue to be private industry and research organizations. Jobs are available in consulting firms, banks, securities and investment companies, labor unions, manufacturing firms, and a host of other industries. With normal rates of economic growth, job opportunities in these areas should grow steadily throughout the 1980s.

Several sources listing present employment opportunities are available for students. The Financial Post and the Financial Times both carry sections listing employment opportunities. By reading the advertisements in these sections, students will have a good idea of which firms are hiring economists, what the educational requirements are, and an idea of salary ranges. Similar employment sections for professionals appear in most big city newspapers daily or weekly.

The American Economics Association publishes a listing of jobs in J.O.E. (Job Opportunities for Economists). J.O.E. contains listings for academic job openings but there is always a section on nonacademic jobs. University Affairs and the C.A.U.T. Bulletin (Canadian Association of University Teachers) also publish listings for academic job openings in Canada.

Canada Manpower offices can provide students with listings of jobs available for economists in various areas of the country, requiring a variety of educational backgrounds and paying a wide range of salaries. Many universities and colleges work closely with Manpower offices in an attempt to help their graduates find employment.

The job outlook for economists in the 1980s is generally seen as good, particularly for those who have earned a master's degree. Jobs will probably continue to be available at all educational levels, but many job market counselors feel that a person with a master's

---

[2]Charles E. Scott, "The Market for Ph.D. Economists: The Academic Sector," American Economic Review 69, May 1979, p. 141.

degree in economics has little difficulty finding a job.

Areas of Primary Employment

As Table 2 shows, respondents working in consulting reported the highest salaries. Not surprisingly, they also had a high standard deviation. Many economists working in this area have salaries that are based on the general state of the economy, so wide salary variations can easily result.

Description of Responsibilities

Almost 39 percent of those who responded said their major responsibilities involved economic analysis: predicting economic decisions or conditions and explaining how these decisions or conditions would be affected by other forces within the economy (see Table 3).

Education, Work Experience, and Age

Ph.D. economists had the highest salaries, and salaries increased, as expected, with years of work experience. The largest number of respondents held master's degrees, but work experience is an important determinant of salary for economists at all levels of education. Age, which is often related to experience, also influenced salary. (See Tables 4, 5, and 6.)

Table 2
Earnings by Sector of Primary Employment

Sector (ranked from numbers 1 to 18)	Responses No.	%	Mean Earnings	Standard Deviation
1 Consulting	41	13.7	46,442	17,877
2 Securities & investments	23	7.7	46,214	21,058
3 Education	12	4.0	46,136	20,955
4 Govt. - Federal	23	7.7	45,754	9,727
5 Energy	61	20.3	42,843	16,706
6 Durable manufacturing	9	3.0	42,811	13,421
7 Non-durable manufacturing	3	1.0	42,000	12,754
8 Trade association	8	2.7	41,850	9,448
9 Non-profit research	10	3.3	41,749	14,336
10 Mining, Forestry	14	4.7	41,550	13,650
11 Communication, Utilities	21	7.0	41,278	11,032
12 Banking	34	11.3	38,193	16,265
13 Transportation	7	2.3	36,343	13,921
14 Other	5	1.7	35,955	16,344
15 Govt. - Provincial	12	4.0	35,383	12,762
16 Agriculture, Fishing	5	1.7	35,127	6,120

Table 2 Continued
Earnings by Sector of Primary Employment

Sector (ranked from numbers 1 to 18)	Responses No.	%	Mean Earnings	Standard Deviation
17 Construction	2	0.7	32,000	7,000
18 Insurance	8	2.7	31,625	10,197

Source: C.A.B.E. Salary Survey, 1981.

Table 3
Earnings by Principal Area of Responsibility

Area	Responses No.	%	Mean Earnings	Standard Deviation
Other	10	3.5	50,910	15,098
Administration	29	10.1	49,765	14,559
Consulting	40	13.9	45,250	17,107
Corporate planning	37	12.8	44,452	15,511
Teaching	7	2.4	43,662	21,285
Financial analysis	26	9.0	41,231	18,714
Market research	14	4.9	39,951	10,682
Economic analysis	112	38.9	38,504	14,317
Econometrics	5	1.7	35,033	10,963
Statistics	8	2.8	31,700	12,523

Source: C.A.B.E. Salary Survey, 1981.

Table 4
Earnings by Education

Education	Responses No.	%	Mean Earnings	Standard Deviation
Ph.D.	36	12.0	55,517	17,407
All doctoral requirements except dissertation	19	6.3	47,572	15,979
Other	3	1.0	42,500	9,721
Master's	156	52.0	40,430	13,297
B.A., Honours or General	86	28.7	37,906	16,798
No degree	0	0.0	0	0

Source: C.A.B.E. Salary Survey, 1981.

Table 5
Earnings by Experience

Years	Responses No.	%	Mean Earnings	Standard Deviation
0-2	43	14.2	27,037	9,231
3-6	77	25.5	35,952	11,359
7-10	78	25.8	41,039	12,202
11-14	45	14.9	46,725	9,789
15-19	22	7.3	57,291	19,767
20 and over	34	11.3	59,369	16,601

Source: C.A.B.E. Salary Survey, 1981.

Table 6
Earnings by Age

Age	Responses No.	%	Mean Earnings	Standard Deviation
24 + under	10	3.4	23,135	2,955
25 - 34	144	48.5	34,553	10,179
35 - 44	96	31.3	48,558	14,698
45 - 54	26	8.9	52,496	18,037
55 + over	23	7.9	59,124	17,281

Source: C.A.B.E. Salary Survey, 1981.

Table 7
Earnings by City

City	Responses No.	%	Mean Earnings	Standard Deviation
Ottawa	27	8.9	47,964	12,584
Toronto	85	28.1	42,857	17,822
Calgary/Edmonton	74	24.5	42,433	16,323
Vancouver/Victoria	56	18.5	41,560	14,161
Other	16	5.3	39,200	14,260
Montreal	44	14.6	37,468	14,675

Source: C.A.B.E. Salary Survey, 1981

Location of Employment

As shown in Table 7, the location of an economist's work made some difference to salary. Ottawa, with its large number of civil servant jobs, ranked the highest.

Conclusion

The salary figures presented here are only rough guides to economists' salary levels. The samples are small and limited to C.A.B.E. membership so it is impossible to say whether the figures are representative of all economists. Nevertheless, a general idea of salary levels and how they relate to area of employment, responsibilities, education, work experience, age, and job location can be had from the C.A.B.E. survey.

USEFUL PUBLICATIONS FOR ECONOMICS MAJORS

The following is offered as a representative, but abridged, list of publications that you should find useful in your studies of economics and in your pursuit of a career involving those studies.

I. Government and OECD Publications
   The following are published by various departments of the government or by the Organization for Economic Cooperation and Development. They contain a wide variety of regularly published statistics pertaining to such areas as national income accounting, money supply data, employment information, population trends, and so on. Most also contain helpful interpretive articles regarding trends and correlations of the various data.
   A. The Bank of Canada Review, published monthly by the Bank of Canada, contains collections of statistics regarding the money supply and related totals. For information write: Bank of Canada, 234 Wellington Ave., Ottawa, Ontario K1A 0G9.
   B. The Economic Review is published yearly by the Federal Government Department of Finance. It contains an excellent survey of Canadian economic experience, with some data going back to 1950. For information write: Department of Finance, 160 Elgin Street, Ottawa, Ontario K1A 0G5.
   C. The Labour Force is published monthly by Statistics Canada (publication no. CS71-001) and provides statistical data on all aspects of the labor force. For information write: Statistics Canada, Ottawa, Ontario K1A 0T6.
   D. The Canadian Statistical Review. Published monthly by Statistics Canada (publication no. CS11-003), it is a collection of the most commonly used statistics. For information write: Statistics Canada, Ottawa, Ontario K1A 0T6.

E. Economic Indicators. Published monthly by the Organization for Economic Cooperation and Development (OECD), it is a collection of statistics from a large number of nations. For information write: OECD, No. 2 Rue Andre Pascal, F-75775 Paris CEDEX 16, France.

II. Newspapers and Magazines
These selected newspapers and magazines concentrate in whole or in part upon the reporting and interpretation of current business and economic news. All are highly readable.
  A. Canadian Business Review. Published by the Conference Board in Canada for a business audience. It contains short articles in nontechnical language. For information write: Conference Board in Canada, Suite 100, 25 McArthur Road, Ottawa, Ontario K1L 6R3.
  B. Challenge, the Magazine of Economic Affairs. Published bimonthly by M.E. Sharpe. Leading economists write articles for readers with little formal training in economics, relating economic theory to current problems and policies. For information write: Challenge, 901 North Broadway, White Plains, New York 10603.
  C. The Economist. Published weekly. Student subscription discount available. This entertaining British publication frequently contains criticisms of American economic policies. For information write: The Economist Newspaper Limited, 25 St. James's Street, London SW1A 1HG, England or P.O. Box 2700, Woburn, Mass. 01888 U.S.A.
  D. The Financial Post. A weekly newspaper reporting items of interest to Canadian business people. Student subscription discount may be available. For information write: Financial Post, 481 University Avenue, Toronto, Ontario M5W 1A7.
  E. Financial Times. A weekly newspaper reporting items of interest to Canadian business people. Student subscription discount may be available. For information write: The Financial Times, Suite 500, 920 Yonge Street, Toronto, Ontario M4W 3L5.
  F. Fortune. Published fortnightly by Time, Inc., 541 North Fairbanks Court, Chicago, Illinois 60611. Student subscription discount may be available on some campuses.
  G. Globe and Mail Business Report. Published from Tuesday to Saturday each week. For information write to The Globe and Mail, 444 Front Street W., Toronto, Ontario M5V 2S9.

III. Selected Professional and Business Journals
The following is a small sample from the large number of journals whose intended readership consists primarily of professional economists or of professionals in related fields. While many articles may be too technical for the beginning economics student, each journal contains writing well within the grasp of the interested student who has completed one school year's study of microeconomic and macroeconomic principles.
  A. American Economic Review. Published quarterly by the American

Economic Association, along with its annual Proceedings of the annual meetings, which is published in May. Student subscription discount available. For information write to the American Economics Association, 1313-21st Avenue South, Nashville, Tennessee 37212. Students should find the Proceedings issue especially useful, because it often contains broad coverage of selected economists' views on current economic issues and government policies.

B. Canadian Journal of Economics. Published quarterly by the University of Toronto Press as a journal for professional economists. Student discount may be available. For information write: University of Toronto Press, Journals Department, 5201 Dufferin Street, Downsview, Ontario M3H 3T8.

C. Canadian Public Policy. Published quarterly, with articles for professional economists concerning public policy issues. Student discount may be available. For information write: University of Toronto Press, Journals Department, 5201 Dufferin Street, Downsview, Ontario M3H 3T8.

D. Harvard Business Review. Published bimonthly by the Harvard University Graduate School of Business Administration, as part of a program in executive education for professional managers. For information write: Harvard Business Review, Subscription Service Department, P.O. Box 9730, Greenwich, Connecticut 06835.

E. Journal of Economics Literature. Published quarterly by the American Economic Association along with the American Economic Review. This publication is a must for any economics researcher. It usually contains a survey article of the latest developments in a field of economics; and also provides reviews of recently published economics books, an annotated listing of new books, contents of selected current economic and business professional journals, and a classification by economics area of articles and abstracts of selected articles in current economic and business journals. See American Economic Review.

F. Journal of Political Economy. Published bimonthly by the University of Chicago Press. Student subscription discount available. For information write: The University of Chicago Press, 5801 Ellis Avenue, Chicago, Illinois 60637.

G. Quarterly Journal of Economics. Published quarterly by John Wiley & Sons, Inc., and by the President and Fellows of Harvard College. For information write: Journal Department, John Wiley & Sons, 605 Third Avenue, New York, New York 10158.

HOW TO USE
THIS STUDY GUIDE

This study guide to <u>Basic Economics</u>, Second Canadian Edition is intended for use as an integral part of your learning program for the first course in economics.

The text, your instructor's lectures, and the study guide each cover the same ground, but they cover it in different, complementary ways. The text is the most comprehensive of the three in its coverage, but because of physical limitations on its size it can usually only offer one or two illustrations of each theory, and one or two examples of each type of problem. Your instructor's lectures and class discussions cannot cover the material as extensively as the text, but they offer new points of view, applications of economic theory to this week's problems of economic policy, and - perhaps most valuable of all - a chance for you to ask questions.

This study guide complements both the text and the lectures. It provides the repeated, additional illustrations, examples, and problems you need to become proficient in the more technical aspects of economics. It provides learning objectives that help you focus on the key concepts presented in the text. And it provides questions and sample test items that not only prepare you for examinations, but show you what questions you should be asking in class.

Different students will use this study guide in different ways, but here are the authors' suggestions for using each section.

Where You're Going

As you approach each new chapter, begin with the text. Read the section entitled "What You Will Learn In This Chapter," and check the terms for review. Then skim quickly through the chapter, looking at headings, key ideas, graphs, and new vocabulary items. All this will give you an overview.

Now turn to the "Where You're Going" section in this study guide, and carefully read through the learning objectives listed there. As you read through the chapter carefully for the first time, keep this list of learning objectives handy, and check them off as you go along. By the end of your first careful reading of the chapter, you should have at least a good preliminary grasp of each objective.

Walking Tour

The "Walking Tour" sections of this study guide provide a further review of what you have learned from the text, but this time in a form that makes you an active participant. The word "active" is important. You will be wasting your time and the money you spent on this study guide unless you carefully cover the answers given in the margin and <u>think</u> about each question before you look at the answer. When you come to graphical or numerical problems, solve the problems yourself before checking the answers. Once you have filled in the blanks and solved the problems, the completed "Walking Tour" section will make a useful supplementary review at exam time.

Self Test

When you have read the chapter carefully and worked through the other sections in the study guide, you are ready for the self test. The items in the self test are real examination items from real tests given at real colleges and universities. They are carefully coordinated with the Basic Economics text, and selected to represent a range of difficulty. Answers to all items and explanations where necessary are given at the end of the study guide. Don't take the self test too early in your program of study for each chapter. It is most useful when you have the material pretty well mastered. If you find yourself missing more than five items per self test, you should study more before using these sections of the study guide.

Hands On

Now that you have studied and reviewed, you are ready for serious exam preparation. There are three kinds of exam questions you need to be prepared for: graphical or numerical problems, essay questions, and multiple choice questions. Each kind receives separate attention in this study guide.

Begin with the "Hands On" graphical and numerical problems that appear in some study guide chapters. Graphical and numerical problems are the hardest part of the course for many students, but this study guide is written with that fact in mind. However, don't look at the answers until you have really worked to answer the problems to the best of your ability.

It is a good idea to always do the graphical problems in pencil and use a straightedge. Work neatly. If you make mistakes go back and carefully correct your own diagram. Then check it a second time against the solution diagram.

Don't Make This Common Mistake!

Here and there throughout the study guide you will find boxes with the caption "Don't Make This Common Mistake!" These boxes are intended to prevent you from making the dozen or so common mistakes our own students have made every term for years. Not one of these mistakes is hard to avoid if you are alert.

Application

Each application section includes material that is not in your text, usually a newspaper article, which relates to the economic theory you have studied in the chapter. Several questions follow to help you apply the theory you have learned to that particular article.

In economics and other fields, new theory often seems clear and uncomplicated until you attempt to apply it yourself. You have mastered the tools of economics only after you are able to apply them to situations outside of your text. This section is designed to help you do this.

Your instructor may use the application section as an assignment or as the basis for class discussion. If your instructor chooses not to use this section for instruction, you may be able to obtain a copy of the answers from him or her.

When Exam Time Comes

When exam time comes, the best thing for you to do would be to read page by page through the whole text and all of your lecture notes. But let's be realistic - unless economics is the only course you are taking, you may not have time to do that much studying during exam week. That is when this study guide can be most valuable. Sit down with the study guide and pick up a pen or pencil with a color you have never before used in the book. Read through each chapter of the study guide, including the "Walking Tour" and "Self Test" sections, which you by now will have completed. As you go along, use your colored pen or pencil to highlight every definition, concept, or problem-solving technique that you have not yet completely mastered. Then use your time selectively to go back over the text and your lecture notes for those selected topics. You can then approach your exam with confidence.

CHAPTER 1

WHAT ECONOMICS IS ALL ABOUT: THE CANADIAN SETTING

WHERE
YOU'RE GOING

When you have mastered this chapter, you will be able to:

- Explain why <u>scarcity</u> is the central concept of economics.

- Identify the factors of production: natural resources, capital, labour, entrepreneurship.

- State the importance of the <u>division of labor</u> to economic production.

- Explain the unique role of geography and <u>staple products</u> in Canada's economic development.

- Distinguish between <u>normative</u> and <u>positive</u> elements in discussions of economic policy.

- Explain the meaning and significance of the following additional terms and concepts:

        scientific prediction
        empirical
        econometrician
        efficiency
        fairness
        economic ideology
        microeconomics
        macroeconomics

In addition, after mastering the appendix to this chapter, you will be able to:

- Associate pairs of numbers with points on a graph, and read common economic <u>graphs</u>.

- Determine the <u>slope</u> of a line or curve drawn on a graph.

- Use graphs efficiently and effectively as a study aid.

- Construct graphs of your own on the basis of verbal instructions.

You have read the chapter at least once and have reviewed the summary in the text. Now you are going to walk through the material step by step, filling in the blanks and answering the questions as you go along. After you have answered each question, check yourself by uncovering the answer given in the margin. If you do not understand why the answer given is the right one, refer back to the proper section of the text.

Scarcity and Choice in Economics

In economics, scarcity is a/an [objective/ subjective] concept. That means that it is properly measured in terms of [objective physical standards/human wants].

    Our economic choices are limited by the factors of production: _____,

_____, _____,

_____. Adam Smith stressed

the importance of the _____ of

_____ for efficient production in

his book _____.

a subjective

human wants

natural resources

labor   capital

entrepreneurship

division

labor

The Wealth of Nations

An Overview of Early Canadian Economic History

Canadian geography dictated both the location and economic development of the early Atlantic coast and St. Lawrence settlements, and played a major role in the pattern of western exploration and economic expansion. Harold Innis stressed the importance of

_____ such as fish, timber,

_____, _____,

_____, _____, and

_____ in Canada's economic

development. Since these natural resources were abundant during Canada's early development, and labor and capital relatively scarce, raw materials were exported and many finished goods imported.

staple products

fur   pulp and paper

minerals   wheat

oil

Economic Science and Economic Policy

Any discussion of economic policy can be stated in the form of a three-step chain of reasoning, as follows:

1. If political party X is elected, policy Y will be instituted, other things being equal.
2. Policy Y is a good (or bad) thing.
3. Therefore, vote for (or against) political party X.

The first step in this chain of reasoning is known as a/an _____. Such a   **a scientific prediction**

statement has the form of a prediction that if A occurs, then B will occur under [all/ specified] conditions. When economists make   specified
scientific predictions, they are said to be practicing _____ economics.   positive

     Methods of resolving disputes over matters of positive economics by looking at evidence based on observations of past experience are known as _____   empirical

methods. Economists who specialize in the statistical analysis of empirical economic data are known as _____.   econometricians

     The second step in the three-step chain of reasoning given above is a statement in _____ economics. Among the   normative

important value standards used in normative economics are _____ and   efficiency

_____.   fairness

_____ means the property   Efficiency
of producing or acting with a minimum of expense, waste, and effort. Fairness is much harder to define. However, two common conceptions are the _____ concept   egalitarian

of fairness which associates fairness with an equitable distribution of income, and the _____ concept of fairness which   libertarian

associates fairness with the right of each individual to act in accordance with private choice, free from force, threat, or coercion by others.
     A person's judgments and interpretations of the value standards used in normative economics constitute a framework of thought that can be called an _____.   economic ideology

Economics as a discipline is divided into
two broad subdivisions. _____ is   Microeconomics

the study of the economic behavior of
[individual/groups of] households and firms   individual
and the determination of the market prices
of [individual/groups of] goods and services.   individual
_____ is the study of [large/   Macroeconomics

small]-scale economic phenomena, especially   large
inflation, unemployment, and economic growth.

APPENDIX TO CHAPTER 1: Working With Graphs

Learning how to work with graphs begins with learning how to associate
points on a graph with pairs of numbers. Exhibit S1.1, for example,
represents graphically the records kept by a small rental firm of the
number of cars rented per day on each of three dates and the rental
price per car on that date. Use the graph to fill in this table:

Date	Number of Cars	Price		
July 1, 1979	_____	_____	10	5
July 1, 1980	_____	_____	7	11
July 1, 1983	_____	_____	5	15

A further examination of the firm's records shows that
on December 31, 1979, eight cars were rented at a price
per car of $7. Add this point to the graph, and label
it accordingly. It lies [above/below/on] a straight   below
line drawn through the three points given in the
table. On the basis of the data given in the graph,
including the point that you have added, it can be
said that for this firm, the number of cars rented
per day tends to decrease as the price [increases/
decreases].   increases

Exhibit S1.1

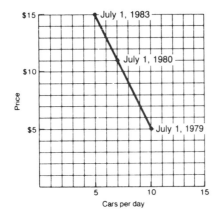

Exhibit S1.2

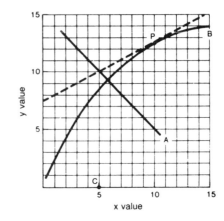

It is also important to be able to determine the slope of a line or curve on a graph. Slope is defined as the ratio of the change in the [x/y] value to the change in the [x/y] value between two points. Look at Exhibit S1.2. Line A in that exhibit has a slope of ___. The slope of a curve at any given point is defined as the slope of a straight line drawn _____ to the curve at that point. The curve B has a slope, at Point P, of approximately ___. Now draw a line from Point C with a slope of 4. This new line passes through Line A at a point having an x value of ___ and a y value of ___.

y
x

-1
tangent

0.5

7
8

Suppose you were asked to draw a graph representing the following proposition: as the quantity of fertilizer used per hectare (x) increases, other things being equal, the yield of corn (y) tends to increase, rapidly at first, and then less rapidly. Your graph would look most like [A/B/C] in Exhibit S1.2.

B

SELF TEST

These sample test items will help you check how much you have learned. Answers and explanations can be found at the end of this book. Scoring yourself: one or two wrong - on target. Three or four wrong - passing, but you haven't mastered the chapter yet. Five or more wrong - not good enough; start over and restudy the chapter.

Multiple Choice

1. Scarcity would cease to exist as an economic problem if
   a. everyone were willing to accept a monastic standard of living.
   b. everyone in the world enjoyed as high a material standard of living as the average worker in Canada.
   c. the population of the planet Earth were reduced to a tenth of its present size and stabilized at that number.
   d. none of the above.

2. Early Canadian economic development concentrated on the export of raw materials because
   a. raw materials were readily available.
   b. European nations were eager to buy raw materials.
   c. Canada had relatively little labor and capital with which to process raw materials into finished goods.
   d. all of the above.

3. The "staples trap" means that an economy or economic region
   a. exports only raw materials.
   b. does not import a significant amount of goods.
   c. concentrates on the export of a few products and fails to develop a wide range of industries.
   d. does not export any goods.

4. Which of the following is not a proposition of positive economics?
   a. Unemployment averaged 12.4 percent of the labor force in 1983.
   b. Other things being equal, interest rates tend to rise when the rate of inflation rises.
   c. If most workers prefer to work during the day rather than during the night, employers are likely to have to pay higher wages to get night shift workers.
   d. It is likely that we would all be happier if federal policymakers paid more attention to econometric forecasts in formulating their economic policy and less attention to the next election.

5. If I think inflation is bad and price controls will make it worse and you think inflation is good and price controls will stop it, then
   a. we will agree that price controls should be tried.
   b. we will agree that price controls should not be tried.
   c. you will think price controls should be tried and I will not.
   d. I will think price controls should be tried and you will not.

6. Efficiency
   a. is the only standard for measuring the performance of an economic system.
   b. and fairness are standards by which economists analyze economic policies.
   c. is defined as equal distribution of income.
   d. is defined as minimum profits for firms.

Note: The remaining questions in this section cover the appendix on working with graphs.

7. Draw a graph with "number of students at university" on the horizontal axis and "tuition, dollars per year" on the vertical axis. On this diagram, the statement "The higher the tuition, the fewer students at university, other things being equal" would best be represented by
   a. a line with a slope greater than zero.
   b. a line with a slope of zero.
   c. a line with a slope less than zero.
   d. a vertical line.

8. Draw a diagram with x on the horizontal axis and y on the vertical axis. Put in Point A at x3 and y4. Put in Point B at x4 and y6. A straight line connecting A and B would have a slope of
   a. ½
   b. 2
   c. -½
   d. -2

9. You are shown a graph with "hours spent studying per week" on the horizontal axis and "student's grade point average" on the vertical axis. The relationship between studying and grades is shown by a line that first rises, reaches a maximum, and then falls. The best interpretation of this graph in words would be that
   a. you can't hurt your grades by studying more.
   b. it's not worth studying; you can get bad grades whether you study or not.
   c. grades depend more on native intelligence than on studying.
   d. up to a point you can improve your grades by studying but if you study so much you don't have time to get a good night's sleep, your grades may suffer.

10. You are shown a graph on which two points, A and B, are marked. Point B lies below and to the right of Point A. A straight line connecting A and B would have a slope of
    a. less than zero.
    b. less than 1 but greater than zero.
    c. greater than 1.
    d. insufficient information given for an answer.

APPLICATION

"Political economy or economics is a study of mankind in the ordinary business of life; it examines that part of individual and social action which is most closely connected with the attainment and with the use of material requisites of well-being. Thus it is on the one side a study of wealth; and on the other, and more important side, a part of the study of man."

*Alfred Marshall, **Principles of Economics**, 8th ed. (London: Macmillan and Co., 1964), p. 1.*

1. How do the concepts of scarcity and choice fit into Marshall's definition of economics?

2. How did Canada's geography and raw materials influence the "attainment and use of material requisites of well-being" in the country's early economic development?

3. Does Marshall's definition of economics allow for a variety of economic ideologies? Explain briefly.

CHAPTER 2
THE BASIS OF TRADE, THE PRICE SYSTEM, AND THE MARKET ECONOMY

WHERE
YOU'RE GOING

When you have mastered this chapter, you will be able to:

- Apply the concept of opportunity cost to familiar economic decisions of the kind you make yourself.

- Explain the basis for specialization of production and trade between nations.

- Explain how the price system functions as a mechanism for transmitting information in a market economy.

- Explain how the market system also provides the incentives necessary to insure that people will make effective use of the information they receive via the price system.

- Explain why the third function of markets, distributing income, cannot be entirely separated from the first two.

- Explain the meaning and significance of the following additional terms and concepts:

    allocation of resources
    production possibility frontier
    homogeneous
    law of increasing costs
    absolute advantage
    comparative advantage
    monopoly power

WALKING TOUR

You have read the chapter at least once and have reviewed the summary in the text. Now you are going to walk through the material step by step, filling in the blanks and answering the questions as you go along. After you have answered each question, check yourself by uncovering the answer given in the margin. If you do not understand why the answer given is the right one, refer back to the proper section of the text.

Opportunity Cost and the Production Possibility Frontier

The cost of attaining any chosen economic objective is the loss of the opportunity to do something else instead with the same time or resources. Cost measured in this way is known as _OPPORTUNITY_ cost. In a production possibility frontier diagram, such as that shown in Exhibit S2.1, opportunity cost

opportunity

Exhibit S2.1

is indicated by the _SLOPE_ of the frontier at any given point. For example, at Point A on the diagram, the opportunity cost per unit of civilian goods (in terms of military goods) is calculated by the slope of a line _TANGENT_ to the _FRONTIER_ at Point A. At Point B, the opportunity cost per unit of civilian goods is approximately _ONE_ unit(s) of military goods. The total opportunity cost of increasing military production from Point A to Point B is approximately _85_ units of civilian goods production.

When the economy is operating at a point like A or B, it is producing _EFFICIENCY_. If it is producing at a point like C, it is producing _INEFFICIENCY_. A point such as D is _IMPOSSIBLE_, given the quantities of resources and the technology available.

The production possibility frontier is a curve because the factors of production are not _HOMOGENEOUS_. That is, all factors of production cannot be substituted for one another in the production process and still produce the same level of output. A curved production possibility frontier illustrates the law of _INCREASING COSTS_, which states that as resources

slope

tangent; frontier

one

eighty-five

efficiently

inefficiently

impossible

homogeneous

increasing costs

are shifted from one use to another, an additional
unit of output of one good requires an [increasing/
decreasing] rate of sacrifice of other goods as   increasing
greater and greater shifts occur.
    However, if all factors of production are
assumed to be homogeneous, the production possibility
frontier would be a _____ line.   straight

Specialization and Trade

Nations and regions within a country often have
different resources that allow them to produce
some goods more cheaply or more easily than
other goods. Because of these differences,
nations or regions may gain from specialization
and trade. In trade theory, _____   absolute
is the ability of a region or country to   advantage
produce a good at an absolutely lower cost,
measured in terms of factor inputs, than its
trading partners. _____ is the   Comparative
ability of a region or country to   advantage
produce a good at a lower opportunity cost,
measured in terms of other foregone goods,
than its trading partners. As long as a
country or region has a _____   comparative
in the production of a good there will   advantage
probably be gains from specialization and
trade. In Canada, specialization and trade
takes place between regions of the country
and between Canada and many other trading
nations.

The Functions of Markets

The three main functions performed by markets are:
1. _____   transmitting information

2. _____   providing incentives

3. _____   distributing income

Of all the various channels for transmitting
information in the market economy, the most
important is the _____ system.   price
Increasing scarcity of a good or service is
signaled by a [rise/fall] in its price relative   rise
to the prices of other goods and services.
Increasing abundance is indicated by a [rise/fall]   fall
in the relative price.
    It is important to understand that relative
prices, not absolute prices, are what count in

transmitting information. For example, if the price
of copper goes up from $1.60 per kilogram to $1.76
per kilogram while all other prices go up by 10
percent, the price of copper relative to the prices
of other goods [has/has not] changed; no signal is   has not
given that copper is more or less scarce than before.
If the price of lumber goes up from $.50 per board
foot to $.75 per board foot while all other prices
go up by 10 percent, the relative price of lumber
has __INCREASED__ . Users will react by using   increased
[more/less] lumber and by using [more/less] brick.   less; more
If the price of barley goes up from $112 per tonne
to $116 per tonne while all other prices go up by
10 percent, the relative price of barley has
__DECREASED__ . Users will respond by using   decreased
[more/less] barley and [more/less] of other grains.   more; less
    Profits, an important source of incentives in
a market economy, account for a very [large/small]   small
percentage of all income earned. They have an
importance out of proportion to their magnitude
because they are the incentive provided to
__ENTREPRENEURS__ for coordinating the contributions   entrepreneurs
of workers and other resource owners.
    The distribution of income in a market economy
may be considered fair for those to whom fairness
means __EQUAL__ opportunity, but it is not   equal
necessarily considered fair to those for whom
fairness means __EQUALITY__ of income.   equality

Imperfections in the Market System

Markets in the real world are far from perfect. In
product markets some firms are able to exercise
__MONOPLY__ power by raising product prices without   monopoly
losing customers. In other cases prices may be
" __FIXED__ " by agreement between a few producers.   fixed
Similar market imperfections exist in labor markets,
financial markets, and agricultural markets.

SELF TEST

These sample test items will help you check how much you have learned.
Answers and explanations can be found at the end of this book. Scoring
yourself: one or two wrong - on target. Three or four wrong - passing,
but you haven't mastered the chapter yet. Five or more wrong - not
good enough; start over and restudy the chapter.

Multiple Choice

1. The opportunity cost of taking a course in biology rather than a
    course in economics would not include:
    a. the cost of any special lab supplies needed for the biology
        course.
    b. the need to spend an extra three hours a week in biology lab.
    c. the cost of the biology text, assuming an equally expensive
        text is needed for the economics course.
    d. a possible reduction in your grade point average, assuming
        the biology course to be harder than the economics course.

2. The discovery of a low-cost method for extracting huge quantities
    of oil from garbage would
    a. permit the economy to reach a point now outside the
        production possibility frontier.
    b. permit the economy to move from a point inside the
        production possibility frontier to one on it.
    c. tend to straighten the curvature of the production possibility
        frontier.
    d. best be represented by a movement along the current production
        possibility frontier.

3. It is possible for Canada to produce tomatoes for the consumer
    market year-round if heated greenhouses are used in the winter.
    However, Canada chooses to import tomatoes from Mexico in the
    winter, because Mexico has
    a. a comparative advantage in the winter production of tomatoes.
    b. an absolute advantage in the winter production of tomatoes.
    c. probably both an absolute and a comparative advantage in the
        winter production of tomatoes.
    d. an agreement with the Canadian government to sell tomatoes
        to Canada in the winter.

4. In Canada it costs $1 to produce one unit of Good A and $2 to
    produce one unit of Good B. In the United States it costs $.25 to
    produce one unit of Good A and $.40 to produce one unit of Good B.
    If there were trade between Canada and the United States, then
    a. Canada would export Good A and import Good B.
    b. Canada would import Good A and export Good B.
    c. the United States would import both Good A and Good B.
    d. there would not be a basis for trade between the United States
        and Canada.

5. The importance of bargaining in a bazaar economy is an indication
    that
    a. profits are very high.
    b. profits are very low.
    c. information is very abundant.
    d. information is very scarce.

6. Adam Smith wrote that the "invisible hand" of the market led the butcher and the baker to promote an end (consumer satisfaction) which was no part of their intention. His point was
   a. that participants in the market system often operate with minimal information.
   b. that the profit motive gives sellers an incentive to do what buyers want.
   c. that the merchants of his day were selfish and greedy.
   d. that a knowledge of economic science, as set forth in The Wealth of Nations, would improve the management of the small businesses on which prosperity ultimately depends.

7. The price system provides incentives
   a. to businesses, through the profit motive.
   b. to workers, through different wages for different jobs.
   c. to consumers, through the relative prices of goods.
   d. all of the above.

8. The distributional function of markets is a source of controversy because
   a. the question of the fairness of distribution is a sensitive normative issue.
   b. there is little empirical evidence on the distribution of income.
   c. it is not known whether the market really has much to do with distribution.
   d. different economists have different definitions of what constitutes a market.

9. If rents on urban housing are held down to make it easier for the poor to afford a decent place to live, then
   a. builders may receive false signals about where to construct new housing.
   b. renters may have an incentive to pass up good jobs in small towns.
   c. owners may have insufficient incentive to maintain their buildings.
   d. all of the above.

10. Monopoly power is an example of
    a. market perfection.
    b. a bazaar economy.
    c. market imperfection.
    d. zero information costs to buyers in a market system.

HANDS ON

Now that you have reviewed the concepts introduced in this chapter, it is time for some hands-on practice with the analytical tools that have been introduced. Work through each problem in this section carefully, and then check your results against those given at the end of the book.

Problem 1.

(a)   When you graduate from university with your degree you are offered
      two different jobs in two different cities. From the list below
      construct a Budget of Out-of-Pocket Costs and a Budget of
      Opportunity Costs involved in accepting the job with the XYZ Corp.
      in Calgary rather than the job with the ABC firm in Halifax.
      Assume your parents expect you to take a job upon graduation and
      that living at home is not an option.

Exhibit S2.2

Salary offer from the XYZ Corp. in Calgary	$15,000
Rent for an apartment in Halifax or Calgary	$4,500
Transportation expenses in either Calgary or Halifax	$1,500
Salary offer from the ABC firm in Halifax	$17,000
Food costs in either Calgary or Halifax	$1,200
Personal expenses in either Calgary or Halifax	$2,500

   (All costs and salaries are on a yearly basis.)

(b)   Construct the same two budgets involved in accepting the job with
      the ABC firm in Halifax rather than the Calgary job.

(c)   Assuming that both jobs offer the same chances for advancement
      and job satisfaction, that both cities offer all the amenities
      you are concerned with, and that all other things (except salary)
      are the same with both jobs, which offer should you accept and why?

Problem 2. Assume that Mexico and Canada both produce oranges and
steel and that Exhibit S2.3 shows the hours of labor required in each
nation to produce a kilogram of oranges and a tonne of steel. All
costs other than labor costs will be ignored for simplicity in this
example. Assume also that labor costs remain constant.

Exhibit S2.3

	Mexico	Canada
oranges (per kilogram)	1 hour	8 hours
steel (per tonne)	8 hours	4 hours

(a)   Which nation has the absolute advantage in producing oranges?
      Which in producing steel? Explain.

(b)   Using the concept of opportunity cost, which nation has the
      comparative advantage in the production of oranges? Which in
      the production of steel? Assume that each country has a total
      of 2,000 hours available for production. Explain your answer.

(c) Assuming no trade takes place between Mexico and Canada, what will be the price ratios for oranges and steel in each country?

(d) Assuming 2,000 hours of labor are available for production in each country, draw a production possibility frontier for Mexico and for Canada; measure steel on the vertical axis and oranges on the horizontal axis.

(e) Without trade Canada chooses to produce 100 kilograms of oranges using (100 x 8) = 800 hours of labor and 300 tonnes of steel using (300 x 4) = 1,200 hours of labor. Mark this combination of output Point C on Canada's production possibility frontier on your graph from part (d). Without trade Mexico produces 1,000 kilograms of oranges using (1,000 x 1) = 1,000 hours of labor and 125 tonnes of steel using (125 x 8) = 1,000 hours of labor. Mark this as Point M on Mexico's production possibility frontier. Now, construct a chart similar to Exhibit 2.5 in your text to show the pretrade equilibrium production for Mexico and Canada. Change the last column to a total for the two countries.

(f) Assume that both Mexico and Canada agree to specialize their production by producing only the product each has the comparative advantage in producing and trading for the other. Draw a posttrade production and consumption exhibit similar to Exhibit 2.6 in your text; assume that the nation with the comparative advantage wants to consume the same amount of the item they produce as they consumed in the pretrade equilibrium. Any remaining production then goes to the other nation. Clearly show the gains to both nations as a result of specialization and trade (i.e., the pre- and posttrade production totals).

A parable of advantage

In a time past, one George the lawyer hired unto himself a splendid young typist named Minnie.

His friends leered and sniggered, because they knew that George was an excellent typist in his own right. In fact, they said, the lawyer could type far faster than this young woman, and he could easily do his own typing and save money.

George ignored them, because his motives were pure. And very practical.

Of course, George could practise law at the going rate of $50 an hour. Given a 40-hour week, he could spend 30 hours on law to earn a whacking $1,500, and then knock off all his typing in the other 10 hours.

Instead, George chose to practise law all 40 hours of the week, to take in $2,000. He paid slow-typing Minnie the going $5 an hour, or $200 for her 40-hour week, leaving himself with a decidedly improved net income of $1,800.

Regardless of George's superior typing skills, it paid him to spend his time doing that which maximized his gains—that is, in the argot of trade, "exporting" legal services and "importing" typing services.

Thus, lawyer George gave mankind the Law of Comparative Advantage. In short, always export the goods you have the *relative* advantage in, and import the rest.

His friends gathered around George in awe—all except one who stood back, frowning.

But what if Minnie should join a powerful wage-fixing cartel? the puzzler asked.

Or what if hard times came, and George could "export" only 20 hours a week of legal services? Clearly, his wisest course then would be to eliminate the "imports" and do his own typing.

The lawyer thought for a moment. And then he replied with a chuckle:

"Silly boy! Who ever heard of such one-sided interventions? And won't there always be full employment? Why let such thoughts muck up a perfectly good theory?"

All exited, laughing.

*From **The Financial Post**, June 28, 1980. Reprinted by permission.*

1. Explain the concept of comparative (or "relative") advantage. What is an absolute advantage and how (if at all) does it differ from a comparative advantage?

2. Who has the comparative advantage in law, George or Minnie? Who has the absolute advantage in typing? Explain.

3. If Minnie joins a powerful wage-fixing cartel, should George consider doing his own typing? If so, at what wage should he begin to type his own material rather than pay Minnie to do it?

4. Give at least four examples of goods or services in which Canada or your particular province has a comparative advantage. In which of these examples does Canada or your province have an absolute advantage?

CHAPTER 3
SUPPLY AND DEMAND—THE BASICS

WHERE
YOU'RE GOING

When you have mastered this chapter, you will be able to:

- State the law of demand and explain the importance of the "other things being equal" assumption.

- Distinguish between changes in quantity demanded, represented by movements along a given demand curve, and changes in demand, represented by shifts in entire demand curves.

- Distinguish between changes in quantity supplied, represented by movements along a given supply curve, and changes in supply, represented by shifts of entire supply curves.

- Explain the meaning of market equilibrium, and show why equilibrium occurs at the price and quantity represented graphically by the intersection of the supply and demand curves.

- Show how equilibrium prices and quantities are affected by given changes in supply or demand.

- Apply supply and demand analysis to determine the effects of minimum and maximum price controls.

- Explain the meaning and significance of the following additional terms and concepts:

  normal good
  inferior good
  substitutes
  complements
  shortage
  surplus

WALKING TOUR

You have read the chapter at least once and have reviewed the summary in the text. Now you are going to walk through the material step by step, filling in the blanks and answering the questions as you go along. After you have answered each question, check yourself by uncovering the answer given in the margin. If you do not understand why the answer

given is the right one, refer back to the proper section of the text.

The Law of Demand

According to the law of demand, the quantity of
any good demanded tends to increase as the price
_____, other things being equal.   decreases
Demand curves thus normally have _____   negative
slopes.

    A change in the quantity demanded means
a [shift in/movement along] the demand curve.   movement along
A change in demand means a [shift in/
movement along] the demand curve. Consumer   shift in
income is one of the "other things" held
equal in the statement of the law of demand,
so a change in consumer income is said to
cause a _____. If an increase in   change in demand
consumer income causes an increase in demand
for the good, it is said to be a/an _____   a normal
good. If an increase in income causes a decrease
in demand for the good, it is said to be a/an
_____ good.   an inferior
    The prices of other goods are also held
equal in the statement of the law of demand.
If an increase in the price of Good X causes
a decrease in the demand for Good Y, the two
goods are said to be _____. If an   complements
increase in the price of Good X causes an increase
in the demand for Good Y, the two goods are said
to be _____.   substitutes

Supply

Supply curves normally have _____   positive
slopes. This indicates that an increase in the
price of a good tends to induce sellers to
increase the [supply/quantity supplied] of   quantity supplied
the good in question. Changes in technology,
input prices, or in the prices of other goods
are potential causes of changes in [supply/
quantity supplied], which causes a [shift of/   supply
movement along] the supply curve.   shift of

The Interaction of Supply and Demand

When the plans of buyers and sellers of a
good exactly mesh, so that the quantity supplied
and the quantity demanded at the prevailing
price are equal, the market is said to be in
_____. At any price higher than the   equilibrium
equilibrium price, there will be a [shortage/
surplus] of the good. Inventories of the good   surplus

will tend to [increase/decrease] and the price will	increase
tend to [rise/fall]. At any price below the	fall
equilibrium price, there will be a [shortage/surplus],	shortage
and the inventories will tend to [increase/decrease].	decrease
This will put [upward/downward] pressure on the price	upward
until equilibrium is restored.	

Supply and demand curves can be used to represent the effects of changing supply and demand conditions. Exhibit S3.1, which shows hypothetical supply and demand curves for oak flooring, provides an exercise. As the diagram is drawn, the equilibrium price is _____ per board foot, and the equilibrium quantity is _____ million board feet (mbf) per year. Suppose that a boom in home construction occurs, raising the demand for oak flooring. This would properly be represented in the exhibit as an [upward/downward] shift in the [demand/supply] curve. Draw in the new demand curve so that it passes through the point D₂ and has the same slope as the original demand curve. The new equilibrium price is

$1.20
160

upward; demand

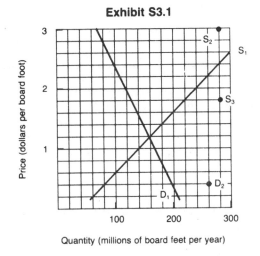

Exhibit S3.1

Price (dollars per board foot)

Quantity (millions of board feet per year)

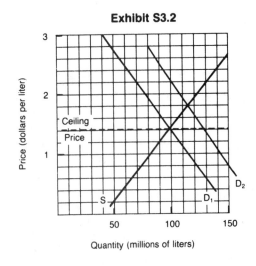

Exhibit S3.2

Price (dollars per liter)

Quantity (millions of liters)

_____. Next, suppose that a strike	$1.60
against a major producer of oak flooring cuts	
the supply. This would best be represented by	
the supply curve shifting so that it passes through	
[S₂/S₃] with the same slope as before. After this	S₂
takes place, the new equilibrium price will be	
_____ per board foot and the equilibrium	$2
quantity will be _____ mbf.	180

The preceding example assumed that the price of flooring was free to vary in response to changes

in supply and demand. The next example, given in Exhibit S3.2, assumes a controlled price for the product, which this time is milk. Initially, the supply and demand curves are in the positions S and D₁, respectively, giving an equilibrium price of _____ per liter. After that price $1.40
is established, the government imposes a price ceiling preventing it from rising any further. With an increased population more milk is consumed, shifting the demand curve to D₂. Without the price ceiling, this increase in demand would push the price up to _____ per $1.80
liter. With the price ceiling in effect, however, there is a shortage of _____ million   30
liters at the $1.40 price. One likely result of the price ceiling is the emergence of a black market in milk. Producers receive only the controlled price of $1.40, but buyers lucky enough to have their orders filled resell the product to less fortunate buyers for whatever the market will bear. As the exhibit is drawn, the black market price could rise as high as _____ per $2.20
liter.

SELF TEST

These sample test items will help you check how much you have learned. Answers and explanations can be found at the end of this book. Scoring yourself: one or two wrong - on target. Three or four wrong - passing, but you haven't mastered the chapter yet. Five or more wrong - not good enough; start over and restudy the chapter.

Multiple Choice

1. The "other things being equal" clause in the law of demand covers
   a. consumer incomes.
   b. the prices of other goods.
   c. consumer tastes and preferences.
   d. all of the above.

2. A rise in the price of coffee is likely to have which of the following effects on the market for tea?
   a. A movement up along the tea demand curve.
   b. A movement down along the tea demand curve.
   c. A leftward shift in the tea demand curve.
   d. A rightward shift in the tea demand curve.

3. If consumer incomes go up while the prices of new cars remain unchanged, which of the following is most likely?
    a. An upward movement along the demand curve for cars.
    b. A downward movement along the demand curve for cars.
    c. A rightward shift in the demand curve for cars.
    d. A leftward shift in the demand curve for cars.

4. Assuming gasoline and tires to be complementary goods, the effect on the tire market of an increase in the price of gasoline (other things being equal) would best be described as
    a. an increase in the demand for tires.
    b. a decrease in the demand for tires.
    c. an increase in the quantity of tires demanded.
    d. a decrease in the quantity of tires demanded.

5. Market equilibrium
    a. is represented graphically by the intersection of the supply and demand curves.
    b. is the condition under which the plans of buyers and sellers exactly mesh when tested in the market.
    c. is the condition under which neither buyers nor sellers have an incentive to change their plans.
    d. includes all of the above.

6. An increase in the price of beef increases the demand for pork. Restoration of equilibrium in the pork market will require
    a. an upward shift of the supply curve.
    b. a downward shift of the supply curve.
    c. a movement up along the supply curve.
    d. a movement down along the supply curve.

7. If the steelworkers' union negotiates a new contract with sharply higher wages, we would expect, once a new equilibrium is reached in the steel market,
    a. a shortage of steel.
    b. a decrease in the demand for steel.
    c. a decrease in the price of steel.
    d. a decrease in the quantity of steel demanded.

8. During a recent visit to Moscow, a Canadian tourist noticed long lines outside every butcher shop. The most reasonable conclusion to be drawn from this observation is that
    a. meat is very expensive in the Soviet Union.
    b. citizens of the Soviet Union are insatiable carnivores.
    c. the clerks in Soviet stores work very slowly.
    d. meat is subject to price controls in the Soviet Union.

9. If the equilibrium price of milk is $1.10 per liter and a price
    ceiling is imposed at $1.45 per liter, the likely result will be
    a. a surplus.
    b. a shortage.
    c. a depletion of inventories.
    d. none of the above.

10. According to supply and demand analysis, the likely effect of a
    minimum wage law would be
    a. a shortage of jobs for low-skill workers.
    b. a shortage of workers to fill low-skill jobs.
    c. increased incomes for all low-skill workers.
    d. decreased incomes for all low-skill workers.

HANDS ON

Now that you have reviewed the concepts introduced in this chapter, it
is time for some hands-on practice with the analytical tools that have
been introduced. Work through each problem in this section carefully,
and then check your results against those given at the end of the book.

Problem 1. Exhibit S3.3 gives supply and demand curves for corn
sweetener, a sugar substitute made from corn. Use it in answering the
questions that follow. Show your work clearly on the diagram. Whenever
you need to show a shift in the supply or demand curve, draw the new
curve parallel to the original one.

Exhibit S3.3

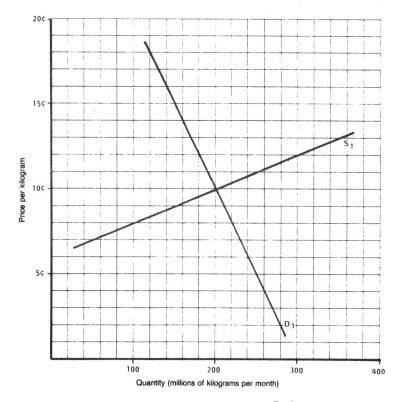

(a) Given the supply curve S_1 and the demand curve D_1, what is the equilibrium price of corn sweetener? What is the equilibrium quantity produced? Label the initial equilibrium point E_1.

(b) An increase in the price of cane sugar improves market conditions for producers of corn sweetener, raising the equilibrium price to 12¢ per kilogram. Would this event best be represented by a shift in the supply curve, the demand curve, or both? Draw in the new curve or curves, labeling them with the subscript 2. Label the new equilibrium point E_2.

(c) After the market has reached E_2, a crop failure increases the price of corn, pushing up production costs for corn sweetener. The price of corn sweetener rises to 15¢ per kilogram. Would this event best be represented by a shift in the supply curve, the demand curve, or both? Draw in the new curve or curves, labeling them with the subscript 3. Label the new equilibrium point E_3.

(d) Given supply curves, how low would the price of corn sweetener have to fall to stop production of the crop altogether?

Problem 2. Exhibit S3.4 shows supply and demand curves for lettuce. Use it in answering the questions that follow.

Exhibit S3.4

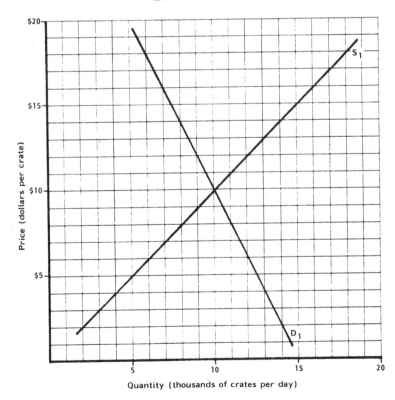

(a) As the diagram is drawn, the equilibrium quantity of lettuce demanded is _____ crates per day. The equilibrium price is $_____ per crate. Label this equilibrium point E_1.

(b) Suppose now that invention of a better mechanical lettuce picker reduces costs. Producers are now willing to supply any given quantity of lettuce for $3 less per crate than previously. What will happen to the equilibrium price of lettuce? Will it fall by the full $3 amount? Explain why or why not by drawing in new supply and/or demand curves as needed. Label the new curve or curves and the new equilibrium point with the subscript 2.

(c) Beginning from the point reached in your answer to part (b) of this problem, suppose a fad for bean sprout salad cuts the demand for lettuce, so that people are now willing to buy only half the lettuce, at any given price, that they would have bought before. What will happen to the equilibrium price and quantity of lettuce? Draw in new supply and/or demand curves, as needed, to illustrate the new situation, labeling the new curve or curves and the new equilibrium point with the subscript 3.

(d) As the sprout fad cuts lettuce-farmers' income, the lettuce farmers send a delegation to Ottawa asking for a bail-out. Parliament responds by imposing an $8 per crate minimum price for lettuce, agreeing to buy all surplus lettuce that farmers can't sell for $8 per crate, using it to make salads for the armed forces. How much lettuce will the government have to buy to stabilize the price at $8 per crate? How much will the program for government lettuce purchases cost the taxpayer? How much more lettuce will be produced than if the price ceiling had not been imposed?

DON'T MAKE THIS COMMON MISTAKE!

The most common mistake on tests covering supply and demand is to mix up shifts in the curves with movements along the curve. Suppose you know, from common sense, that some event will cause people to buy more gasoline--how do you know which curves are shifting and which ones are being moved along? Ask yourself the following key questions:

1. Would the event in question make people buy more even if the price of gasoline did not change? If so, the demand curve is shifting (that is, there is an increase in demand); the demand curve shifts upward to the right.

2. Does the event in question make people buy more only because the price is driven down? If so, there is a movement along an unchanged demand curve (that is, an increase in quantity demanded); there is movement downward to the right along the demand curve.

Example 1: Airline fares go up, causing many people to drive instead of fly on vacation trips. Analysis: With air fares up, people would use more gas even if the price of gas didn't change. Thus, the demand curve is shifting (upward to the right). This shift will, in turn, cause an increase in the price as the market moves along its supply curve.

Example 2: A price war among Arab oil producers pushes the price of crude oil down. Analysis: This event will affect gasoline buying habits only if the cut in the crude oil price is passed through to motorists as a cut in retail gasoline prices. Your diagram should show a downward shift in the supply curve, which then causes a movement (downward to the right) along the demand curve.

APPLICATION

Almond harvest sets a record

By Steve Sherman

The last commercial harvest of almonds set a record at 450 million pounds. It's one reason producers are now marketing almonds more aggressively with advertisements you've probably seen. For consumers this means lower prices, especially on bulk orders of 10 or 20 pounds, at a time when all else seems to be rising.

It couldn't happen to a nicer food. Almonds make friends with nearly every section of a cookbook — from soups to breads, vegetables, meats, fish, and desserts.

*From **The Christian Science Monitor**, February 25, 1982, page 19. Reprinted by permission.*

1. Illustrate graphically how the record almond harvest influenced the market supply and/or demand, relative to normal harvests. Does your graph show a change in supply and/or demand or a change in the quantity supplied and/or demanded? Do not add supply and demand curves to your graph that do not illustrate the record harvest situation.

2. Graphically illustrate the desired results from almond producers' aggressive marketing and advertising. Does your graph show a change in supply and/or demand or a change in the quantity supplied and/or demanded?

3. Combine your graphs from questions 1 and 2 to show lower market prices for almonds. What has happened to the quantity of almonds sold? Be sure your graph actually shows a falling price for almonds.

4. This little article was followed by several recipes using almonds. How might these recipes influence the demand for almonds? Are recipes likely to cause a change in supply and/or demand or a change in the quantity supplied and/or demanded?

5. Graphically illustrate the situation if almond merchants did not advertise or aggressively market their product after a record harvest. Does your graph show a change in supply and/or demand? Does it show a change in the quantity supplied and/or demanded? Explain how your graph is different, if at all, from your graph in question 3.

CHAPTER 4
THE ROLE OF BUSINESS AND GOVERNMENT IN THE CANADIAN ECONOMY

WHERE
YOU'RE GOING

When you have mastered this chapter, you will be able to:

- Distinguish between <u>market coordination</u> and <u>managerial coordination</u> as methods of organizing economic activity.

- Explain why firms exist and what limits the size of the firm in a market economy, in terms of the two principles of coordination.

- Define <u>sole proprietorship</u>, <u>partnership</u>, and <u>corporation</u>, and explain the advantages and disadvantages of each type of business organization.

- Explain why the interests of corporate managers and shareholders may sometimes diverge, and discuss the mechanisms that prevent managers from acting independently of the interests of the shareholders.

- Trace the growth of government in Canadian economic development.

- Explain how power is distributed between levels of government.

- Identify five major economic functions of government and give examples of each.

- Use supply and demand analysis to determine the incidence of simple taxes under given conditions.

- Discuss overall <u>tax incidence</u> for Canada in terms of the concepts of <u>progressive</u>, <u>regressive</u>, and <u>proportional</u> taxes.

- Explain the meaning and significance of the following additional terms and concepts:

      co-operative
      government purchases of goods and services
      transfer payments
      public goods
      stabilization policy

You have read the chapter at least once and have reviewed the summary in the text. Now you are going to walk through the material step by step, filling in the blanks and answering the questions as you go along. After you have answered each question, check yourself by uncovering the answer given in the margin. If you do not understand why the answer given is the right one, refer back to the proper section of the text.

Coordinating Economic Activity

Two major forms of coordinating economic activity are used in the Canadian economy. Market coordination relies on the market to transmit _____ | information

and to provide the necessary _____ . | incentives

Managerial coordination relies on _____ | directives
for communication between managers and subordinates and relies for incentives on the fact that subordinates have pledged obedience, at least within certain limits, as a condition of employment. For each of the following tasks, which form of coordination would be more appropriate?
(a) Deciding which worker sweeps the floors and which washes the windows: _____ . | managerial
(b) Deciding whether a clothing firm should specialize in coats or dresses: _____ . | market
(c) Deciding how investment funds should be divided between farming and industry: _____ . | market
(d) Deciding which plant of a multiplant auto firm should specialize in trucks: _____ . | managerial
    As a general principle, the size of a firm is limited by the number of tasks it can efficiently coordinate by use of the [managerial/market] principle. | managerial

Alternative Forms of Business Organization

Firms differ not only in size and complexity, but also in terms of legal form of organization. A firm owned and managed by one person is known as a _____ . | sole proprietorship
The owner of such a firm is subject to [limited/ unlimited] financial liability. A firm owned jointly | unlimited
by two or more people, each of whom retains unlimited liability, is known as a _____ . A firm | partnership
having ownership divided into many _____ , | shares
with each shareholder having [limited/unlimited] | limited
liability, is known as a _____ . Corporations | corporation
are the most suitable form of organization for [large/ small] business and account for approximately 75 | large
percent of manufacturing firms.
    Another important form of business organization in Canada is the _____ , which gives each | co-operative

member one vote in management decisions. Earnings
not retained by the co-operative are paid out to
the members, according to the amount of business
each member has done with the co-op. The chief
disadvantage of the co-op is the difficulty it may
have in raising funds, because increased investment
by members [does/does not] lead to increased   does not
control. Two examples of co-ops are _____   credit unions
and _____ .   agricultural
                                                                 marketing co-ops,
                                                                 and so on.
Ownership and Control of Corporations

Legally, _____ have the power to control   shareholders
the corporation through their ability to elect the
board of directors. In practice, however, many
[large/small] shareholders are not really in a   small
position to know what goes on within the corporation
and they tend to [accept/reject] management decisions   accept
as best.
      Nevertheless, corporate managers do have
incentives to [maximize/earn an acceptable level of]   maximize
profits. Managers are often involved in _____   profit-sharing
schemes, so increased _____ will benefit   profits
them personally. The fear of a _____   takeover
if share prices fall as a result of low profits may
also encourage managers to [maximize/minimize] profits.   maximize
      Workers have traditionally had [little/great]   little
control over the corporations they work for. This
situation may change in the next decade as union
_____ purchase corporation _____   pension funds;
and hence workers gain control in the decision-making   shares
process. Many firms are also making their shares
available to workers through profit-sharing plans.

Government and the Canadian Economy

Confederation in Canada was a response to political
and economic forces. The desire for an east-west
economic and political union was stimulated by
protective American tariffs, aggressive American
interests who wished to encroach on the Canadian
_____ , and tensions between _____   prairies; French

and _____ language groups. Manitoba and   English
British Columbia were added to Confederation in 1870
with the promise of a _____ , which was   national railway
eventually built across the West. The government
encouraged the economic development of the West
by imposing protective _____ , providing   tariffs

cheap _____ , and encouraging immigration.   land
Private business and government worked closely in
the economic development of Canada.

Government purchases of goods and services in Canada are currently equal to about _____ percent of gross national product. If government payments to individuals not made in return for goods or services currently supplied - that is, _____ - are included, the total is about

20

transfer payments

_____ percent of GNP. Compared to the advanced industrial countries of Western Europe, the size of the government sector in Canada is thus relatively [large/small].

40

Government at federal, provincial, and local levels uses this share of GNP to perform five major functions:

1. _____
2. _____
3. _____
4. _____
5. _____

small

provision of
 public goods;
income transfers;
 economic stabili-
 zation;
regulation of
 private business;
administration of
 justice.

Who Pays for Government?

Governments raise revenue for their expenditures by a variety of taxes. _____ taxes raise the most revenue, followed by _____ taxes and _____ profit taxes. Provincial governments get most of their revenue from _____ taxes, which are collected for them by the federal government. _____ taxes and transfers from the federal government also provide needed funds for the provinces. Municipal governments rely mainly on _____ taxes and transfers from provincial governments to finance their expenditures.

Personal income

sales; corporate

personal income

Sales

property

In relative terms, as a percent of GNP, Canada's government debt [has/has never] been higher than it is today. Compared to many other industrialized nations like West Germany and Japan, Canada's government deficit as a percentage of GNP is [high/low].

has

low

Economists are more interested in who bears the true economic burden of various taxes than in who has the legal obligation to make the tax payments. This is known as the problem of _____. Supply and demand analysis can be used to determine the incidence of any tax, provided the shapes and positions of the curves are given. For example, you can use Exhibit S4.1 to determine the incidence of a 5 cent per box tax on matches collected from manufacturers. Initially, the equilibrium price is _____ cents per box. Imposition of the tax can be

tax incidence

6

represented by a/an [upward/downward] shift in the
supply curve by _____ cents. Draw in the
new supply curve, using the same slope as in S₁, and
label it S₂. The new equilibrium price is
_____ cents per box. Of this, sellers

keep _____ cents per box, and the
government collects _____ cents. The
price to consumers has gone up by _____
cents as a result of the 5 cent tax, and the price
received by sellers has gone down by _____
cent(s). The burden of the tax is thus distributed
unequally between buyers and sellers. If the slope
of the demand curve had been flatter, indicating
that buyers were more sensitive to the price of
matches, then consumers would have borne a [larger/
smaller] share of the burden of the tax. They also
would have borne a smaller share of the tax if the
slope of the supply curve had been [flatter/steeper].

Several important issues in the economics of
taxation concern the incidence of taxes. A tax that
takes a larger percentage of _____ from

people whose incomes are high is a _____
tax. A _____ tax takes a larger percentage
of income from people with low incomes, and a
_____ tax takes a constant percentage of
income from all people. Even though the total tax
burden in Canada is slightly progressive, _____
from government have to be considered to determine
the real tax burden. The _____ of taxation
is defined as the difference between the amount paid
to governments and the amount received from them,
calculated as a percentage of income.

an upward
5

10

5
5
4

1

smaller

steeper

income

progressive
regressive

proportional

benefits

net incidence

Exhibit S4.1

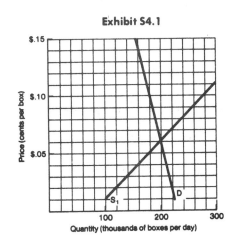

4-5

These sample test items will help you check how much you have learned. Answers and explanations can be found at the end of this book. Scoring yourself: one or two wrong - on target. Three or four wrong - passing, but you haven't mastered the chapter yet. Five or more wrong - not good enough; start over and restudy the chapter.

Multiple Choice

1. Which of the following is not an advantage of the corporate form of organization?
   a. "Double taxation" of corporate income.
   b. Limited liability.
   c. Unlimited life of the firm.
   d. Flexibility in changing managers.

2. Which of the following forms of business has the disadvantage that an individual owner may find it difficult to withdraw capital contributions to invest elsewhere?
   a. Sole proprietorship.
   b. Partnership.
   c. Corporation.
   d. All of the above are about equal in this respect.

3. Which of the following forms of business has the advantage when it comes to raising large amounts of capital from many small investors?
   a. Sole proprietorship.
   b. Partnership.
   c. Corporation.
   d. All of the above are about equal in this respect.

4. Which of the following is probably the least effective as a means of persuading managers to keep shareholders' interests in mind?
   a. Stock option plans.
   b. Takeover threats.
   c. Votes by small shareholders in the annual meeting.
   d. All of the above are equally ineffective.

5. Which of the following statements is not true?
   a. Most Canadian workers have no ownership rights in the corporations in which they work.
   b. Some Canadian companies have made stock available to their workers through "profit-sharing" programs.
   c. Few Canadian corporations have any of their workers sitting on their boards of directors.
   d. Worker control in Canadian corporations has decreased in the last twenty years.

6. Which of the following least fits the concept of a public good?
   a. National defense.
   b. Immunization against epidemic disease.
   c. Public housing construction.
   d. Enforcing highway safety rules.

7. Which of the following is part of the economic stabilization function of government?
   a. Promoting full employment.
   b. Regulating electric utility rates.
   c. Providing public education.
   d. Prosecuting white-collar crime.

8. Which of the following is most important as a source of federal government tax revenue?
   a. Personal income taxes.
   b. Corporate income taxes.
   c. Canada Pension Plan contributions.
   d. Property taxes.

9. Supply and demand analysis suggests that sales taxes
   a. are borne entirely by consumers.
   b. are borne entirely by retailers.
   c. are borne entirely by wholesalers.
   d. are usually borne jointly by buyers and sellers.

10. Which of the following taxes is the most progressive?
    a. Provincial sales taxes.
    b. Property taxes.
    c. Income taxes.
    d. All of the above are regressive.

City's tax bite is small but draws most flak

WINDSOR (Staff) — Mayor Bert Weeks says city administrations are unfairly becoming the target of tax protests, even though property tax is only a minor part of all taxes paid by a citizen.

Mr. Weeks, who was forced to adjourn one council meeting jammed with "an unruly mob until order could be restored," said figures in a report this year by the Fraser Institute show that of all the taxes paid by individuals, income tax accounts for 33 per cent, provincial retail sales tax takes 14 per cent and various federal and provincial hidden taxes on such things as fuel, vehicles, amusement, liquor and tobacco make up 43 per cent.

"Property tax accounts for only 10 per cent, but I dare say we're drawing 90 per cent of the flak because City Hall is highly visible and, for whatever reason, people have become conditioned to reacting vehemently to property tax increases."

Municipal services are being cut this year in Windsor. Some engineering work is being contracted to private firms, the grass in some parks will not be cut, library service is being reduced and the city is cutting back on the summer student program. And although there have been no layoffs in police ranks, the force is now under strength through attrition, the mayor said.

But still, a noisy crowd of taxpayers jammed the council chambers demanding a tax freeze. It is a sign of the city's troubled economy, says Bob Pedler, a realtor and past president of the Ontario Real Estate Board. "High interest rates and layoffs have melded together to become a disastrous force," and the tax protests stem from "a rude awakening of the costs affecting the very existence of people in the city."

Although high unemployment — city officials estimate 16 to 17 per cent — has bedevilled the city, much of the tax protest started from a landlord group. Mr. Pedler said a combination of high interest rates and a 6 per cent vacancy rate means many landlords are unable to survive financially if their mortgages come up for renewal, because tenants will move out rather than pay rent increases.

From **The Globe and Mail**, *May 13, 1982, p. 9. Reprinted by permission.*

1. How do progressive and regressive taxes differ in their incidence? From information in the chapter, are property taxes progressive or regressive?

2. Which property owners do you think are least likely to be able to afford increasing property tax rates during a recession and why?

3. If property taxes account for only 10 percent of all taxes paid by individuals, why do you think property tax increases are so vehemently protested?

4. From the information in the article, do you think Windsor landlords usually bear the entire burden of a property tax increase on their rental properties? Explain your answer.

CHAPTER 5
THE CIRCULAR FLOW OF INCOME AND PRODUCT

WHERE
YOU'RE GOING
_____

When you have mastered this chapter, you will be able to:

- Trace the circular flow of income and product through an economy
  made up of households, business firms, governments, and foreign
  countries.

- Distinguish between stocks and flows and give examples of each.

- Explain why national product is always equal to total
  expenditure when both planned and unplanned expenditure are
  taken into account.

- Explain the meaning of aggregate supply and aggregate demand
  and explain how the economy reacts when the two are not equal.

- Explain why national product is always equal to national
  income.

- Explain what injections and leakages are and why total
  injections are always equal to total leakages.

- Explain the meaning and significance of the following additional
  terms and concepts:

        factors of production
        factor payments
        saving
        fixed investment
        inventory investment
        investment
        net taxes
        deficit
        surplus
        net exports

WALKING TOUR
_____

You have read the chapter at least once and have reviewed the summary
in the text. Now you are going to walk through the material step by
step, filling in the blanks and answering the questions as you go along.
After you have answered each question, check yourself by uncovering

the answer given in the margin. If you do not understand why the answer given is the right one, refer back to the proper section of the text.

The Structure of the Circular Flow

The _____ flow of income and product in   circular
a simple economy measures the flow of goods from
_____ to _____, and factor   firms; households
services from _____ to _____.   households; firms
This flow is counterbalanced by a flow of
expenditures from _____ to   households
_____ and factor payments from   firms
_____ to _____.   firms; households
     In economics, it is important to distinguish
carefully between stocks and flows. For example,
the number of radios that a factory produces per
month would be a _____, while the number   flow
of radios in the warehouse awaiting shipment on
any given date would be a _____.   stock
The distinction between stocks and flows applies
to quantities measured in dollars as well as to
those measured in physical units. For example,
your consumption expenditures, measured in
dollars per month, would be a _____,   flow
while the funds you have accumulated in your bank
account as of a certain date would be a
_____.   stock
     Two of the most important components of the
circular flow of income and product are the total
of all wages, rents, interest, and profits earned
by households, known as _____, and   national income
the total value of all goods and services produced
by the economy, known as _____.   national product
National product is alternatively known as
_____.   aggregate supply
     Households do not immediately spend all of
their income to purchase goods; some of their
income is _____. Firms also do not   saved
spend all of their funds immediately. Some of
their money is used to buy newly-produced
_____ goods. These purchases are   capital
called _____ investment. When firms   fixed
increase the stock of finished products or raw
materials they keep on hand, they are engaged in
_____ investment. Total investment   inventory
by firms is the sum of _____ investment   fixed
and _____ investment.   inventory
     The sum of consumption, planned investment,
government purchases, and net exports - that is,
total planned expenditure - is known as _____.   aggregate demand

When aggregate supply and aggregate demand are equal, the economy is said to be _____. If aggregate demand is not equal to aggregate supply, the difference must be made up by [planned/unplanned] inventory investment. For example, if total planned expenditure exceeds national product, there will be unplanned inventory [accumulation/depletion]. If aggregate supply exceeds aggregate demand, there will be unplanned inventory [accumulation/depletion].

in equilibrium

unplanned

depletion

accumulation

Unplanned inventory changes act as a signal to producers that the production plans they have formulated are not meshing with the expenditure plans of households, business firms, government, and the foreign sector. If unplanned inventory accumulation takes place, producers are likely to react by [cutting/raising] prices and/or output until inventories fall to the desired level. Similarly, producers will tend to raise prices and/or output when inventory changes indicate an excess aggregate [supply/demand].

cutting

demand

Whether the circular flow is in equilibrium or not, national product must always be equal to total expenditure. This can be demonstrated by filling in the missing totals in problem 1 in the Hands On section of this chapter.

When government and a foreign sector are added to the circular flow, the equality between national product and total expenditures (planned plus unplanned) is retained.

The concepts of injections and leakages are useful to the analysis of an economy. Class each of the following transactions as an injection or a leakage (from the point of view of the Canadian economy):

You pay $1 sales tax on a purchase of a dress.

leakage

An accounting firm buys a new Canadian-made typewriter.

injection

The city of Halifax has a street paved.

injection

A private school buys an imported school bus.

leakage

A Canadian worker deposits $25 in a savings account.

leakage

A French firm buys a Canadian-built computer.

injection

When both planned and unplanned investment are taken into account, injections must equal leakages. This [means/does not mean] that saving must equal investment, government purchases must equal net taxes, and imports must equal exports. For example, suppose net exports for a given economy are $500 and the government deficit is $1,000. It follows that saving must [exceed/fall short of] total investment by _____. If saving and planned investment are equal, then unplanned

does not mean

exceed
$1,500

inventory investment will be _____ for   -$1,500
injections to equal leakages. Beginning from this
position, a $250 increase in government transfer
payments, other things being equal, would bring
total unplanned inventory investment to
_____. This unplanned inventory   -$1,750
depletion could be eliminated by an increase in
[imports/exports].   imports

SELF TEST

_____

These sample test items will help you check how much you have learned.
Answers and explanations can be found at the end of this book. Scoring
yourself: one or two wrong - on target. Three or four wrong - passing,
but you haven't mastered the chapter yet. Five or more wrong - not
good enough; start over and restudy the chapter.

Multiple Choice

1. Which of the following is not a flow?
    a. National income.
    b. Exports.
    c. Aggregate supply.
    d. All of the above are flows.

2. A firm that produced $10 million worth of shoes in a year, sold
    $11 million worth of shoes in the year, and purchased $5 million
    in new shoemaking equipment during the year would have made a
    total investment of
    a. $4 million.
    b. $5 million.
    c. $6 million.
    d. $17 million.

3. In an economy in which saving is the only leakage and investment
    the only injection,
    a. saving must always be equal to total investment.
    b. saving must always be equal to planned investment.
    c. saving must always be equal to fixed investment.
    d. none of the above.

4. Aggregate supply minus aggregate demand is equal to
    a. saving.
    b. total investment.
    c. total inventory investment.
    d. unplanned inventory investment.

5. A flow of funds from financial markets to the government indicates
    that
    a. the government budget is in surplus.
    b. the government budget is in deficit.
    c. total injections exceed total leakages.
    d. total leakages exceed total injections.

6. If planned investment equals saving and government purchases
   equal net taxes, then
   a. the economy must be in equilibrium.
   b. imports must equal exports.
   c. both of the above.
   d. none of the above is necessarily true.

7. If national product = 1,000, consumption = 800, planned
   investment = 100, government purchases = 150, exports = 50,
   and imports = 75, then unplanned inventory investment must be
   a. -25
   b. 0
   c. 25
   d. none of the above.

8. Let C stand for consumption, I for total investment, G for
   government purchases, X for exports, M for imports, S for
   saving, and T for net taxes. Which of the following equations
   always holds?
   a. C + I + G + X = C + S + T - M.
   b. C + I + G + X - M = C + S + T.
   c. C - T = I + X - S - M.
   d. None of the above always holds.

9. If the government budget is in surplus by $100 and net exports
   are -$60, then
   a. saving must exceed investment by $40.
   b. saving must exceed investment by $160.
   c. investment must exceed saving by $40.
   d. investment must exceed saving by $160.

10. If planned injections exceed total leakages, then
    a. prices and/or output will tend to rise.
    b. prices and/or output will tend to fall.
    c. prices will tend to rise and output to fall.
    d. output will tend to rise and prices to fall.

HANDS ON

Now that you have reviewed the concepts introduced in this chapter, it
is time for some hands-on practice with the analytical tools that
have been introduced. Work through each problem in this section
carefully, and then check your results against those given at the
end of this book.

Problem 1. Fill in the blanks in the following table, then answer
the questions below.

Output resulting from producers' plans: (1)_____
    Shirts $70,000
    Tennis rackets   80,000
    Drill presses   50,000

Expenditures resulting from buyers' plans
    Total consumption expenditure   (2)_____
        Shirts   70,000
        Tennis rackets   90,000
    Total planned investment expenditure   (3)_____
        Fixed investment   50,000
        Planned inventory investment   0

Total planned expenditure   (4)_____

Total unplanned inventory investment   (5)_____

Summary
National product   (6)_____

Total expenditure   (7)_____

    Planned   (8)_____

    Unplanned   (9)_____

(a) What is the value of aggregate supply? Of aggregate demand?

(b) As the table is constructed, is the economy in equilibrium? How can you tell? If it is not in equilibrium, how would you expect producers to react, and why?

Problem 2. Each of the questions below can be answered by using one or more of the following equations:

$$AD = C + I_p + G + X - M$$

$$AS = AD + I_u$$

$$I + G + X = S + T + M$$

In these equations, AD = aggregate demand, AS = aggregate supply, C = consumption, I_p = planned investment, I_u = unplanned inventory investment, I = total investment, G = government purchases, X = exports, M = imports, and T = net taxes.

(a) Aggregate supply = 1,200, consumption = 800, planned investment = 200, government purchases = 200, exports = 50, and imports = 100. Is the economy in equilibrium? What is unplanned inventory investment?

(b) Aggregate supply = 800, planned investment = 100, consumption = 500, and net exports = 75. What must government purchases equal when the economy is in equilibrium?

(c) If the government budget is in deficit by 100 and net exports are 50, by how much must total investment exceed or fall short of saving? Can the economy be in equilibrium under these conditions?

(d) Is the following statement true or false? Explain. "If planned investment exceeds saving and government purchases exceed taxes, then the economy cannot be in equilibrium unless net exports are negative (a foreign trade deficit)."

DON'T MAKE THESE COMMON MISTAKES!

Many mistakes are made in macroeconomics because of confusion between statements that are <u>identities</u> and statements that are <u>conditional equalities</u>. Both types of statements occur in this chapter.
For example, the statement

$$\text{Aggregate Supply} = \text{Aggregate Demand} + \text{Unplanned Inventory Investment}$$

is an example of an <u>identity</u>. That means the two sides of the equation are equal by definition, or <u>identical</u>. Whether the economy is in equilibrium or not, whether the plans people make work out or not, that relationship will always hold. It holds because, by definition, any part of aggregate supply (that is, national product) that is not used for consumption, <u>planned</u> investment, government purchases, or net exports goes into unplanned inventory investment. (After all, unclaimed goods can't just disappear into thin air.) Similarly, by definition, if the sum of consumption, planned investment, government purchases, and net exports exceeds aggregate supply, demands for those uses can be satisfied only by running down inventories accumulated from production of previous periods - negative unplanned inventory investment. (Goods can't appear out of thin air either.)
But consider, by contrast, the following seemingly similar statement:

$$\text{National Product} = \text{Consumption} + \text{Planned Investment} + \text{Government Purchases} + \text{Net Exports}$$

This one is a <u>conditional equality</u>. It holds only when the economy is in equilibrium, that is, only when the plans of producers of goods just mesh with the plans of users when tested in the marketplace. When plans mesh, nothing unplanned takes place - no unplanned inventory accumulation, no unplanned inventory rundown. Planned investment and total investment are then equal.
Similarly, the statement national income = national product is an identity, at least for the simple economy in this chapter. So is the statement total injections = total leakages. But the statement <u>planned</u>

leakages = total injections is again a conditional equality - it is true only when the economy is in equilibrium.

Many student mistakes in macroeconomics arise from careless use of the term income. As you have learned from this chapter, there are three commonly-used measurements of income: net national income, personal income, disposable income. Unfortunately, in everyday life, the word income is very loosely used. Try to break the habit of this loose usage when speaking the language of economics. Here is an example:
Everyday language: "John has a high income because he earns such a large salary."
Economics language: "John can afford to spend so much because his disposable income is high." People are usually referring to disposable income when they say income, but large tax payments ensure that disposable income is less than personal income for most people. Disposable income is personal income minus personal taxes. Personal income is the total of all income, including transfer payments from government. Net national income is the total income received by a nation's productive factors, including wages and salaries, interest and rent, corporate taxes before profits and income of unincorporated enterprises.
 In short: When you are tempted to use the word income, be precise and state which income total you mean.

APPLICATION

U.S. wins battle for buns

Province Staff Reporter

Vancouver's parks board has decided to award its concession contract for hamburger and hotdog buns to a Seattle bakery rather than to more expensive B.C. bidders.

General manager Vic Kondrosky said Tuesday the board would save $12,150 by buying buns from M and C Bakery rather than from McGavin Foods, the leading Canadian bidder.

The 4-3 vote was protested by the Bakery Workers Union and the Vancouver and District Labor Council.

Doug Evans, labor council first vice-president, said it was a "crying shame, with conditions the way they are now, that we are talking about exporting jobs to the U.S."

Kondrosky said the board's policy was to give local products a five-per-cent preference in tendering but there was a 37½-per-cent price difference between the American and Canadian buns.

*From the **Vancouver Province**, March 13, 1982, page A5. Reprinted by permission.*

1. How will the decision by the Vancouver parks board to buy hamburger and hotdog buns from a U.S. bakery affect Canadian net exports, assuming that all other things stay the same? How will it affect the Canadian national product?

2. How, if at all, will the decision by the parks board affect the U.S. national income, assuming that all other things stay the same? How, if at all, will it affect U.S. aggregate demand?

3. In what way is the Seattle contract "exporting jobs to the U.S." if the parks board is importing the buns?

4. Is the total of U.S. and/or Canadian injections or leakages affected by the parks board decision? Explain.

CHAPTER 6
NATIONAL INCOME AND NATIONAL PRODUCT

WHERE
YOU'RE GOING
_____

When you have mastered this chapter, you will be able to:

- Distinguish between <u>nominal</u> and <u>real</u> measurements of economic quantities.

- Define <u>gross national product</u> and explain how the <u>expenditure approach</u> is used to measure it.

- Explain how the <u>income approach</u> is used to measure national income, and reconcile the income and expenditure approaches.

- Calculate <u>GNE deflators</u> and <u>consumer prices indexes</u> from simple sets of data, and use price indexes to convert nominal data from different years into dollars of constant purchasing power.

- Explain the meaning and significance of the following additional terms and concepts:

    final goods and services
    personal income
    personal disposable income

WALKING TOUR
_____

You have read the chapter at least once and have reviewed the summary in the text. Now you are going to walk through the material step by step, filling in the blanks and answering the questions as you go along. After you have answered each question, check yourself by uncovering the answer given in the margin. If you do not understand why the answer given is the right one, refer back to the proper section of the text.

Measuring Nominal National Income and Product

The questions in this section are all based on data given in Exhibit S6.1, which follows:

Depreciation...$130
Change in business inventories................................. -20
Compensation of employees..................................... 930
Contributions to social insurance............................. 110
Corporate profit taxes.. 50
Dividends... 30
Exports... 150
Fixed investment... 220
Government purchases.. 380
Imports... 125
Indirect business taxes....................................... 140
Net interest.. 175
Personal consumption expenditures............................. 975
Personal taxes.. 170
Proprietors' income... 90
Rental income... 25
Transfer payments... 210
Undistributed corporate profits............................... 10

Begin by using the expenditure approach to compute gross national product. This is the sum of personal consumption of $975, total private investment of _____ (which is _____ investment plus change in business _____), government purchases of $380, and net exports of _____. GNP totals _____. From this total, the net national income of _____ is derived by subtracting the capital consumption allowance (depreciation) of $130 and the _____ of $140.

$200
fixed
inventories
$25
$1,580
$1,310

indirect
business taxes

Next, using the income approach, compute net national income. This is the sum of compensation of employees of $930, rental income of $25, net interest of $175, corporate profits before taxes of _____ (which is the sum of corporate profit taxes of _____, dividends of _____, and undistributed corporate profits of $10), and proprietors' income of $90. NNI totals _____.

$90
$50
$30

$1,310

The next statistic to compute on the basis of Exhibit S6.1 is personal income. This is obtained by first subtracting contributions for social insurance, corporate profits taxes, and undistributed corporate profits from net national income and then adding transfer payments. PI totals

_____. Disposable personal income is $1,350

_____, which is found by subtracting $1,180
personal taxes from personal income.

Measuring Real Income and Prices

The next set of questions is based on Exhibit S6.2:

Exhibit S6.2

	1970 Quantity	1970 Price	1984 Quantity	1984 Price
Plastic Bowls	2,000	$ 2.50	4,000	$ 4.00
Radios	200	20.00	300	40.00
Hamburger (kilograms)	1,000	1.00	1,100	2.50

For all of the following problems, 1970 will
be considered the base year and 1984 the current
year. The first task will be to calculate real
GNE in 1984. Real GNE is defined as [current/base]   current
year output evaluated at [current/base] year prices.   base
The evaluation must be made one product at a time;
the resulting figures are then summed to give total
real GNE for the current year. Beginning with plastic
bowls, multiply the current year quantity
(_____) by the base year price   4,000

(_____ per bowl) to get _____ $2.50; $10,000
as the current year quantity of bowls evaluated at
base year prices. Proceeding in the same way, you
can find the current year quantity evaluated at the
base year price to be _____ for radios $6,000
and _____ for hamburger. Adding these $1,100
together gives a 1984 real GNE of _____. $17,100
     The next task is to determine the GNE deflator
for 1984. The GNE deflator is the ratio of current
year _____ GNE to current year _____   nominal; real
GNE, times 100. 1984 real GNE has already been
calculated. To get current year nominal GNE, compute
the sum of _____ year quantities valued at   current

_____ year prices. For 1984, this gives   current

_____. The GNE deflator for 1984 is thus $30,750

found to be _____.   179.8
     Finally, use the data from Exhibit S6.2 to
calculate a consumer price index (CPI) for 1984. The
CPI is defined as the ratio of the _____   base

year market basket valued at _____ prices   current

to the _____ year market basket valued at   base

_____ year prices, times 100. The base   base
year market basket valued at current prices comes
out to _____. The same market basket $18,500
valued at the prices at which the goods were actually
sold comes out to _____. The CPI for 1984 $10,000

is thus _____.   185

SELF TEST
_____

These sample test items will help you check how much you have learned.
Answers and explanations can be found at the end of this book. Scoring
yourself: one or two wrong - on target. Three or four wrong - passing,
but you haven't mastered the chapter yet. Five or more wrong - not
good enough; start over and restudy the chapter.

Multiple Choice

1. Gross national product is officially measured by
   a. multiplying the quantity of each good and service
      produced by the price at which it is sold and adding the
      totals.
   b. adding the quantities of domestically-produced final goods
      and services purchased by all economic units.
   c. adding together the totals of all incomes received by households
      from the sale of productive services.
   d. none of the above.

2. Which of the following would be counted as a final good or
   service in calculating GNP?
   a. An automotive brake unit sold by a Canadian company to Ford
      Motor Company of Canada for use in a new car.
   b. A truckload of fertilizer sold to a Manitoba farmer.
   c. A used typewriter purchased by a real estate agent.
   d. A haircut purchased by a retired bank teller.

3. Which of the following would not be counted as an investment for
   purposes of computing GNE?
   a. Construction of a new movie theater.
   b. Purchase by an appliance dealer of a newly-produced refrigerator,
      which the dealer subsequently fails to sell to a consumer
      during the year in question.
   c. Construction of a new, single-family house.
   d. Purchase of 1,000 shares of Alcan stock by a union pension fund.

4. Net national income is
   a. always greater than GNP.
   b. personal income plus capital consumption allowances
      (depreciation).
   c. equal to GNP minus capital consumption allowances and indirect
      business taxes.
   d. personal disposable income plus personal taxes.

5. Which of the following is included in personal income but not in disposable personal income?
   a. Employee contributions to social security.
   b. Undistributed corporate profits.
   c. Transfer payments.
   d. Personal taxes.

6. Let P_c stand for current year prices, P_b for base year prices, Q_c for the current year market basket of goods, and Q_b for the base year market basket. Then the correct formula for the consumer price index is:
   a. (Q_c valued at P_c/Q_b valued at P_b) x 100
   b. (Q_c valued at P_b/Q_b valued at P_b) x 100
   c. (Q_b valued at P_c/Q_b valued at P_b) x 100
   d. (Q_c valued at P_c/Q_c valued at P_b) x 100

7. If 1972 quantities valued at 1972 prices are 150; 1972 quantities valued at 1984 prices are 300; 1984 quantities valued at 1972 prices are 200; and 1984 quantities valued at 1984 prices are 600; the GNE deflator for 1984, using 1972 as the base year, is
   a. 200
   b. 300
   c. 400
   d. impossible to calculate with the information given.

8. One way the consumer price index differs from the GNE deflator is that the CPI
   a. uses current year quantities.
   b. includes all final goods and services.
   c. includes only goods bought by typical urban consumers.
   d. includes services as well as physical goods.

9. Suppose a typical automobile tire cost $20 in 1935 and $40 in 1980 and that the 1935 tire had a useful life of 16,000 kilometers, whereas the 1980 tire had a useful life of 64,000 kilometers. If no adjustment is made for changes in quality, then
   a. the CPI would overestimate inflation between the two years.
   b. the CPI would underestimate inflation between the two years.
   c. the CPI would accurately measure inflation between the two years.
   d. it is not possible to judge how well the CPI would measure inflation between the two years without knowing how the quantity sold changed.

10. Which of the following categories are not included in the calculation of the CPI?
    a. Food consumed away from home.
    b. Expenditures on public transportation.
    c. Health and personal care expenditures.
    d. All of the above are included in the calculation of the CPI.

Problem 1. The list below is an attempt to compile an approximate "market basket" of goods and services that would be purchased on a fairly regular basis by a typical Canadian youth between the ages of 12 and 17. It is assumed youth incomes come from allowances, paper routes, babysitting, odd jobs, etc.

KIDS' CONSUMER MARKET BASKET

		1979	1981	1983
1.	Wpg. Jets general admission hockey ticket	$6.50	$7.25	$8.50
2.	Youth (14-17) ticket to a movie	2.75	3.75	4.00
3.	Package of chewing gum	.15	.20	.25
4.	Record album	7.00	8.00	8.50
5.	Candy bar	.15	.25	.40
6.	McDonald's hamburger, small fries, small Coke	1.35	1.40	1.70
7.	Can of soft drink (from vending machine)	.40	.50	.60
8.	Ice-cream bar	.10	.15	.25
9.	Bus ride (Winnipeg Transit Student Fare)	.15	.15	.25
10.	Running shoes (Adidas)	22.00	25.00	30.00

	1979	1981	1983
Kids' Price Index	___	___	___
Consumer Price Index (All items)	182.7	225.1	264.3

The prices in the table come from Winnipeg company records or are the "best guess" of people who sold that good or service in those years.

(a) Add up the prices of this "market basket" of ten goods or services regularly purchased by kids in 1979, 1981, and 1983 to get a Kids' Price Index.

(b) Restate both the Kids' Price Index (KPI) and the regular CPI, using 1979 as a base year, i.e., 1979 = 100. The two indices can now be compared directly. Who fared better over each period, kids or adults?

(c) Note that the market basket for the KPI consists of one of each item listed. That makes the KPI a simple average of prices, whereas the regular CPI is a weighted average. This means that items with a small unit price get low weights in the KPI, even though they might be purchased often and might represent a large part of total expenditures. Take food, for example. In the 1979 base year, the five food items on the list accounted for only $2.15 of the $40.55 total. Do you think kids spend more (or less) than 5 percent of their incomes on food? Did the kids' food index rise faster or slower than the whole KPI? What would a greater weight for food in the index do to the whole picture of kids and inflation?

(d) The KPI, like the regular CPI, can be used to deflate nominal quantities to any desired base year. Earnings provide an example. If nominal earnings per customer for a Winnipeg paper boy or girl rose from 44¢ per customer per six-day week in 1979 to 71¢ in 1983, what happened to real earnings, stated in constant 1979 dollars, deflated by the KPI? What happened to real hourly earnings of babysitters, assuming that the going wage was $1.00 per hour in 1979, $1.25 in 1981, and $1.60 per hour in 1983? What if the babysitter spent all of his or her income on food? Deflate by the kid food index to find out how such a babysitter would have fared in real terms. (Hint: To deflate nominal earnings for any year, divide that year's nominal earnings figure by the ratio of that year's price index to the base year price index.)

What does tourism mean to you?

To Canadians it means one million jobs

- It's 100,000 businesses, from the largest hotel complex to the independent cabbie.
- It's almost 300,000 hotel and motel rooms, more than 30,000 restaurants.
- It's the waiter, the doorman, the bank teller, the salesperson, the policeman—all walks of Canadian life.

To Canada it means over $12.3 billion annually

- It's five per cent of our Gross National Product.
- It's the sixth largest earner of foreign exchange—about $2.9 billion.

Reach out a friendly hand

TM©

Tourism is important to all of us

TOURISM INDUSTRY ASSOCIATION OF CANADA
L'ASSOCIATION DE L'INDUSTRIE TOURISTIQUE DU CANADA

1. The advertisement says tourism is five percent of the Canadian GNP. Is tourism also included in Gross National Expenditure (GNE)? If so, in what part(s) of GNE is it included? If not, why isn't it included?

2. Is tourism reflected in net national income (NNI) and/or personal income (PI)? If yes, give at least three examples of how it is included in NNI and/or PI. If no, explain why it is not included.

3. The advertisement values tourism in Canada at over $14.8 billion annually. Is this likely to be the nominal or real value of tourism? Under what circumstances is it valuable to use a price deflator for such figures as the value of tourism?

CHAPTER 7
THE GOALS OF STABILIZATION POLICY
AND THE PERFORMANCE OF THE CANADIAN ECONOMY

WHERE
YOU'RE GOING

_____

When you have mastered this chapter, you will be able to:

- Identify the main goals concerning unemployment outlined in the
  White Paper of 1945 and the revisions that have since been made
  to those goals.

- Define the unemployment rate and contrast the official definition
  of unemployment with the commonsense notions of "not working" and
  "can't find a job."

- Describe, in general terms, unemployment trends in Canada since
  1950 and identify population groups most and least affected by
  unemployment.

- Describe, in general terms, inflation trends in Canada since
  1950 and identify population groups most and least affected by
  inflation.

- Determine nominal, expected, and realized real rates of interest,
  given the necessary data.

- Use the production possibility frontier to illustrate the concepts
  of economic growth and potential real output.

- Use economic analysis to evaluate arguments about the desirability
  and possibility of economic growth.

- Discuss the problem of balanced regional development in Canada
  and the efforts made by the federal and provincial governments
  to achieve regional development balance.

- Explain the meaning and significance of the following additional
  terms:

      labor force
      full employment
      indexing

You have read the chapter at least once and have reviewed the summary in the text. Now you are going to walk through the material step by step, filling in the blanks and answering the questions as you go along. After you have answered each question, check yourself by uncovering the answer given in the margin. If you do not understand why the answer given is the right one, refer back to the proper section of the text.

Full Employment

The White Paper of 1945 stated that the federal government should not set a target lower than full employment. A more "realistic" goal of "acceptable" unemployment has been formulated in the 1970s and 1980s acknowledging that a [higher/lower] rate of unemployment may be inevitable at the present time.

higher

As measured by Statistics Canada, the _____ is defined as the percentage of people in the labor force who are actively looking for employment but who are not currently employed. People under _____ years of age, those not seeking work, military personnel, and certain institutionalized persons are not counted as part of the _____, and therefore not counted as employed or unemployed.

unemployment rate

15

labor force

The burden of unemployment does not fall equally on all groups in the economy. People aged [15-24/over 25] are more likely to be unemployed, as are [women/men], and those with little formal education. Different regions of Canada often have higher rates of unemployment. The _____ provinces generally have high levels of unemployment while Alberta and Saskatchewan have had relatively low levels in the last few years.

15-24
women

Atlantic

Price Stability

Inflation rates in the 1970s and early 1980s were [higher than/lower than/the same as] those experienced in Canada in the 1950s and 1960s. High rates of inflation have brought renewed interest in the question of who gains and who loses from inflation. As a general rule, wage and salary income is relatively [well/poorly] protected against inflation. Transfer income is relatively well protected against inflation, partly because many transfers are paid in kind and partly because social security benefits are

higher than

well

                _____ - that is, automatically   indexed
adjusted for inflation.

     Traditionally, inflation has been thought
to injure [creditors/debtors] and benefit   creditors
[creditors/debtors]. Now, it is recognized   debtors
that this is true only for inflation that is
[expected/unexpected]. For example, suppose   unexpected
the Royal Bank is willing to give you a new
car loan at a 14 percent nominal rate of
interest when it expects 10 percent inflation,
which will give it an expected real rate of
interest of _____ percent. If,   4
instead, it expects inflation to accelerate
to 12 percent per year, it has to get a
_____ percent nominal rate to   16
maintain the same expected real rate. If
you too expect a 12 percent rate of inflation,
you may consider a 16 percent nominal rate
reasonable and take out the loan. If the rate
of inflation then unexpectedly accelerates to
15 percent per year, the realized real rate of
interest on the loan will be _____   1
percent. You will thus have benefited at the
bank's expense. However, if the rate of
inflation over the period of the loan unexpectedly
turns out to be 9 percent, the realized real rate
turns out to be [higher/lower] than the expected   higher
real rate, and the bank will benefit at your
expense.

     The tax system plays an important role in
determining the distributional effects of
inflation. In the early 1970s, corporate profits
before and after tax [increased/decreased] much   increased
[faster/slower] than average weekly wages and   faster
salaries of workers. But by 1975 when the federal
government imposed income controls, corporate
profits were [increasing/decreasing] and average   decreasing
weekly wages and salaries were [increasing/
decreasing].   increasing

     Government tax revenues are also affected
by inflation. _____ personal and   Progressive
corporate income taxes [rise/fall] steadily with   rise
inflation-induced income and profit increases.
Even _____ of personal income taxes   indexing
does not remove all of the inflationary bias.
However, government expenses for nominal interest
payments, wages, salaries, and other costs also
[rise/fall] during inflationary periods.   rise

Economic Growth

The real output that the economy could produce
if resources were fully employed is known as

_____. Given improvements in   potential real
technology and the growth of the labor force,   GNP or output
real output in Canada could have grown by
_____ percent annually, but it   4
actually increased at an average of less than
_____ percent between 1974 and 1981.   3
Actual GNP is [often/rarely] below potential real   often
GNP and [often/rarely/never] above it.   rarely

    Today, not everyone considers further economic
growth to be possible or desirable. In evaluating
the debate over economic growth, it is important
to distinguish between the size of real output and
its _____. If the composition of output   composition
remains unchanged, economic growth [will/will not]   will
result in increased environmental problems. By
adjusting the composition of output in favor of
environmentally "clean" goods and services, however,
pollution can be controlled without the
curtailment of growth.

    Other things being equal in the short run,
economic growth may provide the [most/least] benefits   most
to the [employed/unemployed] through job creation   unemployed
and reduced unemployment rates.

Balanced Regional Development

The Economic Council of Canada stated in its first
Annual Review that, "Ever since Confederation the
notion of balanced regional development has been
an implicit, if not explicit, objective of national
policy." The Equalization Program of 1957
officially used _____ sharing to improve   tax
the imbalance between provinces. Since then, other
sharing programs have been established. There have
been numerous disagreements between the
_____ and the federal government concerning   provincial
the calculation of relative needs and wealth used   governments
for intergovernmental transfers.

SELF TEST
_____

These sample test items will help you check how much you have learned.
Answers and explanations can be found at the end of this book. Scoring
yourself: one or two wrong - on target. Three or four wrong - passing,
but you haven't mastered the chapter yet. Five or more wrong - not
good enough; start over and restudy the chapter.

Multiple Choice

1. The unemployment rate in Canada is
   a. the percentage of people 15 years and over in the labor force who are actively looking for work but who are not presently employed.
   b. the percentage of people 18 years and over in the labor force who are actively looking for work but who are not presently employed.
   c. the percentage of the labor force currently receiving unemployment insurance benefits.
   d. the percentage of people not in the labor force, for whatever reason.

2. Which of the following, on average, experience the highest unemployment rates?
   a. Teenagers.
   b. Women.
   c. Married men.
   d. Married women.

3. Between 1971 and 1981, wage and salary income in Canada
   a. rose roughly at the same rate as consumer prices.
   b. increased much more slowly than prices on average.
   c. rose more slowly than prices for workers in the forestry, mining, transport, and financial sectors.
   d. was not indexed to inflation for any workers.

4. Families heavily dependent on transfer payments have been protected from inflation to a considerable extent because
   a. many social welfare benefits are indexed.
   b. many transfers are made in kind.
   c. total transfer payments increased in real terms in the 1970s.
   d. all of the above are true.

5. If the expected real rate of interest is 2 percent and the expected rate of inflation is 8 percent, the nominal rate of interest must be
   a. 2 percent.
   b. 4 percent.
   c. 10 percent.
   d. The question cannot be answered unless the actual rate of inflation is known.

6. If the actual rate of inflation exceeds the expected rate of inflation, then
   a. the nominal rate of interest will be lower than the realized real rate of interest.
   b. the realized real rate of interest will be lower than the expected real rate of interest.
   c. the realized real rate of interest must be negative.
   d. creditors will gain at the expense of debtors.

7. The federal government
   a. pays lower wages and salaries during inflationary periods.
   b. benefits directly from inflation.
   c. has never indexed personal income taxes.
   d. both a and b.

8. Growth of potential real GNP is
   a. represented graphically by an outward shift of the production possibility frontier.
   b. estimated to be about 7 percent per year at present.
   c. possible only when prices are relatively stable.
   d. possible only when resources are fully employed.

9. If nominal GNP grows at a rate of 10 percent per year and inflation proceeds at a rate of 6 percent per year, real output will grow at a rate of
   a. 4 percent per year.
   b. 6 percent per year.
   c. 10 percent per year.
   d. 16 percent per year.

10. The idea of balanced regional development
    a. is rejected by many provincial governments because of its potentially destabilizing effects on the economy.
    b. has been an implicit goal of Canadian national policy since Confederation.
    c. has recently involved transferring tax revenues from the Maritimes to Alberta and Saskatchewan.
    d. has always won unanimous agreement from provincial governments.

HANDS ON

The Canadian labor force is defined as all members of the noninstitutionalized population over the age of 15, who are either officially employed or who are seeking employment (i.e., unemployed). The unemployment rate is calculated by dividing the number of unemployed persons in the labor force by the total labor force. The labor force participation rate is reached by dividing the labor force total by the population 15 years and older.

(a) Fill in the blanks below and calculate the participation and unemployment rates for each division of the labor force.*

---

* Source: The Labour Force, Statistics Canada, March 1983, Table 3, p. 24.

Labor Force
(Thousands)

	Population 15 Years and Over	Total =	Employ-ment	+ Unemploy-ment	% Parti-cipation Rate	% Unem-ployment Rate
Males						
15-24 years	2,251	_____	1,068	411	_____	_____
25 years and over	6,933	_____	4,844	614	_____	_____
All males 15 years and over	_____	_____	_____	_____	_____	_____
Females						
15-24 years	2,187	_____	1,080	247	_____	_____
25 years and over	7,375	_____	3,244	386	_____	_____
All females 15 years and over	_____	_____	_____	_____	_____	_____
Both sexes 15 years and over	_____	_____	_____	_____	_____	_____

(b) From your general knowledge of the labor force, why is the unemployment rate higher for persons 15 to 24 years of age than for those 25 and over?

Ottawa ready to pump millions into creating jobs in B.C.

Province News Services

VICTORIA — Federal Manpower Minister Lloyd Axworthy says he's willing to pump millions of job-creating dollars into B.C. to help people now collecting unemployment insurance benefits.

And if the provincial government isn't willing to share the cost of the program, Ottawa may go it alone.

"The money can be allocated with provincial support and agreement, which is certainly my preference, or we can work directly through federal departments where we have sole jurisdiction," he said.

Referring to the programs of other departments, Axworthy said total job-creation spending for 1981–82 was $351 million. Preliminary estimates released a year ago anticipated spending of $143 million — the rest came from supplementary estimates during the year.

"Main estimates for 1982–83 are, therefore, only a portion of the story," he said.

Axworthy said summer student employment programs will add $100 million to the total and another $25 million will come from job-creation plans announced last December. The government also expects to spend another $40 million under a work-sharing program and another $20 million in job-creation under the Unemployment Insurance Act.

This brings the real 1982–83 expected total to $386 million, he said.

Following a Victoria meeting with B.C. Labor Minister Jack Heinrich, Axworthy told reporters that new jobs could be in such areas as reforestation, environment, mining, parks and fishing.

A similar scheme in Ontario recently saw Ottawa contribute $11 million, matched by about the same amount from the province. The federal government claims about 3,000 jobs were created by the move.

Here's how the federal scheme works.

Axworthy said Ottawa has a pool of about $75 million taken from the unemployment insurance commission development fund. The money will be used to pay unemployment insurance recipients an extra $50 a week to go and work in areas designated by a province and Ottawa. In Ontario, most of the workers are doing reforestation jobs.

The extra $50 provided by Ottawa is expected to be "topped up" by a province.

*From the **Vancouver Province**, February 26, 1982, page A1. Reprinted by permission.*

1. List the four goals of economic stabilization policy and indicate which, if any, of these goals the federal government's job-creation programs are likely to help.

2. Why do you think the government is especially interested in summer student employment programs?

3. Is the government program mentioned in the last two paragraphs likely to increase the size of the labor force because of the extra $50 a week?

4. Do you think any of the programs mentioned in the article are designed to promote balanced regional development? Explain your answer.

CHAPTER 8
THE DETERMINANTS OF PLANNED EXPENDITURE

WHERE
YOU'RE GOING

When you have mastered this chapter, you will be able to:

- Draw a consumption schedule, given values for autonomous consumption and the marginal propensity to consume.

- Draw a saving schedule, given a corresponding consumption schedule.

- Distinguish between changes in economic conditions that cause movements along the consumption schedule and those that cause shifts in the schedule.

- Discuss the determinants of planned investment in terms of the expected real rate of return and the expected real rate of interest.

- Explain marginal efficiency of investment, and the determinants of planned investment.

- Distinguish between changes in economic conditions that cause movements along the planned investment schedule and those that cause shifts in the schedule.

- Describe the growth of government purchases of goods and services.

- Explain the determinants of net exports in the Canadian economy.

- Explain the meaning and significance of the following additional terms and concepts:

        dissaving
        marginal propensity to save
        lump sum taxes
        marginal propensity to import

WALKING TOUR

You have read the chapter at least once and have reviewed the summary in the text. Now you are going to walk through the material step by step, filling in the blanks and answering the questions as you go along.

After you have answered each question, check yourself by uncovering the answer given in the margin. If you do not understand why the answer given is the right one, refer back to the proper section of the text.

Consumption

As a general rule, consumers tend to devote part, but not all, of any increase in income to consumption. In numerical terms, this implies that their marginal propensity to consume is greater than _____   zero
but less than _____. This kind of   1
consumption behavior can be expressed in the form of a table such as the following:

Disposable Income	Consumption	Saving
1,000	1,400	-400
2,000	2,200	-200
3,000	3,000	0
4,000	3,800	200
5,000	4,600	400

This table incorporates a marginal propensity to
consume of _____ and a marginal propensity   0.8

to save of _____. Although not shown   0.2
explicitly in the table, autonomous consumption
can be determined to be _____. This is   600
the level of consumption that would prevail if
disposable income were to fall to _____.   zero
      In Exhibit S8.1, graph the consumption and
saving schedules given in the table above. Begin by
drawing in Exhibit S8.1(a) a 45° reference line -
that is, a straight line passing through the origin
with a slope of +1. Now draw the consumption
schedule; if correctly drawn, it intersects the
vertical axis at _____ and intersects $600
the 45° reference line at a disposable income of
_____. Next draw the saving schedule $3,000
in Exhibit S8.1(b). The saving schedule, if
correctly drawn, intersects the vertical axis at
a level of _____ and intersects the   -$600
horizontal axis at a disposable income of

_____. $3,000
      Changes in disposable income, other things
being equal, can be represented graphically as
[shifts in/movements along] a consumption schedule,   movements along
such as the one in Exhibit S8.1(a). A change in
consumer wealth or expectations can be represented
by a [shift in/movement along] the schedule. A   shift in
single permanent increase in the general price level
would produce a/an [upward/downward/uncertain] shift   an upward

in the consumption schedule. A change in the rate
of inflation tends to produce a/an [upward/downward/
uncertain] shift in the nominal consumption schedule,   an uncertain
although to the extent that an increase in inflation
triggers anticipatory buying, the direction of the
shift tends to be [upward/downward].   upward

Exhibit S8.1

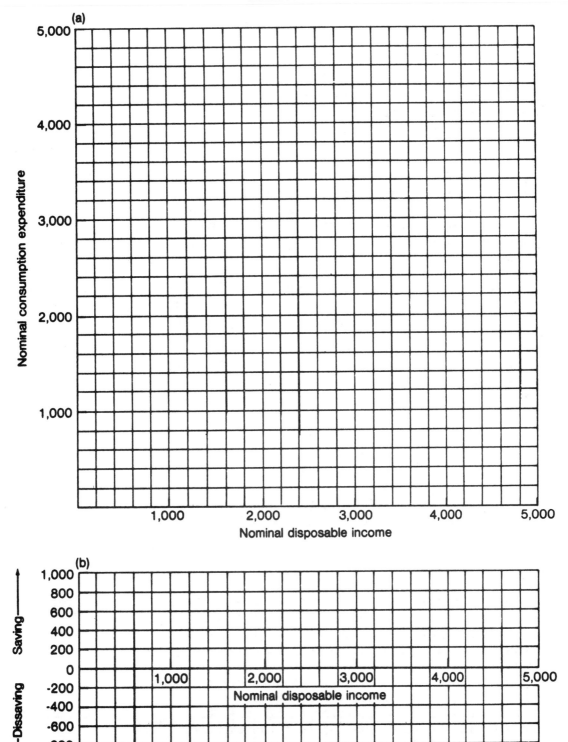

_____ taxes do not vary as income
varies, but they do [reduce/increase] the amount
of nominal national income that is available for
consumption and _____. That is, lump
sum taxes (and a proportional income tax) make
disposable income [greater/less] than nominal
national income.

A Simple Theory of Investment

In addition to consumption, planned investment
expenditure is a major component of aggregate
demand. Whether a firm is acquiring new fixed
investment capital or inventories, investment
always involves an _____ cost. The
opportunity cost of investment depends on the
_____ rate that must be paid for
borrowed funds, or the income that could be
earned by investing the firm's own funds elsewhere.
    As a firm's annual investment expenditures
[increase/decrease], the expected rate of return
from the last dollar invested tends to fall.
Expressed in economic terms, the _____
of investment [increases/decreases] as annual
investment increases. Therefore, it is profitable
for a firm to expand its annual investment [up to/
beyond] the point where the marginal efficiency
of investment falls below the _____
cost of capital, as represented by the market rate
of interest.
    Other things being equal, planned investment
is greater, the greater the expected real rate of
_____ and less, the greater the rate of
_____. The relationship between planned
investment and the rate of interest for the entire
economy can be represented graphically in a diagram
such as Exhibit S8.2. For example, the planned
investment schedule I_1 in that exhibit shows total
planned investment of _____ when the rate
of interest is 4 percent. Beginning from that
point, a 4 percentage point increase in the interest
rate, other things being equal, would [increase/
decrease] the amount of planned investment by
_____. This would be represented by a
[movement along/shift in] the planned investment
schedule. From that point, an increase in the
expected rate of inflation, with no further change
in the interest rate, would [increase/decrease]
planned investment expenditure and would be
represented by a [movement along/shift in] the
schedule I_1. Finally, suppose that the expected
rate of return on investment were to increase as

Lump sum
reduce

saving

less

opportunity

interest

increase

marginal efficiency
decreases

up to
opportunity

return

interest

$100

decrease
$50
movement along

increase

movement along

the result of an expected improvement in general
business conditions. This would produce a
[movement along/shift in] the planned investment   shift in
schedule. The final position of the planned
investment schedule after this shift would best be
represented by [I_2/I_3]. I_3

Exhibit S8.2

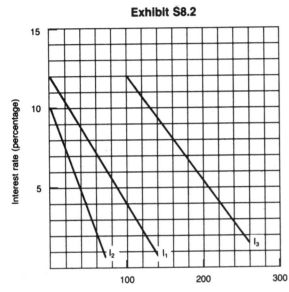

Planned investment (billions of dollars)

Other Types of Expenditure

A third major component of aggregate demand (the
first two components being consumption and planned
investment, as discussed already in this chapter)
is government purchases of goods and services.
Government spending has been [increasing/
decreasing] for a number of years, and is now   increasing
growing more [rapidly/slowly] than national output.   rapidly
    The fourth component of aggregate demand is
_____, which represents the difference   net exports
between the value of goods and services exported
to foreigners and the value of goods and services
imported from foreign countries. Foreign trade
is important to the Canadian economy and accounts
for approximately _____ percent of   25
GNP annually.
    Imports are generally determined by national
income, the _____ of foreign goods, and   price
the foreign exchange rate. The [higher/lower] the   lower

value of the Canadian dollar relative to the U.S. dollar, the fewer the goods and services likely to be imported from the United States by Canadians. _____ are generally determined by the national incomes of other countries, relative prices, and exchange rates.

Exports

The _____ to import is the proportion of each added dollar of disposable income that goes to added imports. Since the model in the text expresses the difference between disposable income and _____ (which is represented by the letter Y) as a _____ tax, the marginal propensity to import is also expressed as the proportion of each added dollar of national income that goes to added imports.

marginal propensity

national income

lump sum

In the textbook model, imports (M) are expressed by the formula $M=Ma+m(Y-T)$, where Ma is _____, the value of imports when Y is zero, m is the _____, and T is _____.

autonomous imports

marginal propensity to import; net taxes

Imports tend to [increase/decrease] as nominal national income rises, while our model assumes that exports [rise/fall/remain constant] as Y increases. Net exports are defined as _____ minus _____. Therefore, the net export schedule [rises/falls/remains constant] as Y increases.

increase

remain constant

exports; imports
falls

SELF TEST

These sample test items will help you check how much you have learned. Answers and explanations can be found at the end of this book. Scoring yourself: one or two wrong - on target. Three or four wrong - passing, but you haven't mastered the chapter yet. Five or more wrong - not good enough; start over and restudy the chapter.

Multiple Choice

1. According to Keynes, when disposable income increases, consumption increases
   a. but not by the full amount of the increase in disposable income.
   b. and saving decreases.
   c. by at least 90 percent of the increase in income.
   d. and saving increases by an equal amount.

2. If the marginal propensity to consume is 0.8, the marginal propensity to save
   a. is 0.2.
   b. is also 0.8.
   c. is 1/8.
   d. cannot be determined without more information.

3. If autonomous consumption is zero, then
   a. the marginal propensity to consume is 1.
   b. the marginal propensity to consume is zero.
   c. the consumption schedule lies entirely below the 45° reference line.
   d. saving is less than zero for all income levels.

4. Using MPS to stand for the marginal propensity to save and MPC to stand for the marginal propensity to consume, we can write
   a. MPS=MPC.
   b. MPS=1-MPC.
   c. MPC=MPS-1.
   d. MPS=$1/$MPC.

5. Which of the following events would not produce a shift in the consumption schedule, other things being equal?
   a. An increase in consumer wealth.
   b. An increase in autonomous consumption.
   c. An increase in the number of consumers expecting hard times in the near future.
   d. An increase in nominal disposable income.

6. If the consumption schedule is drawn on a diagram having nominal national income on the horizontal axis, an increased lump sum tax
   a. will increase the slope of the consumption schedule.
   b. will decrease the slope of the consumption schedule.
   c. will cause an upward parallel shift in the consumption schedule.
   d. will cause a downward parallel shift in the consumption schedule.

7. The opportunity cost of capital for an investment project
   a. is the interest rate that must be paid for borrowed funds.
   b. is the amount a firm could earn if it invested its own funds elsewhere.
   c. is not important to a firm's investment decisions.
   d. both a and b, depending on whether the firm borrows funds or uses its own money.

8. The planned investment schedule will shift upward if
   a. interest rates rise.
   b. interest rates fall.
   c. the expected rate of return on investment decreases.
   d. the expected rate of return on investment increases.

9. Government purchases are considered given for the purposes of elementary analysis, because
   a. the government is immune to inflation.
   b. government purchases are usually stated in nominal terms.
   c. the government does not have to pay interest on funds it borrows from the public.
   d. even though government purchases may be indirectly affected by national income and interest rates, the effects are too complex to be analyzed easily.

10. An increase in imports, other things being equal,
   a. adds to aggregate nominal demand.
   b. reduces aggregate nominal demand.
   c. increases the slope of the consumption schedule.
   d. does none of the above unless exports also change.

HANDS ON

Problem 1.

(a) Calculate the values for savings, marginal propensity to consume, and marginal propensity to save at various levels of nominal disposable income in the table below.

Nominal Disposable Income	Nominal Consumption Expenditure	Nominal Savings	Marginal Propensity to Consume	Marginal Propensity to Save
0	50			
200	210			
400	370			
600	530			
800	690			
1,000	850			
1,200	1,010			

(b) What is the value of autonomous consumption? What is the slope of the consumption schedule? The slope of the savings schedule?

(c) Graph the consumption schedule on the grid below. Draw in the 45° reference line and clearly indicate areas of dissavings and positive savings, as well as the point of zero savings.

Exhibit S8.3

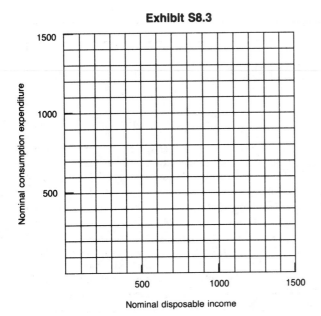

Nominal consumption expenditure (y-axis)
Nominal disposable income (x-axis)

Problem 2.

(a) Assuming that (m), the marginal propensity to import, is 0.10, and that autonomous imports are $50, calculate values for imports (M), using the values of nominal disposable income in Problem 1. Since net taxes (T) are zero in this example, nominal disposable income is equal to nominal national income.

(b) What is the slope of the import schedule in this example?

(c) Assuming exports remain constant at $100 for all levels of nominal national income, plot both exports and imports on grid a. Calculate net exports and plot the values on grid b, clearly indicating where net exports are positive, negative, and equal to zero.

Exhibit S8.4

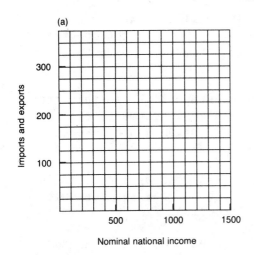

(a)

Imports and exports (y-axis)
Nominal national income (x-axis)

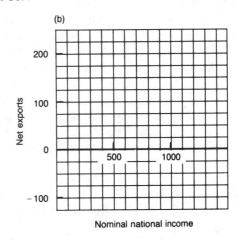

(b)

Net exports (y-axis)
Nominal national income (x-axis)

How to coax the consumer is the problem

By Frances Phillips

RETAILERS AND ANALYSTS are banking on the consumer to lead us out of the recession, but nobody is predicting a wild upswing later this year, or next year, or the year after.

"People have long memories. We won't see a big buying splurge, even if interest rates do come down," says George Hartman, vice-president and director of brokerage firm Brown Baldwin Nisker Ltd. in Toronto. "The consumer will come out of this period with very different priorities; he will be much more cautious," Hartman says.

The latest figures out of Statistics Canada demonstrate just how reluctant Canadians are to part with their money. After growing by 9.1% in 1980, and 12.5% in 1981, retail sales have slowed to a crawl. First-quarter 1982 sales were up only 2.7% from a year earlier and April sales not much better, at 3.2%. Taking price increases into account, that means a significant decline in "real" spending.

While April sales, totaling $8 billion, were somewhat affected by unseasonably cool temperatures, nothing could have lifted the spirits and spending habits of Canadians who appear to have lost confidence in the government's ability to put the economy on a recovery course.

Particularly hard hit are cars, appliances, furniture and sporting goods.

"The thing that's holding us back is not so much a lack of money, but a lack of confidence," says Leonard Kubas of Kubas Research Consultants in Toronto. "We are looking at a deterioration in consumer confidence the likes of which I haven't seen since the 1930s."

The severity of the recession has caused many retailers to panic. Depleted inventories have not been updated, orders for summer clothes were slashed, and the merchandise went on sale before summer even arrived. Consumers who have delayed purchasing something for the hot, sultry days ahead will be faced with a limited selection when, and if, they venture out into the shopping malls.

"If the savings rate would come down only a half of a percent, we would get a bit of a push," says Charles Barrett, vice-president and director of economic research at the Conference Board of Canada.

"If" is the operative word, especially since the mania for salting cash away shows no signs of subsiding.

*From **The Financial Post**, June 26, 1982, p. 1. Reprinted by permission.*

1. According to the article, how has the recession affected consumption in the Canadian economy? Would this best be illustrated by a movement along the consumption function or a shift in the function? In which direction has a movement or shift occurred? Give an explanation of your answer.

2. How has the recession affected planned investment? Would this best be illustrated by a movement along the planned investment schedule or by a shift in the schedule? In which direction has a movement or shift occurred? Explain your answer.

3. How, if at all, has the savings rate been affected by the recession? Do you think there has been a movement along the savings schedule or a shift in the schedule and in what direction?

4. Explain how the recession has affected aggregate demand in Canada.

CHAPTER 9
THE MULTIPLIER THEORY OF NATIONAL INCOME DETERMINATION

WHERE
YOU'RE GOING

When you have mastered this chapter, you will be able to:

- Draw an <u>aggregate nominal demand schedule</u> for an economy, given a consumption schedule and values for planned investment, government purchases, and net exports.

- Explain why the <u>aggregate nominal supply schedule</u> is always a 45° line passing through the origin.

- Determine the equilibrium level of nominal national income for the economy, using either the <u>Keynesian cross</u> or the leakages-injections approach.

- Explain what is meant by the <u>multiplier effect</u> and calculate the value of the <u>multiplier</u> for a given aggregate nominal demand schedule.

WALKING TOUR

You have read the chapter at least once and have reviewed the summary in the text. Now you are going to walk through the material step by step, filling in the blanks and answering the questions as you go along. After you have answered each question, check yourself by uncovering the answer given in the margin. If you do not understand why the answer given is the right one, refer back to the proper section of the text.

The Aggregate Demand and Supply Schedules

Exhibit S9.1 provides a space for you to construct a Keynesian cross diagram for a hypothetical economy similar, but not identical, to the one on which the numerical examples and diagrams of the text are based. Begin by drawing in the aggregate nominal supply schedule. This schedule begins at _____   the origin

and continues at an angle of _____ .   45°
    Next, construct the aggregate demand schedule. Assume a marginal propensity to consume domestic output of 0.5, a marginal propensity to import of 0, autonomous consumption of $2,500, net taxes of zero, planned investment of $1,000, government purchases of $1,500, exports of $800, and total imports of $300. The result should be a schedule that intersects the

vertical axis at _____ and intersects $5,500
the aggregate nominal supply schedule at an
equilibrium nominal national income of
_____. $11,000
        Remember that aggregate nominal demand is the
total of planned _____, which is   expenditure
C+I+G+(X-M). Consumption (C) is equal to autonomous
consumption (a) [plus/minus] the marginal propensity   plus
to _____ (b) times nominal disposable   consume
income (DI) or, what is the same thing as in our model,
nominal national income (Y) [plus/minus] net taxes   minus
(T). In algebraic terms, C=a+b(Y-T). Since net
taxes are _____ in this example, Y is   zero
equal to DI, or C=a+b(Y).

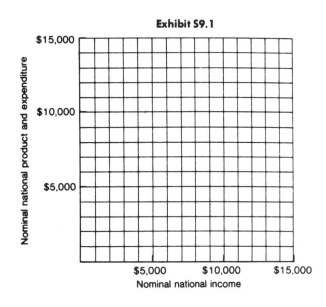

Exhibit S9.1

Finding the Equilibrium Level of Nominal National Income

Exhibit S9.2 provides a space in which to solve a
different income determination problem, using the
injections-leakages approach. Begin by drawing in a
saving schedule, assuming autonomous consumption of
$2,500 and a marginal propensity to consume domestic
output of 0.5 as before. (Marginal propensity to
import is zero.) This schedule should be a straight
line intersecting the vertical axis at _____   -$2,500

and intersecting the horizontal axis at _____. $5,000
Next, adjust for net taxes of $1,000 and imports of
$1,000 to give a total leakages schedule. This
schedule should intersect the vertical axis at
_____ and the horizontal axis at   -$500

_____. $1,000

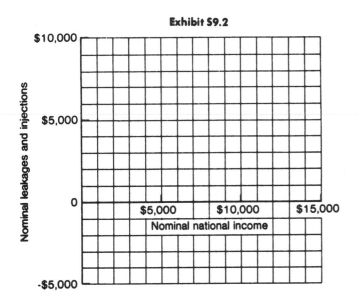

Exhibit S9.2

Now, construct a planned injections schedule,
assuming planned investment of $2,000, government
purchases of $2,000, and exports of $1,000. This
planned injections schedule should be a [horizontal/
vertical/45°] line intersecting the vertical axis at
_____.

        horizontal
        $5,000

The intersection of the leakages and injections
schedules as drawn in Exhibit S9.2 shows the
equilibrium level of nominal national income to be
_____ under the assumptions used. At a
nominal national income of $15,000, leakages would
[exceed/fall short of] injections by _____.
This would result in unplanned inventory [accumulation/
depletion], which in turn would tend to cause national
income to [rise/fall]. On the other hand, at a
nominal national income of $9,000, leakages would
[exceed/fall short of] injections, which would tend
to cause nominal national income to [rise/fall] as
inventories were [building up/drawn down].

        $11,000

        exceed; $2,000

        accumulation
        fall

        fall short of
        rise
        drawn down

Changes in Nominal National Income and the Multiplier Effect

Beginning from the position now represented in Exhibit
S9.1, any change in autonomous consumption, planned
investment, government purchases, or exports will
produce a [shift in/movement along] the aggregate
nominal demand schedule. For example, suppose
exports were to fall from $800 to $300. This would
produce a/an [upward/downward] shift of
_____ in the aggregate nominal demand
schedule. The new schedule (label it D2) would
intersect the vertical axis at _____

        shift in

        a downward
        $500

        $5,000

and would intersect the aggregate nominal supply
curve at an equilibrium nominal national income
of _____. $10,000
        Comparing the new and old equilibria in
Exhibit S9.1, you can see that a $500 decrease
in aggregate nominal demand has produced a
_____ decrease in equilibrium $1,000
nominal national income. It follows that the
value of the multiplier for this economy is
_____. This value could have been   2
calculated directly from the multiplier formula,
which is:
        Multiplier = _____ $1/(1-MPC_D)$

SELF TEST
_____

These sample test items will help you check how much you have learned.
Answers and explanations can be found at the end of this book. Scoring
yourself: one or two wrong - on target. Three or four wrong - passing,
but you haven't mastered the chapter yet. Five or more wrong - not
good enough; start over and restudy the chapter.

Multiple Choice

1. Which of the following would produce an upward shift in the aggregate
    nominal supply schedule?
    a. An increase in nominal GNP.
    b. An increase in real GNP.
    c. An increase in the marginal propensity to consume.
    d. None of the above.

2. When nominal national income exceeds its equilibrium value, there
    will be
    a. unplanned inventory depletion.
    b. unplanned inventory accumulation.
    c. a government budget deficit.
    d. a government budget surplus.

3. Whatever the actual level of nominal national income,
    a. the slope of the aggregate nominal demand curve must equal the
        slope of the leakages schedule.
    b. the gap between the aggregate nominal supply and demand curves
        must equal the gap between the injections and leakages schedules.
    c. injections must exceed leakages if aggregate nominal supply
        exceeds aggregate nominal demand.
    d. none of the above is true for all levels of nominal national
        income.

4. Other things being equal, an increase in imports will cause
   a. an increase in equilibrium nominal national income.
   b. a downward shift in the injections schedule.
   c. an upward shift in the leakages schedule.
   d. none of the above.

5. Beginning from an equilibrium position, an increase in planned investment expenditure would cause
   a. unplanned inventory depletion.
   b. an upward movement of prices, real output, or both.
   c. an upward shift in the injections schedule.
   d. all of the above.

6. If the marginal propensity to consume domestic output is 0.9, a $100 increase in planned investment expenditure, other things being equal, will cause an increase in equilibrium nominal national income of
   a. $90.
   b. $100.
   c. $900.
   d. $1,000.

7. If the marginal propensity to save is 0.1, and the marginal propensity to import is 0.3, the value of the multiplier must be
   a. zero.
   b. 2.
   c. 2.5.
   d. infinity.

8. If the marginal propensity to consume domestic output is 0.75, a $50 decrease in exports, other things being equal, would cause equilibrium nominal national income to
   a. increase by $50.
   b. decrease by $50.
   c. increase by $200.
   d. decrease by $200.

9. Suppose that for some economy, GNP = $2,000, consumption = $1,500, planned investment = $300, government purchases = $300, exports = $100, and imports = $200. It follows that
   a. the economy is in equilibrium.
   b. there must be unplanned inventory depletion.
   c. prices and/or real output will tend to rise.
   d. insufficient information is given for an answer to be reached.

10. If an economy is experiencing both inflation and rapid real economic growth, then
    a. it must have too large a multiplier.
    b. government purchases must exceed planned investment.
    c. nominal national income must be growing.
    d. all of the above must be true.

Problem 1. Assume autonomous consumption of $150, net taxes (T) of zero, planned investment (I) of $200, government purchases (G) of $200, exports (X) of $125, autonomous imports (Ma) of $50, a marginal propensity to consume (MPC) of 0.6, and a marginal propensity to import (MPM) of 0.1. Remember that the formula for imports (M) is $M=Ma+m(Y-T)$, where m represents the MPM. Also recall that since nominal national income (Y) minus T equals disposable nominal income (DI), Y=DI in this problem. In the space provided in Exhibit S9.3, construct a Keynesian cross diagram and use it to answer the questions that follow.

Exhibit S9.3

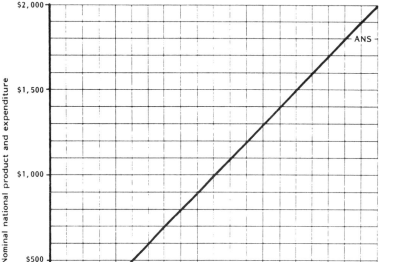

(a) What is the value of consumption (C) when DI is zero? When Y is zero? At what level does the consumption schedule intersect the vertical axis? What is the slope of the consumption schedule? At what point does the aggregate nominal demand schedule intersect the vertical axis? What is the slope of the aggregate nominal demand schedule?

(b) What is the equilibrium level of nominal national income as you have drawn your diagram? At a nominal national income of $1,500, would there be unplanned inventory accumulation or depletion? At a nominal national income of $900?

(c) Suppose aggregate nominal demand were to increase by $200, shifting the aggregate nominal demand schedule upward by that amount. Draw the new schedule and label it AND$_2$. What would be the new equilibrium level of nominal national income? What is the value of the multiplier for this economy?

Problem 2. Assume autonomous consumption of $250, net taxes (T) of zero, autonomous imports (Ma) of $50, planned investment (I) of $125, government purchases of $100, exports of $75, a marginal propensity to consume (MPC) of 0.6, and a marginal propensity to import (MPM) of 0.1. Using the injections-leakages approach and the space provided in Exhibit S9.4, answer the questions that follow. Remember that, as in Problem 1, nominal national income (Y) is equal to disposable nominal income (DI), since net taxes are zero.

Exhibit S9.4

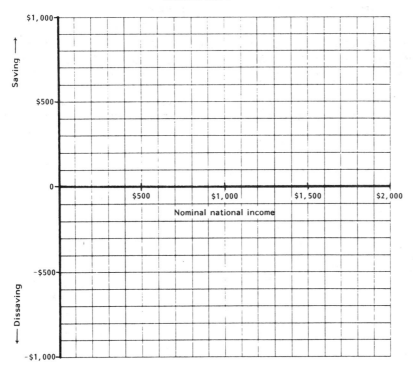

(a) What is the value of savings when DI is zero? When nominal national income is zero? What are the total leakages when nominal national income is zero? What is the marginal propensity to save (MPS)? What is the slope of the leakages schedule? Draw the leakages schedule and label it L_1.

(b) What are the total planned injections when nominal national income is zero? What is the slope of the injections schedule? Draw the planned injections schedule and label it J_1.

(c) What is the equilibrium level of nominal national income as your graph is drawn?

(d) Suppose that planned injections decreased by $100. Draw the new injections schedule and label it J_2. What is the new level of equilibrium nominal national income? What is the value of the multiplier?

(e) Return to the original starting point where L_1 and J_1 intersect. Suppose now that autonomous imports fall to $25. Draw the new leakages schedule and label it L_2. What is the new equilibrium level of nominal national income?

DON'T MAKE THIS COMMON MISTAKE!

Believe it or not, an amazing number of students lose marks on their exams because they don't learn how to calculate the multiplier. The formula, as you should remember, is:

Multiplier = $1/(1 - MPC_D)$ or $1/(MPS + MPM)$ or $1/1 - (MPC - MPM)$

'Buy Canadian' push fends off imports

By Frances Phillips

AS THE economy falters and unemployment becomes a major issue, both the public and private sectors are asking Canadians to check the label as well as the price tag. "Buy Canadian" is the catchword.

Following hard on the heels of advertisements placed by the private sector, which urged car buyers to favor North American automakers, federal and provincial governments, public institutions, and municipalities across Canada have hopped onto the bandwagon with import replacement programs of their own.

Latest figures show that $1.5-billion worth of furniture and fixtures, appliances, laboratory and scientific equipment, sporting goods, nonprinted educational supplies and materials, and audio-visual equipment used by Canadian government offices is imported each year.

"Our goal is to achieve a 10% reduction on imports by replacing them with Canadian goods of comparable price and quality," said Ontario Industry & Trade Minister Gordon Walker when he announced the cooperative effort in the Ontario Legislature earlier this year.

"Success in achieving this goal will garner $150 million in orders for Canadian manufacturers and generate at least 1,200 new jobs," says the minister.

The Buy Canadian initiative in Ontario is backed by a directory of Canadian manufacturers, and meetings around the province where local suppliers can meet government and institutional purchasing agents on a one-to-one basis.

As well, the Ontario government is continuing its 10% price preference policy, whereby purchasing agents pledge to buy Canadian-made products, even if they cost 10% more than comparable imports.

Stelco has been fighting the battle on imports from the other side of the fence.

To display its concern over the federal government's policy on auto imports, the company spent $500,000 on print advertisements to get the word across on North American cars. The underlying theme behind the comparison ads: "Buying North American cars is good for the economy."

No further advertisements are in the works, but Stelco has designed a sticker for North American car manufacturers, their dealers and related industries. The message reads: "Drive the cars that drive Canada's economy!" The company is also producing a 25-minute film which drives home the point that one in seven manufacturing jobs in Canada is directly or indirectly related to the auto industry.

From **The Financial Post**, *May 29, 1982, p. 14. Reprinted by permission.*

1. If the 'Buy Canadian' campaign is successful, which component (or components) of aggregate nominal demand will be affected? Will total aggregate nominal demand increase or decrease?

2. Will the multiplier for the Canadian economy increase, decrease, or remain the same if the 'Buy Canadian' campaign is successful? Explain your answer.

3. Other things being equal, do you think Canada would prefer to have a larger or smaller multiplier and why?

4. In what way is "Buying North American (in particular Canadian) cars ... good for the economy?"

CHAPTER 10
FISCAL POLICY AND THE MULTIPLIER THEORY

WHERE
YOU'RE GOING
_____

When you have mastered this chapter, you will be able to:

- Explain the control of aggregate demand by means of government fiscal policy.

- Define deflationary and inflationary gaps.

- Use the Keynesian cross to determine the size of the deflationary or inflationary gap (if any) prevailing in the economy, given demand conditions and an income target.

- Calculate the size and direction of change in government purchases or net taxes required to fill any given deflationary or inflationary gap.

- Calculate the net tax multiplier corresponding to any given marginal propensity to consume domestic output.

- Explain the difference between discretionary fiscal policy and automatic stabilizers.

- Describe the balanced budget multiplier.

- Critically evaluate arguments concerning the burden of the national debt.

In addition, after mastering the appendix to this chapter, you will be able to:

- Express the multiplier theory of national income determination in algebraic form.

- Use the algebraic form of the theory to calculate the fiscal policy measures required to achieve given policy objectives.

WALKING TOUR
_____

You have read the chapter at least once and have reviewed the summary in the text. Now you are going to walk through the material step by step, filling in the blanks and answering the questions as you go along. After you have answered each question, check yourself by uncovering the answer given in the margin. If you do not understand why the answer given is the right one, refer back to the proper section of the text.

Fiscal Policy in Action

Fiscal policy begins with the specification of a nominal income target thought best to serve the policy goals of full employment, price stability, real economic growth, and balanced regional development. Suppose that for the economy represented in Exhibit S10.1, the income target is $1,000. This target is [above/below] the equilibrium   below
level of nominal national income, which is
_____, as the figure is drawn. There is $2,000
thus a/an [inflationary/deflationary] gap of   an inflationary
_____ that must be overcome. Unless some $500
action is taken to eliminate the inflationary gap,
unplanned inventory [buildup/depletion] will occur   depletion
at the target income, preventing equilibrium from

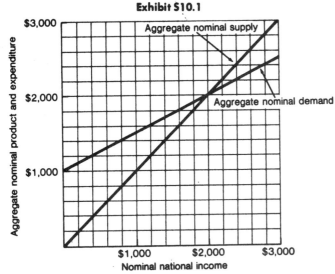

Exhibit S10.1

being achieved there. This unplanned inventory
depletion implies that injections will [exceed/fall
short of] leakages at the target nominal income.   exceed
    One fiscal policy action that could be used to
eliminate the inflationary gap in question would be to
[increase/decrease] government purchases by   decrease
_____. Given the multiplier of $500

_____ implied by the aggregate demand   2
schedule in Exhibit S10.1 (figured from the slope
of AND), this policy action would produce a
_____ decrease in equilibrium to the $1,000
target level of income.

Alternatively, the desired policy objective could be achieved by [raising/lowering] net taxes. For the economy shown in Exhibit S10.1, assuming a marginal propensity to consume of 0.75 (Calculate the MPC_D from the multiplier above or the aggregate nominal demand schedule in Exhibit S10.1.), the net tax multiplier is _____, indicating

raising

-1

that a _____ increase in taxes would be required to move equilibrium national income to the target level. Alternatively, the same thing could be accomplished with a $500 increase in taxes and a/an _____ [increase/ cut] in transfer payments. (Remember that transfer payments are multiplied by the net tax multiplier to determine their effect on nominal national income.)

$1,000

a $500 cut

If the government cut its purchases by $1,000 and decreased taxes by $1,000 at the same time, a _____ multiplier effect would occur. The resulting change would be to [raise/lower] nominal national income by _____.

balanced budget
lower
$1,000

Exhibit S10.2 presents another fiscal policy problem. The figure shows an economy with a marginal propensity to consume domestic output of _____, a multiplier of

0.8

_____, and an equilibrium nominal

5

national income of _____, under the demand conditions shown.

$700

Suppose now that policymakers set $1,200 as their nominal income target. Under the demand conditions shown, there is a/an [inflationary/ deflationary] gap of _____ at the target level of nominal national income. One

a deflationary
$100

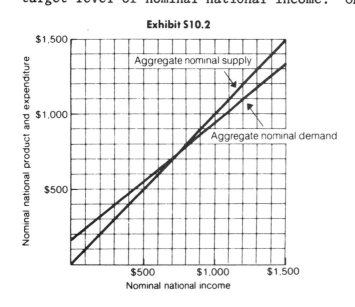

Exhibit S10.2

fiscal policy action that could fill the deflationary
gap would be a _____ [increase/decrease]
in government purchases. Alternatively, assuming
a marginal propensity to consume domestic output of
0.8, a tax [decrease/increase] of _____
would do the job. Finally, an increase of $25 in
social security payments to retired workers together
with an _____ increase in highway
construction would put income at the target level.

$100; increase

decrease; $125

$80

Exhibit S10.2 is drawn on the assumption of no
automatic stabilizers. Suppose, however, that the
assumed lump sum taxes were replaced by an income
tax that took $.20 of each dollar of added income for
all taxpayers. For each $1.00 increase in national
income, then, disposable income would increase by
_____ and consumption of domestic output

$.80

by _____. With such an income tax in
effect, government purchases required to raise the
equilibrium level of nominal national income by any
given amount would be [increased/reduced].

$.64 = (0.8 x 80¢)

increased

Discretionary Fiscal Policy and Automatic Stabilizers

When policymakers adjust taxes and government
spending to vary the level of aggregate demand in
the economy, they are using _____ fiscal
policy. An example of this policy is the tax
concessions made by the then Minister of Finance
John Turner in 1972.

discretionary

Fiscal policy measures that occur without special
action by Parliament are called _____.
This nondiscretionary policy causes changes in
_____ and _____ to occur
automatically as nominal GNP rises or falls.
Automatic stabilizers are a useful supplement to
discretionary policy and are not usually able to
provide full employment or price stability on
their own.

automatic stabilizers

taxes; transfers

Fiscal Policy and the National Debt

In order to move toward the goals of fiscal
policy, which are _____,

_____, _____, and

_____, it may be necessary for the
government to run deficits or acquire surpluses.
Arguments against growing deficits are often
heard from people arguing for "fiscal responsibility,"
but there are four arguments showing that no one need
be hurt by a growing national debt. If the trend is

full employment;
price stability;
economic growth;
balanced regional
  development

for the debt to [increase/decrease] relative to GNP,   decrease
as it has been in Canada since the end of World War II,
there should be little concern. A second argument
for not being concerned with the size of the national
debt is that the federal government will never go
bankrupt as long as it has the _____ of   power
_____. A third argument states that we   taxation
owe the debt to _____, and the fourth   ourselves
position states that we "can't build _____   today's houses
with _____," or that real goods and   tomorrow's bricks
services cannot be transferred from the future to the
present. It is important that the national debt not
be compared to _____ debt, since a private   private
individual cannot be compared accurately to the
government.

While the four arguments for not being concerned
about the national debt are good as far as they go,
unlimited debt creation is not wise for the following
four reasons: (1) If the [downward/upward] post World   downward
War II trend of national debt relative to GNP is
reversed, the debt could become a concern. Recent
[high/low] interest rates have also [increased/decreased]   high; increased
the proportion of GNP required to service the national
debt. (2) There are _____ to how high   limits
taxes can be raised to repay the national debt.
(3) Since the amount of the Canadian national debt
that is held by foreigners has [increased/decreased]   increased
in the 1970s, it is less true that the debt is
something Canadians owe to themselves. (4) The
national debt may impose a burden on _____   future
if government borrowing begins to crowd out private   generations
_____, on which future economic growth   investment
depends.

Your text concludes that "excessive short-run
reliance on _____ spending as a means of   deficit
promoting full employment may in the long run threaten
the ability of the economy to achieve price
_____ and real economic _____."   stability;
                                                         growth

Appendix to Chapter 10: Algebraic Approach
to Income Determination and the Multiplier (Optional)

Problem S1: Let autonomous consumption (a) be $200, lump sum net taxes
(T) be $125, planned investment (I) be $150, government purchases (G)
be $75, exports (X) be $75, autonomous imports (Ma) be $25, the
marginal propensity to consume (b) be 0.8, the marginal propensity to
import (m) be 0.2, and the marginal propensity to consume domestic
output (b_d) be 0.6. What is the equilibrium level of nominal national
income?

Solution: The equilibrium level of nominal national income is given by the formula

$$Y^* = 1/(1-b_d)\ [a-bT+I+G+X-(Ma-mT)].$$

Alternatively,

Y* = aggregate expenditure
$$Y^* = C+I+G+(X-M).$$

Substituting the given values into either version of the formula gives

Y* = _____, $1,000

where Y* is the equilibrium level of nominal national income.

Problem S2: Using the solution to Problem S1 as a starting point, find how large a tax cut would be required to achieve a target level of nominal national income of $1,300.

Solution: The gap between the current equilibrium level of income and the target level = $1,300 – $1,000 = _____. Let k stand for the $300
net tax multiplier.

$$-k \cdot \Delta T = \Delta Y$$
$$-1.5 \cdot \Delta T = 300$$
$$\Delta T = 300/{-1.5}$$
$$\Delta T = \underline{\qquad}$$ -$200

SELF TEST
_____

These sample test items will help you check how much you have learned. Answers and explanations can be found at the end of this book. Scoring yourself: one or two wrong - on target. Three or four wrong - passing, but you haven't mastered the chapter yet. Five or more wrong - not good enough; start over and restudy the chapter.

Multiple Choice

1. If the target level of nominal national income is $2,000, the equilibrium level of nominal national income is $2,500, and the marginal propensity to consume domestic output is 0.5, there is an inflationary gap of
    a. $500.
    b. $250.
    c. $125.
    d. none of the above.

2. If an inflationary gap were eliminated entirely through a fall in the equilibrium price level, with no change in equilibrium real output, policymakers would be
   a. delighted.
   b. disappointed.
   c. neither; the gap could not possibly be eliminated without a change in real output.
   d. neither; if real output did not change, prices would have to rise to eliminate an expansionary gap.

3. If the equilibrium level of nominal national income is $1,600, the target level of nominal national income is $2,000, and the marginal propensity to consume domestic output is 0.75, how large an increase in government purchases would be required to eliminate the deflationary gap?
   a. $75.
   b. $100.
   c. $400.
   d. None of the above; there is an inflationary gap.

4. If the target level of nominal national income exceeds the equilibrium level by $1,000 and the marginal propensity to consume domestic output is 0.8, which of the following changes in net taxes would eliminate the gap?
   a. A $200 cut.
   b. A $250 cut.
   c. A $200 increase.
   d. A $250 increase.

5. If the marginal propensity to consume is 0.7, and the marginal propensity to consume domestic output is 0.6, the value of the net tax multiplier must be
   a. -1.5
   b. -3
   c. -4
   d. -10

6. Which of the following would act as an automatic stabilizer?
   a. A progressive income tax.
   b. A law that automatically increases unemployment benefits when the unemployment rate rises above 6 percent.
   c. A tendency for imports, but not exports, to increase when nominal national income increases.
   d. All of the above.

7. Which of the following characterizes the Canadian national debt at the end of the 1970s?
   a. Smaller in relation to GNP than at the end of World War II.
   b. Owed increasingly to foreigners.
   c. Still a subject of debate among economists.
   d. All of the above.

The remaining questions in this section can be solved either graphically or by use of the algebraic approach described in the optional appendix to Chapter 10.

8. Let autonomous consumption equal 200; net taxes, 200; planned investment, 150; government purchases, 100; exports, 50; autonomous imports, 25; the marginal propensity to consume, 0.8; and the marginal propensity to import, 0.1. The equilibrium value of nominal national income is then closest to
   a. 290
   b. 826
   c. 1,116
   d. 2,117

9. Let autonomous consumption equal 400; net taxes, 200; planned investment, 500; exports, 100; autonomous imports, 200; the marginal propensity to consume, 0.6; and the marginal propensity to import, 0.1. To achieve a target level of nominal national income of 2,000, government purchases must equal
   a. 100
   b. 150
   c. 300
   d. none of the above.

10. Let autonomous consumption equal 600; planned investment, 250; government purchases, 400; exports, 100; autonomous imports, 50; the marginal propensity to consume, 0.80; and the marginal propensity to import, 0.05. In order to achieve an income target of 4,000, net taxes must be set at
   a. 65
   b. 400
   c. -400
   d. -1,600

HANDS ON

Now that you have reviewed the concepts introduced in this chapter, it is time for some hands-on practice with the analytical tools that have been introduced. Work through each problem in this section carefully, and then check your results against those given at the end of the book.

Problem 1.

Exhibit S10.3

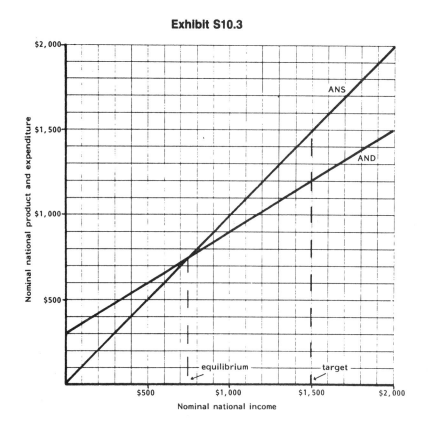

(a) As the exhibit is drawn, what is the marginal propensity to consume domestic output? What is the value of the multiplier?

(b) At the target level of nominal national income, is unplanned inventory accumulation or depletion occurring? Is there an inflationary or deflationary gap at the target income level? If so, what is the size of this gap?

(c) What change in government purchases would be necessary to attain the nominal national income target? What is the net tax multiplier? What change in net taxes would be required to reach the income target?

(d) If the federal budget is in balance at the equilibrium level of nominal national income, what policy could allow the income target to be reached without disturbing the balance? (Use changes in government purchases and net taxes; ignore the effects of automatic stabilizers.) What is the effective multiplier in this situation?

The deficit: Not as bad as some think

By Clarence L. Barber

WINNIPEG — Like a dark cloud which keeps growing larger, the federal deficit overhangs all of Ottawa's policy initiatives. Why is the federal deficit so large? Why does it keep growing? Is there nothing we can do about it?

Economists who advocate deficit spending have long been prone to neglect the fact that governments must pay interest on the debt these deficits create. When interest rates were only 3% or 4% this scarcely seemed to matter. Interest expense grew slowly and when the economy recovered, the deficits often disappeared. The federal budget was in surplus in seven of the 11 years from 1964 through 1974 and accumulated a net surplus of $3.1 billion over this period.

When interest rates are 12%–14% or higher it is quite a different story. At 12%, the interest expense on last year's deficit alone accounts for more than half of the forecast rise in the deficit. Applied to the increased debt created by the government over the past five years, interest at 12% adds about $4 billion to annual interest costs and increases the deficit by a similar amount. Is deficit finance under current circumstances a self-defeating process under which the government rapidly paints itself into a corner where it has little room to manoeuvre?

In fact, the picture is really not as dark as that. Some of our difficulties are simply those of perception. Consider how different the deficit picture would look if the government issued fully indexed bonds, bonds on which interest and principal would increase each year at the same rate as the consumer price index. Such bonds might well carry a coupon rate of 3% or lower. Interest costs would be one quarter or less of their present level. Total government spending would at once fall by $6 billion, and the deficit would suddenly become little more than half of its present size.

Thus, in a fundamental economic sense the government's deficit is not nearly as large as it seems. Current interest rates contain a large inflation premium which serves to protect the bondholder against the decline in the buying power of his bonds as prices rise. No one knows exactly how large this inflation premium is but it may well be 9% or more. Interest expense corresponding to this inflation premium really should be removed from the government's current budget. Financing of this part of interest costs has no more economic significance than refunding bonds or treasury bills which come due for redemption.

What can our government do to present a clearer picture of its finances? One solution would be to publish an inflation-adjusted budgetary statement. In this statement, debt interest would be adjusted to remove that part judged to represent the inflation premium.

An alternative would be to gradually replace all or a large part of the government's current bond issues with fully indexed bonds. Such a step would have other advantages as well. If Canada Savings Bonds were indexed the small saver would be protected against the effects of inflation and the government would no longer have to face the problem of large redemptions whenever interest rates move to higher levels.

Finally, it is worth noting that by international standards the Canadian deficit is not all that high. In 1979, Canada's deficit (all levels of government) was 2.2% of GNP; West Germany's deficit was 3.1% of GNP, Japan's 4.9% and Italy's 11.1%. No one is advocating deficits of this size for Canada. But these figures help put our own picture into proper perspective.

*From **The Financial Post**, July 5, 1980. Reprinted by permission.*

NOTE: A bond is a promise, given in recognition of a loan, to make a fixed annual or semiannual payment (sometimes called a coupon payment) over a period of years plus a final repayment equal to the principal sum initially borrowed.

1. The text mentions that economists hold a variety of opinions on government debt and deficits, and one opinion is presented in this article. Explain in your own words what changes Professor Barber

is suggesting for the way in which government deficit totals should be calculated.

2. Is the idea of removing the interest expense corresponding to the inflation premium similar to the GNE deflator that the text discussed earlier? Explain your answer.

3. Since Canada's deficit is considerably smaller than that of West Germany and Italy, should we cease to be concerned about the present size of the Canadian government deficit? What aspects of the government debt must be taken into consideration to answer this question?

4. The article says that in the past "deficits often disappeared" during periods of economic recovery. Why do you think this might happen?

UPDATE: In 1981, Canada's deficit was 0.7% of GNP, West Germany's deficit was 4.4% of GNP, Japan's 3.6%, and Italy's 9.4%.* By 1982, Canada's deficit had grown to 5.25% of GNP.
(*Economic Review, April 1982.)

CHAPTER 11
CHARTERED BANKS
AND OTHER FINANCIAL INTERMEDIARIES

WHERE
YOU'RE GOING

When you have mastered this chapter, you will be able to:

- List the main types of financial intermediaries and explain their position in the economy in terms of the circular flow.

- Explain the significance of chartered bank reserves and required reserve ratios.

- Understand and explain the meaning of the major entries on the balance sheet of a chartered bank.

- Briefly describe the structure and function of the Bank of Canada and the banking system.

- Discuss the nature and functions of the major types of near banks and contractural savings institutions.

- Explain the functions of the insurance industry as a supplier of protection against risk and as a financial intermediary.

- Distinguish between primary and secondary securities markets and explain the functions of each.

- Explain the meaning and significance of the following terms and concepts:

    assets
    liabilities
    net worth

WALKING TOUR

You have read the chapter at least once and have reviewed the summary in the text. Now you are going to walk through the material step by step, filling in the blanks and answering the questions as you go along. After you have answered each question, check yourself by uncovering the answer given in the margin. If you do not understand why the answer given is the right one, refer back to the proper section of the text.

Chartered Banks

A chartered bank is a financial _____ ,   intermediary

whose major function is to channel _____   funds

from savers to _____ . A good way to   investors or
                                                          borrowers
understand the functions of a chartered bank (or
any other financial intermediary) is to look at its
balance sheet. The balance sheet of the Brandon
National Bank consists of the following items:

Demand deposits	$500
Loans	500
Other assets	50
Reserves	150
Securities	300
Savings deposits	200
Notice deposits	200

In the space that follows, put these entries in
balance sheet form.

First divide the space into two columns. The left-
hand column will contain all of the things to which
the bank holds legal claim, that is, its
_____ . Label it accordingly. The   assets
right-hand column will contain financial claims
against the bank, or _____ , and also the   liabilities
difference between assets and liabilities, or

_____ .   net worth
    Now begin by filling in the assets column. The
two items from which the bank earns the majority of
its income are _____ and _____ .   loans; securities
Funds kept on deposit with the Bank of Canada and
vault cash are included here under _____ .   reserves
Tangible assets, such as the bank's buildings and
office equipment, are listed as _____ .   other assets
Total assets of the Brandon bank thus come to

_____ . $1,000
    Moving to the right-hand side of the balance

sheet, begin by listing chequing accounts, more exactly known as _____ deposits. Next come _____ and _____ deposits. These are interest-paying accounts at chartered banks, against which it is not ordinarily possible to write cheques. Draw a line under this list of deposits and add them up, labeling the sum as total liabilities. On a line below this enter the bank's net worth, which in this case is _____. Note that assets equal liabilities plus net worth; this is the fundamental equality underlying your balance sheet, which is now complete.

demand

notice; savings

$100

The Bank of Canada

The Bank of Canada is the central bank of Canada and was established in 1934 as a result of growing demands for better monetary leadership. The Bank of Canada is managed by a governor, a deputy governor, _____ directors, and the deputy minister of finance, who advises but has no vote in decision making.

twelve

The Bank of Canada is expected to make and execute _____ for the nation, and it is designed to be fairly free from political influence.

monetary policy

The Banking System

The Canadian banking system resembles the [British/ United States] system more closely than it does the [British/United States] system, which has approximately 15,000 separate banks. Many of Canada's banks are large and have [no/few/many] branches.

British
United States

many

Nonbank Financial Intermediaries

Many financial institutions such as _____, _____, _____, _____, and _____ perform many of the same functions as banks. These institutions act as go-betweens for [savers/ investors] with funds to lend and [investors/ savers] who want to borrow.

caisses populaires;
trust companies;
mortgage-loan
 companies;
credit unions;
consumer loan
 companies
savers
investors

Insurance companies act as financial intermediaries and also sell _____. The lag between the time premiums are paid in and and the time claims are paid out gives the companies

risk protection

a large pool of funds, which they use to acquire
such assets as _____, _____,   stocks; bonds
and _____.   commercial
                                                             mortgages

The markets in which stocks and bonds are sold also
play a key role in channeling funds from savers to
investors. Sales of newly-issued securities from firms
to households and other financial and nonfinancial firms,
through brokers and underwriters, take place in
_____ securities markets. Markets like   primary
the Toronto Stock Exchange, where previously
issued securities are traded among asset holders,
are known as _____ securities markets.   secondary

SELF TEST

These sample test items will help you check how much you have learned.
Answers and explanations can be found at the end of this book. Scoring
yourself: one or two wrong - on target. Three or four wrong - passing,
but you haven't mastered the chapter yet. Five or more wrong - not
good enough; start over and restudy the chapter.

Multiple Choice

1. In Canada, financial intermediaries include
   a. chartered banks.
   b. credit unions and caisses populaires.
   c. insurance companies and securities markets.
   d. all of the above.

2. In Canada, the word "bank" is used by
   a. a variety of financial intermediaries.
   b. institutions that receive a special charter and operate under
      the Bank Act.
   c. any institution that uses savers' funds to make loans.
   d. seven institutions in Canada.

3. If a bank has assets of $100 and liabilities of $80, its net worth is
   a. $20.
   b. -$20.
   c. $180.
   d. none of the above; by definition, assets must equal liabilities.

4. Which of the following is not an important asset of chartered banks?
   a. Reserves.
   b. Loans.
   c. Securities.
   d. Demand deposits.

5. Liabilities of chartered banks include
   a. deposits with foreign banks.
   b. loans to foreigners.
   c. mortgages.
   d. Canadian savings or notice deposits.

6. Reserves of chartered banks
   a. include only deposits the banks hold in the Bank of Canada.
   b. must equal 50 percent of all demand deposits held by the banks.
   c. include cash and non-interest-bearing deposits held with the Bank of Canada.
   d. varies for each bank according to what the individual manager thinks is necessary.

7. The Bank of Canada is
   a. a division of the Treasury department.
   b. part of the Department of Finance.
   c. owned by the chartered banks.
   d. a relatively independent central bank.

8. The Canadian banking system is
   a. very similar to the American banking system.
   b. a branch banking system.
   c. a system with approximately 4 separate banks.
   d. all of the above.

9. Insurance companies earn income in part by
   a. selling risk protection.
   b. buying corporate securities and commercial mortgages.
   c. selling annuities.
   d. all of the above.

10. Newly-issued securities are sold for the first time through
   a. primary securities markets.
   b. secondary securities markets.
   c. either of the above.
   d. neither of the above.

APPLICATION

Note: Although this article refers to a specific period in banking history (i.e., the article was published on July 14, 1980), it is worth studying because of the generalities it contains about the banking business.

Banks' image tarnished

OTTAWA (CP) — The wildly-fluctuating interest rates of the [first half of 1980] probably have not made new friends for the chartered banks.

Consumers deferred major purchases and businessmen shelved expansion plans as the cost of money soared.

And accusations of gouging by the banks have intensified as interest levels began falling.

Yet the public image of bankers is not the only casualty of the current round of ups and downs in interest rates.

Financial analysts say the banking industry is in its worst slump in years and isn't making windfall profits at the expense of its clients.

"It's a classic example of perception versus reality," says Hugh Brown, a banking specialist with Burns Fry Ltd. in Toronto.

Here's how Brown and other experts respond to some of the questions raised by the continuing debate on bank profits and interest rates:

How can banks complain about hard times when they make hundreds of millions of dollars a year in profits?

The experts agree bank profits look mind-boggling to the average Canadian but they say clear profits haven't kept pace with the growth in domestic assets of the banks.

Why were the banks quick to raise interest rates [in the fall of 1979] and why are they so slow about lowering them [in the summer of 1980]?

The banks are said to be trying to improve the spread between what they earn on loans, mortgages and other investments and what they pay on deposits and their own borrowings in the money markets.

There seems to be no simple way, however, to calculate the spread of a particular bank from the interest rates that prevail at any given time.

That's because the mix of assets and liabilities of the banks changes all the time. Some transactions carry fixed interest rates while others rise and fall with the prevailing market.

The experts don't all agree the banks were squeezed severely as interest rates moved up to record levels [in 1980]. But the consensus in the financial community is that the squeeze is on as rates fall.

The banks began the [third] quarter [of 1980] chained to short-term funds they borrowed when interest rates were still high. As those funds are replaced by lower-cost money, the banks will be in a better position to lower the rates they charge on loans.

Most analysts see the rates on all kinds of loans falling in the [second half of 1980 and 1981] and the profits of banks improving as a result.

"If we had to give a rule of thumb, it is that rising rates hurt the banks and falling rates help the banks," says Victor Koloshuk of McLeod Young Weir Ltd. of Toronto.

From **Winnipeg Free Press**, July 14, 1980. Reprinted by permission of Canadian Press.

1. Chartered banks are businesses like any others that try to make a profit. According to the article, how do banks earn their profits?

2. Based upon what you know about banking and what you have learned from the article, name at least three costs incurred by the banking business.

3. Why were bank profits falling at the time this article was written?

4. Would you expect nonbank financial intermediaries to try to steal business from chartered banks at this particular time? If so, how would they try to attract business?

CHAPTER 12
THE SUPPLY OF MONEY

WHERE
YOU'RE GOING
_____

When you have mastered this chapter, you will be able to:

- Define money in terms of the functions it performs and explain why
  money is the most liquid asset.

- Explain how M_1 and M_2 are defined and discuss the problems with
  these definitions that have led some economists to recommend new
  ways of measuring the money supply.

- Define and give examples of near money.

- Explain the relationship between credit cards and money.

- Explain the required reserve ratio that the Bank of Canada imposes
  on chartered bank deposits.

- Trace the progress of expansion or contraction of the money supply
  in response to a change in chartered bank reserves, using balance
  sheets for a simplified banking system.

- Calculate the money multiplier for a simplified banking system and
  explain why the money multiplier for the actual Canadian economy
  is subject to variation over time.

- Describe the five monetary policy instruments used by the Bank of
  Canada: open market operations, moral suasion, draw downs and
  redeposits, the bank rate, and changes in required reserve ratios.

- Describe the nature of the money growth targets set by the Bank of
  Canada and explain why the Bank of Canada does not always maintain
  actual money growth within the prescribed target ranges.

- Explain the meaning and significance of the following additional
  terms and concepts:

      currency
      demand deposits
      notice deposits
      excess reserves

You have read the chapter at least once and have reviewed the summary in the text. Now you are going to walk through the material step by step, filling in the blanks and answering the questions as you go along. After you have answered each question, check yourself by uncovering the answer given in the margin. If you do not understand why the answer given is the right one, refer back to the proper section of the text.

Money and Its Functions

Throughout history many things have served as money, but to be serviceable, money must serve the following three functions: (1) _____;

(2) _____; and (3) _____.

means of payment; store of purchasing power; unit of account power

Any asset that can be used directly as a means of payment (or easily converted into a means of payment) and which runs little or no risk of change in nominal value is termed _____. Using this definition, rank the following assets in order of their liquidity (1 = most liquid):

liquid

Corporate stocks   5
Ninety-day certificate of deposit   4
Coins   1
Passbook savings deposit   3
Chequing account   2
Real estate   6

Measuring the Quantity of Money

The most widely used measure of the money supply, consisting of currency plus demand deposits in chartered banks, is the quantity known as
_____. Adding savings and notice deposits at chartered banks gives a broader measure of the money supply known as _____.

M_1

M_2

Creation of Money by the Banking System

One way to understand how the banking system works and how the Bank of Canada controls the supply of money is to look at a simplified banking system in which demand deposits are the only form of money and the only chartered bank liability.

Suppose that demand deposits are subject to a uniform 20 percent required reserve ratio and that banks keep no _____ reserves. Initially, all banks in the system

excess

look like this:

Bank A

Assets		Liabilities	
Reserves	$20,000	Demand deposits	$100,000
Required $20,000			
Excess 0			
Loans	50,000		
Securities	30,000		
Total assets	$100,000	Total liabilities	$100,000

Suppose now that the Bank of Canada makes an open market purchase of $1,000 in government securities for the purpose of [increasing/decreasing] reserves available to the banking system. The seller of the securities is paid with a cheque drawn on the Bank of Canada; when this cheque is deposited in a chartered bank, for instance the Royal Bank, the effect will be to make its balance sheet, which initially looked like the one above, look like this:

increasing

	Assets	Demand deposits	Liabilities
Reserves	(1) _____		(2) _____
Required (3) _____			
Excess (4) _____			
Loans	50,000		
Securities	30,000		
Total Assets	(5)_____	Total liabilities	(6)_____

Answers: (1) $21,000   (2) $101,000   (3) $20,200
          (4) $800   (5) $101,000   (6) $101,000

The Royal Bank could now increase its earnings by using its excess reserves to finance _____ in new loans or to buy the equivalent in additional securities. Suppose that it chooses to make the loan and that the borrower writes a cheque for the amount of the loan, which is subsequently deposited in the Toronto Dominion Bank. After all of these transactions have taken place, total reserves at the Royal Bank will be _____, _____ of which will be

$800

$20,200; all

required reserves, given the _____ $101,000
in demand deposits. Assuming that the Toronto
Dominion Bank starts with the same initial
balance sheet, its deposits will now be
_____. Its total reserves will be $100,800
_____, of which _____ $20,800; $20,160
will be required and _____ excess. $640
That means that it can add earning assets of
_____ in the form of loans or $640
securities. As the process continues, more and
more of the initial $1,000 in reserves injected
into the banking system by the Bank of Canada
will be converted into required reserves. When
the money expansion process is complete, total
demand deposits of all banks (and hence the total
money supply) will have increased by
_____. The value of the money $5,000
multiplier for this simplified economy is
_____, and can be calculated from   5
the formula 1/_____.   required reserve
    ratio

Instruments and Problems of Monetary Policy

In the example given above, the Bank of Canada
was able to set in motion an expansion of the
money supply by making an open market [purchase/
sale].   purchase

     Despite the variety of policy instruments
available, the Bank of Canada is not able to
exercise perfect control over the money supply.
One reason is that as funds are shifted from one
type of account to another, from chartered banks
to other nonbank financial intermediaries, or from
bank accounts to currency, the _____   money multiplier
varies.

     Besides open market operations, the Bank of
Canada has four other instruments of monetary policy.
These are _____, whereby the Bank attempts   moral suasion
to persuade the chartered banks to follow certain
policies; _____ and _____,   draw downs;
which are transfers of government deposits between   redeposits
the Bank of Canada and chartered banks;
_____ changes that vary the interest   bank rate
rate paid by chartered banks who borrow reserve
funds from the Bank of Canada; and changes in the
_____ ratio for chartered banks.   required reserve

     The cash or _____ reserve ratio   primary
is set by the Bank Act and cannot be varied as a
_____ policy tool. However, the Bank   monetary

of Canada can vary the _____ reserve   secondary
ratio, which determines the percentage of chartered
bank _____ that must be held in the form   deposits
of [liquid/illiquid] interest-bearing assets.   liquid

    Even with the monetary instruments available
to the Bank of Canada, real world problems make it
very difficult to meet announced monetary policy
objectives. The Bank of Canada generally regards
actual M_1 growth rates within _____ .   2
percent of the target as successful.

SELF TEST

Multiple Choice

1. Which of the following assets is least liquid?
   a. Coins.
   b. Demand deposits.
   c. Notice deposits.
   d. Chequing accounts.

2. To function properly, money must be
   a. a unit of account.
   b. a medium of exchange.
   c. a store of purchasing power.
   d. all of the above.

3. Since 1945, all currency in Canada has been issued by
   a. the federal government.
   b. the chartered banks.
   c. the Bank of Canada.
   d. The Department of Finance.

4. In a simplified banking system, in which all banks are subject to
   a uniform 20 percent reserve requirement, and in which demand
   deposits are the only form of money, a $2,000 open market purchase
   by the Bank of Canada would cause the money supply to
   a. increase by $2,000.
   b. decrease by $2,000.
   c. increase by $10,000.
   d. decrease by $10,000.

5. In a simplified banking system, in which all banks are subject to uniform reserve requirements, in which demand deposits are the only form of money, and in which the initial quantity of money is $100 million, an increase in the required reserve ratio from 10 percent to 20 percent would cause the money supply to
   a. fall to $50 million.
   b. fall to $20 million.
   c. rise to $200 million.
   d. rise to $500 million.

6. In a simplified banking system, in which all banks are subject to a uniform reserve requirement of 20 percent, and in which demand deposits are the only form of money, a bank receiving a new deposit of $10,000 would be able to extend a maximum of what amount in new loans? (Remember that this problem asks for only the initial effect.)
   a. $2,000
   b. $8,000
   c. $9,000
   d. $10,000

7. If a bank subject to a 10 percent required reserve ratio has $20,000 in excess reserves, it can purchase, at a maximum, which amount of new securities?
   a. $2,000
   b. $18,000
   c. $20,000
   d. $200,000

8. If Bank A is subject to a 10 percent required reserve ratio on demand deposits and Bank B is subject to a 20 percent required reserve ratio, a shift of funds from Bank A to Bank B would
   a. tend to cause the money supply to fall.
   b. tend to cause the money supply to rise.
   c. have no effect on the money supply.
   d. tend to cause <u>a</u> in the simplified system, <u>b</u> in the real world.

9. The rate of interest charged to chartered banks by the Bank of Canada for reserves borrowed from the Bank of Canada is known as
   a. the federal funds rate.
   b. the bank rate.
   c. the repurchase rate.
   d. the near money rate.

10. The real world money multiplier (the M_1 multiplier)
    a. is identical to the money multiplier used in the text's simplified banking system.
    b. varies when funds shift from chartered banks to near banks.
    c. varies because chartered banks sometimes keep excess reserves.
    d. both <u>b</u> and <u>c</u>.

Now that you have reviewed the concepts introduced in this chapter, it is time for some hands-on practice with the analytical tools that have been introduced. Work through each problem in this section carefully, and then check your results against those given at the end of the book.

Problem 1. The following questions refer to Exhibit S12.1, which shows the balance sheet of a typical bank in a simplified banking system.

Exhibit S12.1
Balance Sheet of Sycombeville National Bank

Assets			Liabilities	
Reserves		$ 25,000	Demand Deposits	$250,000
Required	$25,000			
Excess	0			
Loans		225,000		
Total assets		$250,000	Total Liabilities	$250,000

(a) What is the required reserve ratio for the bank shown? If all banks have the same required reserve ratio, what is the money multiplier for this banking system?

(b) If this bank received a new deposit of $50,000, what would it do with the funds in order to maximize profit?

(c) The Bank of Canada makes an open market sale of $100,000. The buyer pays for the sale by writing a cheque on the Sycombeville National Bank. What is the immediate impact on Sycombeville's reserve position? What would this bank do in response to the change in its reserve position? What would be the effect of the open market sale on the money supply as a whole once the banking system had returned to equilibrium?

Problem 2. The following questions refer to Exhibit S12.2, which shows the balance sheet of a typical bank in a different simplified banking system.

Exhibit S12.2
Balance Sheet of Random National Bank

Assets			Liabilities	
Reserves		$ 20,000	Demand Deposits	$100,000
Required	$25,000			
Excess	-5,000			
Loans		80,000		
Total Assets		$100,000	Total Liabilities	$100,000

(a) What is the required reserve ratio for this bank? What is the money multiplier for this banking system?

(b) Is the bank in a position of equilibrium as the balance sheet is shown? If not, what would it do to achieve equilibrium in the simplified banking system? In the real world, what other options would a similarly situated bank have in trying to achieve equilibrium?

(c) Assume that this bank makes the necessary adjustments to return to balance sheet equilibrium. Then the Bank of Canada makes a $10,000 open market purchase. The party selling securities to the Bank of Canada deposits the funds in the Random National Bank. What is the immediate impact on Random's reserve position? What actions would Random take to attain equilibrium? What would be the effect on the money supply once the banking system as a whole had attained equilibrium?

Problem 3. The following questions are based on Exhibit S12.3, which shows an incomplete balance sheet for a typical bank in a third simplified banking system.

Exhibit S12.3
Balance Sheet of Tylertown National Bank

Assets			Liabilities	
Reserves		$_____	Demand Deposits	$500,000
Required	$_____			
Excess	5,000			
Loans		370,000		
Total Assets		$_____	Total Liabilities	$500,000

(a) Begin by filling in the blanks in the balance sheet. What is Tylertown's required reserve ratio? Assuming other banks in the system have the same required reserve ratio, what is the money multiplier for the system?

(b) Is Tylertown in balance sheet equilibrium as shown? If not, what would it do to attain balance sheet equilibrium? In the real world, what other options to attain equilibrium would a similarly situated bank have?

(c) Beginning from just the position shown, suppose a new Bank Act cuts the required reserve ratio to 20 percent. What would be the immediate impact on Tylertown's reserve position? What would it do to attain equilibrium? If the complete banking system consists of 10 banks just like Tylertown, with exactly the beginning balance sheet shown, what will the total money supply be after the reserve requirement is cut and all banks have achieved equilibrium?

DON'T MAKE THESE COMMON MISTAKES!

Many student mistakes in macroeconomics arise from careless use of the word money. As you have learned in this chapter, money has a single, specialized meaning in the language of economics--an asset serving as a means of payment, a store of value, and a unit of account. Unfortunately, in everyday life, the word money is used very loosely. Try to break the habit of these loose usages when speaking the language of economics. Here are some examples:

Everyday language: "After Joan got the promotion, she earned a lot more money than before." Economics language: "After Joan got the promotion, she earned a higher income than before." Income is a flow, a measure of the value of what Joan is paid. Maybe she decides, after her promotion, to save part of her income, adding to the stock of money she has in her chequing account; maybe she spends it all, adding to her stock of consumer goods; we don't know without more information.

Everyday language: "The federal government's defense spending plans will pump so much money into the economy that inflation will become a real danger." Economics language: "The federal government's defense spending plans will add so much to planned expenditure that inflation will become a real danger." What starts as a slip of terminology here could grow into a confusion between fiscal and monetary policy. Defense spending adds to the flow of aggregate demand; it is a fiscal policy action. Such spending does not add directly to the stock of money which is under control of the Bank of Canada. Think of an electric mixer beating a bowl of cake mix. Fiscal policy is like turning up the speed on the mixer--the batter in the bowl flows around faster than before, but there is still the same amount of it. Monetary policy adds to the stock of money in the economy just as a cook might add to the quantity of batter in the bowl by breaking in another egg.

In short: Whenever you are tempted to use the word money, do you really mean to refer to the stock of one of those special kinds of assets that go into M_1 and M_2? Or do you really mean income, demand, investment, spending, saving, or some other specialized word referring to an economic flow? Be precise!

The single most common and least necessary mistake on exams covering this chapter is to confuse the effects of open market sales and open market purchases.

An open market sale is a sale of bonds (or other government securities) by the Bank of Canada to the public. Members of the public pay for these bonds with money that would otherwise stay in the private banking system and be available as bank reserves.

Remember: An open market SALE of bonds by the Bank of Canada moves money OUT OF the banking system INTO the Bank of Canada, thus LOWERING reserves and LOWERING the money supply.

Similarly, in an open market purchase, the Bank of Canada buys bonds from the public. How does it pay for them? With money that then becomes available to the banking system to provide new reserves.

Remember: An open market PURCHASE of bonds by the Bank of Canada injects money INTO the banking system, thus INCREASING reserves and INCREASING the money supply.

In short, when the Bank of Canada sells bonds to the public on the open market, reserves come out of the banking system; when it buys bonds from the public on the open market, reserves go into the banking system. It is the quantity of reserves in the banking system, not the number of bonds in the hands of the public, that determines the level of the money supply.

APPLICATION

Issue of card money justified

In 1685, de Meulle, the intendant, found himself in great straits to provide for the sustenance of the troops. The device to which he resorted in the issue of card money was explained in his letter of 24th September, 1685. It was a purely financial matter, the cards being issued, not to furnish a medium of exchange, but simply as a temporary means for paying the troops and purchasing supplies. A forced issue of paper currency seemed to afford the most effective remedy. The lack of suitable paper and printing materials led him to resort to the only available substitutes, the packs of playing cards, obviously imported by the merchants to meet a popular demand.

My Lord—

I have found myself this year in great straits with regard to the subsistence of the soldiers. You did not provide for funds, My Lord, until January last. I have, notwithstanding, kept them in provisions until September, which makes eight full months. I have drawn from my own funds and from those of my friends, all I have been able to get, but at last finding them without means to render me further assistance, and not knowing to what saint to pay my vows, money being extremely scarce, having distributed considerable sums on every side for the pay of the soldiers, it occurred to me to issue, instead of money, notes on [playing] cards, which I have had cut in quarters. I send you My Lord, the three kinds, one is for four francs, another for forty sols, and the third for fifteen sols, because with these three kinds, I was able to make their exact pay for one month. I have issued an ordinance by which I have obliged all the inhabitants to receive this money in payments, and to give it circulation, at the same time pledging myself, in my own name, to redeem the said notes. No person has refused them, and so good has been the effect that by this means the troops have lived as usual. There were some merchants who, privately, had offered me money at the local rate on condition that I would repay them in money at the rate in France, to which I could not consent as the King would have lost a third; that is, for ten thousand écus he would have paid forty thousand livres; thus personally, by my credit and by my management, I have saved His Majesty thirteen thousand livres.*

[Signed] de Meulle.

Quebec, 24th September, 1685.

* The last sentence is an attempt by de Meulle to justify his actions to the King. Understanding of this explanation is not necessary to answer the following questions.

From **Canadian Currency, Exchange and Finance During the French Period**, edited by Adam Shortt, Vol. 1 (Burt Franklin: Research Source Works Series #235, New York: 1968). Introductory paragraph on p. xlix; letter on pp. 73 and 76.

1. The introduction says that playing cards were not issued "to furnish a medium of exchange," but given de Meulle's report to France, do you think the cards became a medium of exchange? Explain.

2. Were the playing cards money by the definition given in the text? Justify your answer.

3. Why did the troops, merchants, and ordinary citizens in the French colony of Quebec accept the playing cards when precious metals were used in France, and had recently been used in Quebec?

4. Does the card money of seventeenth-century French Quebec have anything in common with the paper money issued by the Bank of Canada today? Explain your answer.

CHAPTER 13
THE DEMAND FOR MONEY
AND THE MONEY MARKET

WHERE
YOU'RE GOING

When you have mastered this chapter, you will be able to:

- State and explain the significance of the equation of exchange, including the concept of velocity of money.

- Discuss the importance of liquidity in a portfolio.

- Explain why the nominal rate of interest is the proper measure of the opportunity cost of holding money.

- Explain why a rise in the nominal interest rate is associated with a fall in the price of bonds, and a fall in the interest rate with a rise in the price of bonds.

- Give examples of how the price of a bond is affected by a change in the interest rate.

- Draw a typical money demand schedule and explain why the demand for money varies directly with nominal income and inversely with the nominal interest rate.

- Explain the need to hold money in terms of the transactions, precautionary, and speculative motives.

- Using money supply and money demand curves, trace the reactions to an excess supply or demand for money and explain why only one nominal rate of interest is consistent with equilibrium in the money market.

- Using money supply and money demand curves, trace the effects of an increase or decrease in the supply of money, assuming that nominal national income does not change.

- Using money supply and money demand curves, trace the effects of an increase or decrease in nominal national income, assuming that the money supply does not change.

WALKING TOUR

You have read the chapter at least once and have reviewed the summary in the text. Now you are going to walk through the material step by step, filling in the blanks and answering the questions as you go along. After you have answered each question, check yourself by uncovering the answer given in the margin. If you do not understand why the answer given is the right one, refer back to the proper section of the text.

The Demand for Money

The demand for money is the demand for a [stock/flow], since it represents the share of total _____ that people would like to hold in the form of money at any one time.

stock

wealth

The equation of _____, MV=Py, where M represents the _____, V the _____, P the _____, and y _____, presented one early view of the demand for money. V, the velocity of circulation of money, is defined as the ratio of _____ to _____.

exchange

money stock
velocity of money;
 price level
real income

nominal national
 income; money
stock

One reason people want to hold money is for use as a means of payment; this is known as the _____ motive for holding money. Another reason people want to hold money is to maintain liquidity in case unforeseen situations arise; this is known as the _____ motive. Finally, people sometimes want to hold money to avoid capital losses, if they think the nominal value of other assets may fall; this is known as the _____ motive.

transactions

precautionary

speculative

The collection of assets of all kinds that a person holds is known as a _____. A portfolio may contain _____ assets such as money and _____ assets such as stocks and bonds. Offsetting the advantages of holding money is the disadvantage that money, at least in the traditional forms of currency and demand deposits, pays no interest. The opportunity cost of holding money is thus the _____ rate of interest that could be earned on other assets.

portfolio

liquid

illiquid

nominal

Some aspects of the demand for money can be understood more clearly in an economy where there are only two assets, money and bonds. Because bondholders receive periodic payments that are fixed in _____ terms, an increase in the market price of already issued bonds is equivalent to a/an [increase/decrease] in the nominal rate of interest, and vice versa.

nominal

a decrease

In this simplified economy, other things being

equal, an increase in nominal national income causes people to [increase/decrease] the quantity of money they want to hold in their portfolios, because of the _____ motive. Given the level of nominal income, an increase in the nominal rate of interest tends to [increase/decrease] the amount of money they want to hold, because it raises the opportunity cost of holding money. Thus, if a money demand schedule is drawn on a set of axes with the quantity of money on the horizontal axis and the nominal interest rate on the vertical axis, it has a [positive/negative] slope. Other things being equal, an increase in the nominal rate of interest causes a [shift in/movement along] such a money demand schedule. An increase in nominal income causes the schedule to shift [upward to the right/ downward to the left], and a decrease in nominal income causes it to shift [upward to the right/ downward to the left].

increase

transactions

decrease

negative

movement along

upward to the
 right
downward to
 the left

The relationship between money and income is also expressed in terms of the concept of velocity. When nominal interest rates rise, velocity [rises/falls]; people economize on the use of money because its opportunity cost has risen.

rises

Equilibrium and Disequilibrium in the Money Market

The money market can be represented diagrammatically by drawing a money supply and a money demand curve on the same diagram, as in Exhibit S13.1. The curves drawn there indicate an equilibrium nominal interest rate of _____ percent. Given a constant level of nominal national income at a lower nominal rate of interest, say 8 percent, the quantity of money people want to hold will _____ the quantity supplied by about _____. At this low interest rate, people will try to get the additional money they want by [buying/selling] bonds; this activity will drive the price of bonds [down/up] and drive the nominal interest rate [down/up]. Equilibrium will eventually be restored. In the process, the total quantity of money [will/ will not] change.

10

exceed

$40 million

selling
down
up

will not

A diagram such as Exhibit S13.1 can be used to illustrate the effects of a change in monetary policy, assuming that nominal national income remains constant. Draw in a new money supply curve, MS$_2$, representing a doubling of the money supply to $200 million.

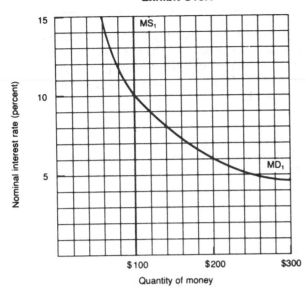

The immediate effect of this policy action is to cause
an excess [supply/demand] of money. People will react   supply
by [buying/selling] bonds, thus causing the price of   buying
bonds to [rise/fall] and the nominal interest rate to   rise
[rise/fall]. Throughout this process the quantity of   fall
money remains constant at its new level of $200
million. Equilibrium will be restored when the
interest rate has fallen to _____ percent,   6
which is low enough to make people willing to hold
$200 million worth of money in their portfolios.

   The same diagram can be used to trace the
effects of a change in nominal national income,
assuming the quantity of money remains unchanged
at MS_2. Draw a new money demand curve, MD_2, in
Exhibit S13.1, corresponding to an increased level
of nominal national income. This new demand curve
should lie to the [right of and above/left of and below]   right of and above
the old one. Assume that the money supply
remains at its new value of $200 million. The
initial effect of the increase in income will be
to [increase/decrease] the transactions demand   increase
for money, thus causing an excess [supply/demand].   demand
People will react to this excess demand by
[buying/selling] bonds in an attempt to get the   selling
money they want. This [will/will not] increase   will not
the total quantity of money available. It will,
however, [increase/decrease] the price of bonds   decrease
and cause the nominal interest rate to [rise/fall].   rise
The new equilibrium interest rate will thus be
[above/below] 6 percent.   above

These sample test items will help you check how much you have learned. Answers and explanations can be found at the end of this book. Scoring yourself: one or two wrong - on target. Three or four wrong - passing, but you haven't mastered the chapter yet. Five or more wrong - not good enough; start over and restudy the chapter.

Multiple Choice

1. According to the equation of exchange, if the money supply is $1 billion and the velocity of money is 5, nominal national income must be
   a. $5 billion.
   b. $200 billion.
   c. $1 billion times the price level.
   d. $5 billion divided by the price level.

2. The speculative motive for holding money is likely to be at its strongest when
   a. bond prices are at historically low levels.
   b. bond prices are low but are expected to recover soon.
   c. the nominal interest rate is low but is expected to rise.
   d. the nominal interest rate is judged equally likely to rise or fall in the near future.

3. The opportunity cost of holding money is best measured by
   a. the nominal rate of interest.
   b. the expected real rate of interest.
   c. the realized real rate of interest.
   d. the expected rate of inflation.

4. If a currently-issued long-term bond with an annual payment of $100 can be purchased now for $1,000, a bond issued last year having a $50 annual payment will have a current price closest to which of the following?
   a. $50
   b. $500
   c. $950
   d. $2,000

5. The quantity of money that people want to hold in their portfolios can be expected
   a. to increase as the nominal interest rate increases and decrease as nominal national income increases.
   b. to decrease as the nominal interest rate increases and increase as nominal national income increases.
   c. to increase both as the nominal interest rate increases and as nominal national income increases.
   d. to decrease both as the nominal interest rate increases and as nominal national income increases.

6. A graph illustrating the relationship between the quantity of money demanded and nominal national income, given a fixed nominal interest rate,
   a. would have a positive slope.
   b. would have a negative slope.
   c. would be perfectly horizontal.
   d. could not be drawn from the information given.

7. If the money demand schedule is drawn in the usual way, with the nominal rate of interest on the vertical axis and the quantity of money on the horizontal axis, an increase in nominal national income will be represented graphically by
   a. a movement up along the money demand curve.
   b. a movement down along the money demand curve.
   c. a rightward and upward shift in the money demand curve.
   d. a leftward and downward shift in the money demand curve.

8. If the money multiplier tended to increase as the nominal interest rate increased (for example, because of a tendency of banks to reduce their excess reserves as the nominal interest rate increased), and if the Bank of Canada did not take action to offset this tendency, then the money supply curve
   a. would have to be drawn with a negative slope.
   b. would have to be drawn with a positive slope.
   c. would have to be drawn as a horizontal line.
   d. would be none of the above; it would still be a vertical line.

9. If nominal national income increases, other things being equal, which of the following is not expected to be a consequence?
   a. A decline in bond prices.
   b. An increase in the nominal interest rate.
   c. An increase in the equilibrium quantity of money supplied.
   d. All of the above are normal consequences of an increase in the level of nominal national income.

10. Other things being equal, an open market sale of securities is likely to have which of the following consequences?
    a. A lower equilibrium price for bonds.
    b. A higher equilibrium nominal interest rate.
    c. Both of the above.
    d. None of the above.

HANDS ON

Now that you have reviewed the concepts introduced in this chapter, it is time for some hands-on practice with the analytical tools that have been introduced. Work through each problem in this section carefully, and then check your results against those given at the end of the book.

Problem 1. The questions that follow refer to Exhibit S13.2, which shows money supply and demand curves for a hypothetical economy.

Exhibit S13.2

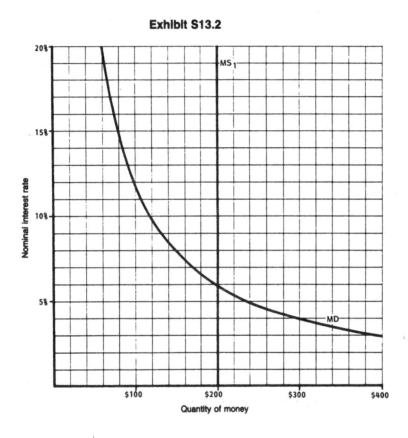

(a) As the diagram is drawn, what is the equilibrium nominal interest rate?

(b) Beginning from the equilibrium position shown, suppose the Bank of Canada uses open market operations to reduce the money supply by half. Draw in the new money supply curve and label it MS$_2$.

(c) Assuming a two-asset economy with noninterest-bearing money and bonds, will the supply curve shift produce an excess supply of or demand for money? An excess supply of or demand for bonds? What kind of portfolio adjustments will people attempt in order to return to equilibrium?

(d) Assume that there is no change in nominal national income as the economy moves to its new equilibrium. What will happen to the price of bonds on the way to the new equilibrium? What will the new equilibrium interest rate be?

Problem 2. The questions that follow refer to Exhibit S13.3, which shows a money supply curve and two possible money demand curves for a hypothetical economy.

Exhibit S13.3

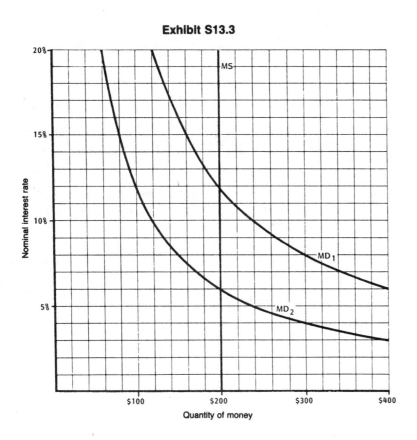

Quantity of money

(a) With the money supply as shown and with money demand curve MD$_1$ in effect, what would be the equilibrium rate of interest?

(b) Beginning from equilibrium at the intersection of MS and MD$_1$, suppose a decrease in nominal national income shifted the money demand curve to the new position MD$_2$. Assuming a two-asset economy, would the shift have the immediate effect of producing an excess supply of money or an excess demand for money? An excess supply of or an excess demand for bonds? What kind of portfolio adjustments will people attempt in order to restore equilibrium?

(c) Assume that the money supply does not change. As the economy moves to a new equilibrium, what will happen to the price of bonds? To the nominal interest rate?

APPLICATION

1. Using a money supply and demand diagram, how would you illustrate the situation described above, in which "the Bank of Canada jammed on the monetary brakes?"

2. What was the likely result of such a "stringent monetary policy" for nominal interest rates? Clearly mark any change in nominal interest rates on your graph from question 1.

3. If such stringent monetary policy were to result in reduced nominal national income, how would money demand and the nominal interest rate be affected with a given level of money supply? If the Bank of Canada wanted to further reduce nominal national income, what changes in the money supply would you suggest and why?

CHAPTER 14
THE INTERACTION OF MONEY AND THE MULTIPLIER

WHERE
YOU'RE GOING

When you have mastered this chapter, you will be able to:

- Distinguish between partial equilibrium analysis and general equilibrium analysis.

- Identify the major channels of interaction between the money market and the circular flow of income and product (as represented by the Keynesian cross).

- Explain why there is one unique pair of equilibrium values for nominal national income and the nominal interest rate, under given conditions, in a general equilibrium framework.

- Explain the crowding out effect and how it modifies the multiplier analysis of Chapter 10.

- Trace the effects of various types of monetary policy (including accommodating monetary policy) in a general equilibrium framework.

- List the main areas of disagreement between monetarist and Keynesian economists.

- Show, in general terms, how the general equilibrium framework used in the early part of this chapter can be modified to take inflationary expectations into account.

In addition, after mastering the appendix to this chapter, you will be able to:

- State the general equilibrium model of nominal income determination in algebraic form.

- Use the algebraic form of the general equilibrium model to solve problems in monetary and fiscal policy.

WALKING TOUR

You have read the chapter at least once and have reviewed the summary in the text. Now you are going to walk through the material step by step, filling in the blanks and answering the questions as you go along. After you have answered each question, check yourself by uncovering the answer given in the margin. If you do not understand why the answer given is the right one, refer back to the proper section of the text.

_____ equilibrium analysis asserts that   Partial
if Event X occurs, the effect in Market Y will be Z,
provided that the _____ of all other   equilibrium
markets is not disturbed. _____   General
equilibrium analysis, which is introduced in this
chapter, asserts that if Event X occurs, the effect
in Market Y will be Z, provided that other markets
adjust [fully/partially] to the event in question.   fully

Exhibit S14.1

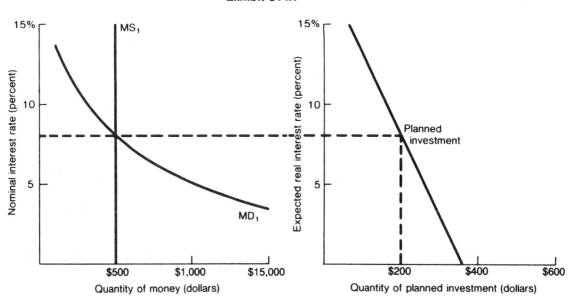

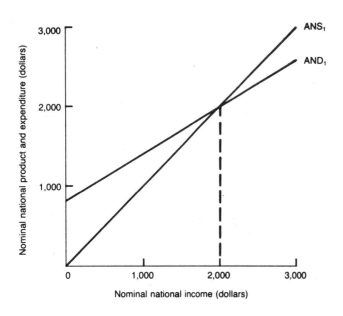

The Interaction of Money and National Income

Exhibit S14.1 shows money supply and demand curves, a planned investment schedule, and aggregate nominal supply and demand curves for a hypothetical economy. As the figure is drawn, the economy is in equilibrium; the interest rate is _____ percent,   8

planned investment is _____, and nominal $200

national income is _____. It can be $2,000
shown that this pair of equilibrium values is
unique, given the assumptions underlying the
exhibit. Consider the possibility, for example,
that there might be another equilibrium with a
lower level of nominal national income. Sketch in
a new aggregate nominal demand curve that would
give a lower equilibrium nominal national income,
and label it AND$_2$. AND$_2$ lies [above/below] AND$_1$.   below
The new level of nominal national income, in turn,
affects the money market; to be specific, it shifts
the money [demand/supply] curve [upward to the right/   demand
downward to the left]. Sketch in the approximate   downward to
location of the new money demand curve, and label   the left
it MD$_2$. The equilibrium interest rate implied by
MD$_2$ is [higher/lower] than before. This new lower   lower
interest rate in turn will cause planned investment
to [increase/decrease]. The effect on aggregate   increase
demand of this increased investment will be to
cause an [upward/downward] shift of the aggregate   upward
nominal demand curve from its initial position, AND$_1$.
But this is not consistent with the initial
assumption that the aggregate nominal demand curve
shifted downward; the assumption of a pair of
equilibrium values for national income and the
interest rate other than $2,000 and 8 percent has
thus led to a contradiction.

The general equilibrium framework developed
in this chapter makes it necessary to revise the
analysis of the effects of fiscal and monetary policy
given in Chapter 10. (In tracing through the
following examples, you may find it helpful to
refer to Exhibit S14.1, sketching in new curves as
appropriate. However, this type of diagram is not
well suited to calculating exact numerical solutions
to policy problems - if you want to be able to do
that, study the algebraic version of the general
equilibrium model given in the appendix to this
chapter.)

Problem 1. In the economy shown in Exhibit S14.1,
the marginal propensity to consume domestic output
is _____. The net tax multiplier   0.6

is _____. According to the partial
equilibrium analysis of Chapter 10, a $400 tax
increase would [raise/lower] the equilibrium
level of nominal national income by _____.
Trace the effects of this policy action in a
general equilibrium framework to determine whether
the change would be larger or smaller than the
partial equilibrium analysis predicts.

Solution: The tax increase, other things being
equal, would shift the aggregate nominal demand
curve [upward/downward] by _____.
This would cause nominal national income to
begin to [expand/contract]. As this change in
national income took place, the money [supply/
demand] curve would shift [upward to the right/
downward to the left]. With a constant money
supply the nominal interest rate is pushed
[upward/downward]. Assuming no inflation is
expected, this change in the nominal interest
rate would induce a [shift in/movement along]
the planned investment schedule, and planned
investment would [increase/decrease]. The
change in planned investment would thus [limit/
add to] the downward shift in the aggregate
demand schedule that resulted from the tax
increase. As a result, the eventual decrease
in equilibrium nominal national income resulting
from the tax increase would be [less/greater]
than the $600 predicted by partial equilibrium
analysis.

Problem 2: The Bank of Canada makes an open
market sale, thereby [increasing/decreasing]
the money supply. What will be the effects of
this policy on the nominal interest rate and
on the equilibrium level of nominal national
income?

Solution: The decrease in the money supply
shifts the money supply curve to the left,
causing an excess [supply of/demand for]
money. In order to restore their portfolios
to balance, people will begin [buying/selling]
bonds. This will tend to [raise/depress] the
price of bonds, and the nominal interest rate
will [rise/fall]. Assuming zero expected
inflation, this change in the nominal interest
rate will cause planned investment to [increase/
decrease]; this in turn will produce a/an
[upward/downward] shift in the aggregate nominal
demand schedule. Firms will react to the
resulting unplanned inventory [accumulation/
depletion] by [raising/lowering] output and/or
prices. Nominal national income will thus fall.

-1.5

lower
$600

downward;
 $240=(0.6 x $400)
contract

demand
downward to
 the left
downward

movement along

increase

limit

less

decreasing

demand for

selling
depress

rise

decrease
a downward

accumulation;
 lowering

This in turn will cause a leftward [shift in/ movement along] the money demand curve, cutting short the rise in the nominal interest rate. In the final equilibrium, the nominal interest rate will thus be somewhat [higher/lower] than before the change in the money supply, and nominal national income will be somewhat [higher/lower].

shift in

higher

lower

Appendix to Chapter 14: The Elementary Algebra of Money and Income

Problem 3: Let a=100, b=0.90, c=150, d=-500, e=80, m=0.30, f=0.2, g=-400, G=250, T=50, MS=250, X=110, and Ma=140. Calculate the equilibrium values of nominal national income and the interest rate, given the initial data.

Solution: Begin by substituting the given values into Equations 14A.4 and 14A.5 from the text (page 266). This gives

$$MD = 80 + 0.2Y - 400r$$

for the money demand equation, and

$$AND = 100 + 150 + 0.9(Y - 50) - 500r + 250 + 110 - 140 - 0.3Y$$
$$= 425 + 0.6Y - 500r$$

for the aggregate nominal demand equation.

In equilibrium, money demand must equal money supply and aggregate nominal demand must equal nominal income. Remember that MS equals 250 in this example. Substituting these equilibrium conditions (MD=MS and AND=Y) into the equations given above and then setting them equal to zero gives these equations:

$$250 = 80 + 0.2Y - 400r$$
$$170 - 0.2Y + 400r = 0$$

and

$$Y = 425 + 0.6Y - 500r$$
$$-1062.5 + Y + 1250r = 0$$

To solve for r, multiply the second MD equation by 5 and add it to the second Y equation. This gives the single equation in one unknown

$$-212.5 + 3250r = 0$$

which gives as its solution (rounded to the nearest one-thousandth) r = _____.

0.065

Using this result (rounded to the nearest one-thousandth) to solve one of the original equations for Y gives the result Y = _____.

981.25 using
the AND formula
and 980 using the
MD formula, due
to rounding

These sample test items will help you check how much you have learned. Answers and explanations can be found at the end of this book. Scoring yourself: one or two wrong - on target. Three or four wrong - passing, but you haven't mastered the chapter yet. Five or more wrong - not good enough; start over and restudy the chapter.

Multiple Choice

1. A full understanding of the effects of monetary and fiscal policy requires general equilibrium analysis because
   a. the demand for money depends on the level of nominal national income.
   b. the level of planned investment depends, other things being equal, on the nominal interest rate.
   c. the level of aggregate nominal demand depends on the level of planned investment.
   d. all of the above are true.

2. In a general equilibrium framework, an increase in the money supply is likely to
   a. lower both the interest rate and nominal GNP.
   b. raise both the interest rate and nominal GNP.
   c. raise the interest rate and lower nominal GNP.
   d. lower the interest rate and raise nominal GNP.

3. In a general equilibrium framework, which of the following would not be expected to increase planned investment expenditure?
   a. An increase in the money supply.
   b. An increase in net taxes.
   c. An increase in net exports.
   d. A cut in transfer payments.

4. If expected inflation is assumed to be zero, a government that wants to stimulate aggregate demand and at the same time keep interest rates low would be best advised to rely on
   a. monetary policy.
   b. government purchases policy.
   c. tax policy.
   d. any of the above; there is no difference in the effects of these policies.

5. According to general equilibrium analysis, an open market purchase by the Bank of Canada will cause a new equilibrium in which
   a. both the money supply and money demand curves shift to the left.
   b. the money supply curve, but not the money demand curve, shifts to the left.
   c. the money supply curve shifts to the left and the money demand curve shifts to the right.
   d. both the money supply curve and the money demand curve shift to the right.

6. An accommodating monetary policy could best be represented graphically by
   a. a horizontal money demand curve.
   b. a horizontal money supply curve.
   c. a horizontal planned investment schedule.
   d. a vertical planned investment schedule.

7. Which of the following would be sufficient to eliminate the crowding out effect?
   a. A vertical planned investment schedule.
   b. A horizontal money demand curve.
   c. A horizontal money supply curve.
   d. Any of the above would be sufficient.

8. According to the monetarists, which of the following might be part of the mechanism that transmits changes in monetary policy to the rest of the economy?
   a. Effects on bond prices.
   b. Effects on stock prices.
   c. Effects on purchases of consumer durables.
   d. All of the above.

9. In a general equilibrium framework in which expected inflation is taken into account, which of the following conclusions about monetary policy may not hold?
   a. Open market purchases will cause the money supply to grow.
   b. The long-run effect of a sustained increase in the rate of money growth will be a reduction in the nominal rate of interest.
   c. Sustained growth of the money supply will result in growth of nominal GNP.
   d. Part of any increase in nominal GNP that takes place in the long run may take the form of inflation rather than increase in real output.

10. If perfect inflation forecasting were possible, changes in the money supply might have no effect on
    a. the nominal rate of interest.
    b. the expected real rate of interest.
    c. the rate of growth of nominal GNP.
    d. the position of the money demand curve.

HANDS ON

Now that you have reviewed the concepts introduced in this chapter, it is time for some hands-on practice with the analytical tools that have been introduced. Work through the problem in this section carefully, and then check your results against those given at the end of the book.

Problem 1.

Exhibit S14.2

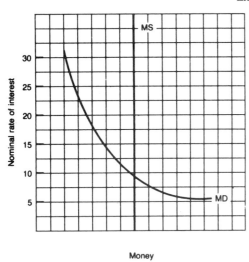

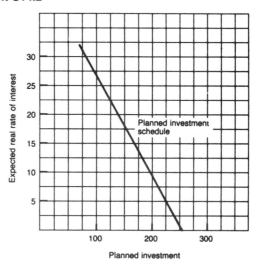

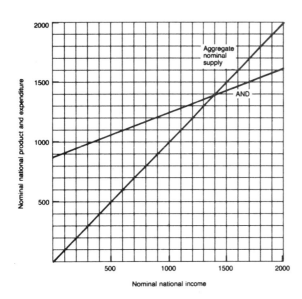

(a) Given the graphs in Exhibit S14.2, what is the interest rate in this economy? At this interest rate, what is the level of planned investment? What is the equilibrium level of nominal national income? Would the economy be in equilibrium at the same level of nominal national income with an interest rate of 6 percent? Explain.

(b) Use your graph to illustrate the effect on aggregate nominal demand of a decrease in government purhcases of $200 with taxes left unchanged. Label your new aggregate nominal demand curve AND$_1$. Does this change in aggregate nominal demand result in unplanned inventory accumulation or depletion? As a result of this policy does the level of nominal national income start to rise or fall? Would you expect a crowding out effect as a result of this

14-8

government policy? Why or why not?

(c) In a general equilibrium analysis what effect is contractionary fiscal policy likely to have on money demand and why? Illustrate your answer with a new money demand curve labeled MD_1. Given a fixed money supply, what will happen to the interest rate as a result of the policy? To planned investment? Show the direction of any changes on the money demand and planned investment graphs.

(d) How will nominal national income be affected by the changes you mentioned in Part (c)? Use the nominal national income graph to illustrate the direction of any changes in AND, labeling your new curve AND_2.

(e) If the government wanted a more powerful contractionary effect on AND than that indicated by your answer to Part (d), what could the Bank of Canada do to the money supply to accommodate the fiscal policy? Indicate the direction of the needed change in the money supply on your graph and label the new curve MS_1. What effect will this change in the money supply have on AND? Illustrate your answer with a new curve AND_3 that shows the direction of the resulting change in AND.

APPLICATION

Some policy recommendations

By Russell E. Harrison

It seems abundantly clear that, although we are always going to be subject to surprises and shocks from the outside world, we Canadians do have considerable power to influence our economic fortunes — as long as we have the will to do so. What, then, are the broad policy options open to us?

A major contribution can be made by government simply following more stable and predictable demand management policies. While governments cannot shield us from all uncertainties (and without a certain amount of risk and uncertainty life could become unbearably dull) at least government should not itself be knowingly adding to instability.

Monetary policy has a key role to play in this connection. To stabilize expectations and rebuild confidence, it is important that the Bank of Canada adhere to non-inflationary limits of money supply growth. The aim must be to reduce these limits expeditiously. We must ensure that this process is not allowed to be so drawn out that it causes a building-in of new inflationary expectations.

As the economy recovers from the present downturn, it is urgent that there be a reduction in the federal government's budget deficit and cash requirements. It has become customary for the government to run large deficits both in good years and in bad. Such a practice is incompatible with maintaining any reasonable degree of monetary stability.

A helpful first step would be for our federal government to establish, and publish on a regular basis, its medium-term economic and fiscal projections. A case could even be made for some form of required budgetary restraint when the inflation rate rises above a certain level. Certainly it is essential that the government, through its policies, should temper the expectations of Canadians regarding real income growth. Only by reducing such growth will there be any possibility of narrowing our present large budgetary deficits as well as the huge deficit on the current account in our balance of payments. Reducing these deficits would be the first clear indication that we have begun to live within our means.

*From "Change, Choice and Challenge: Canada's Economy in the 1980s," **Spectrum**, Canadian Imperial Bank of Commerce Newsletter, Vol. I, No. 2, pp. 10–11. Reprinted by permission.*

1. How could money supply growth cause "a building-in of new inflationary expectations?"

2. If the federal government decreased its budget deficit by increasing net taxes, what is the likely effect on nominal GNP and nominal interest rates in a general equilibrium framework?

3. Why might the author feel that a large federal deficit is "incompatible with maintaining any reasonable degree of monetary stability?" Would you expect the money supply to increase or decrease with an increase in the federal budget deficit?

4. The author says that it would be a good idea for the federal government to publish "medium-term economic and fiscal projections." How do you think this might help to restore and maintain economic prosperity?

CHAPTER 15
INTERNATIONAL TRADE AND THE BALANCE OF PAYMENTS

WHERE
YOU'RE GOING

When you have mastered this chapter, you will be able to:

- Explain the benefits from international trade that can be derived from nations following their comparative advantages.

- Provide arguments for a policy of free trade.

- Define protectionism and provide four arguments for restrictive trade policies.

- Explain the general goals of General Agreements on Tariffs and Trade (GATT).

- Explain the purpose of the balance of payments and the three categories into which it is divided: current account, capital account, and the official reserve account.

- Explain the meaning and significance of the following additional terms and concepts:

        tariff
        import quota
        capital inflow
        capital outflow

WALKING TOUR

You have read the chapter at least once and have reviewed the summary in the text. Now you are going to walk through the material step by step, filling in the blanks and answering the questions as you go along. After you have answered each question, check yourself by uncovering the answer given in the margin. If you do not understand why the answer given is the right one, refer back to the proper section of the text.

An International Application of Comparative Advantage

Trade between regions or countries can be economically advisable when one has a _____ advantage in   comparative
the production of some goods. A comparative advantage
exists when one region or country can produce a good at
a [higher/lower] _____ cost, measured in   lower; opportunity

terms of other foregone goods.

Imagine two countries called, for the sake of example, England and Portugal. These are the only two countries in the world, and they produce only two products, wool and cheese. The only factor of production is labor. In England it takes six labor hours to produce a kilogram of wool and three labor hours to produce a kilogram of cheese; in Portugal three labor hours will produce a kilogram of wool and just one labor hour a kilogram of cheese. Under these conditions, England is said to have a comparative advantage in _____ and Portugal to have   wool

a comparative advantage in _____. Note,   cheese

incidentally, that Portugal has a/an _____   an absolute
advantage in both products.

Suppose that each country has 1,200 labor hours available to it and that each divides these labor hours equally between the two products. This would give England a production of _____   100

kilograms of wool and _____ kilograms of   200

cheese and Portugal a production of _____   200

kilograms of wool and _____ kilograms   600
of cheese. Total world production of wool would be
_____ kilograms and total world production   300

of cheese _____ kilograms.   800

In England, the opportunity cost of a kilogram of wool is _____ kilograms of cheese, and   two
in Portugal, the opportunity cost of a kilogram of
    is _____ kilograms of cheese. This   three
difference in opportunity costs is what creates a possibility of mutually advantageous trade between the two countries. England will give up a kilogram of wool if it can get anything more than _____   two
kilograms of cheese in return, whereas Portugal will
export up to _____ kilograms of cheese if   three
it can get a kilogram of wool in return. Any trading ratio between 2 for 1 and 3 for 1, then, will potentially benefit both parties.

To demonstrate this possibility of mutual advantage, suppose a trading ratio of 2.5 kilograms of cheese per kilogram of wool is decided on. England decides to make an initial export shipment of, say, six kilograms of wool. To produce the six kilograms of wool for export, it must withdraw _____   thirty-six
labor hours from the production of cheese, which
means foregoing production of _____   twelve
kilograms of cheese. When it sends the six kilograms of wool to Portugal, however, it receives

_____ kilograms of cheese in exchange,   fifteen
more than compensating for the loss in domestic
production. To produce the fifteen kilograms of
cheese for export to England, Portugal must shift
_____ hours of labor from producing   fifteen
wool to producing cheese. This means foregoing
production of _____ kilograms of wool.   five
However, in return for the fifteen kilograms of
cheese it exports, it receives _____   six
kilograms of wool from England, more than making
up the loss in domestic production. Both
countries are thus better off than before trade;
England has just as much _____   wool

and more _____ than before, whereas   cheese

Portugal has just as much _____ and   cheese

more _____. Note also that total   wool
world production of both products has increased:
total world output of wool is now _____   301
kilograms, and total world production of cheese
is now _____ kilograms. Further trade   803
at the same ratio would bring still further gains
in production and consumption.

Protectionism and Free Trade

Even though the theory shows advantages from free
trade, many nations establish _____   protectionist

policies such as _____ and   tariffs

_____ to restrict the importation of   quotas
goods. Four basic arguments are used to justify
protectionist trade policies: 1) The
_____ argument sees trade restrictions   terms of trade
allowing a nation to establish more favorable terms
of trade agreements than would be determined with
competitive _____ trade. 2) The   free

_____ distribution argument sees   income
protectionist measures insuring jobs and incomes
for certain groups in an economy by restricting
[imports/exports] that compete with goods they
produce. 3) The _____ interest   imports
argument sees trade restrictions allowing a nation   national
to build a broad _____ base and a   industrial

defense industry. 4) The _____   infant
industry argument says that trade restrictions
are necessary to allow all _____   new
industries to develop until they are mature
enough to compete in world markets.
    No matter what the reason for protectionist

15-3

policies, other nations may _____ by
creating trade restrictions of their own. There
are many difficult problems in evaluating free trade
and protectionist policies, and opinions concerning
free trade vary widely.

retaliate

Balance of Payments

Since Canada exports about 29 percent of the goods
and services that it produces and imports about 31
percent of the goods and services it consumes, the
balance of payments is very important. The accounts
are divided into _____ sections, the

three

_____, the _____, and the

current account;
 capital account
official reserve
 account

_____.

        The _____ measures transactions in
goods and services produced in the current year and
is usually in [surplus/deficit] for Canada because
of the normally large deficits in the service
transactions section. The _____
measures transactions in short- and long-term
securities and bonds and is usually in [surplus/
deficit] because good investment opportunities in
Canada cause an [inflow/outflow] of foreign funds.
The _____ section measures changes in
official foreign currency reserves held by Canada.
When all sources and uses of foreign currency are
added up, the balance of payments overall net
balance is always _____.

current account

deficit

capital account

surplus
inflow
official reserves

zero

SELF TEST
_____

These sample test items will help you check how much you have learned.
Answers and explanations can be found at the end of this book. Scoring
yourself: one or two wrong - on target. Three or four wrong - passing,
but you haven't mastered the chapter yet. Five or more wrong - not
good enough; start over and restudy the chapter.

Multiple Choice

1. Suppose John can sew four shirts per day or knit six caps per day,
    whereas Jane can sew three shirts per day or knit four caps per day.
    It can then be said that
    a. John has a comparative advantage in sewing shirts.
    b. John has a comparative advantage in knitting caps.
    c. both of the above are true.
    d. neither of the above are true.

2. According to international trade theory, a country should
   a. export goods in which it has a comparative advantage.
   b. never export goods in which it has an absolute advantage.
   c. never import goods in which it has an absolute advantage.
   d. import goods in which it has a comparative advantage.

3. It takes five labor hours to produce a tonne of steel in Japan and three labor hours in the United States, and it requires twenty labor hours to produce a car in Japan and only fifteen labor hours in the United States. If Japan and the United States were the only two countries involved in trade, we would expect
   a. Japan to import cars and export steel.
   b. Japan to export cars and import steel.
   c. Japan to export both cars and steel.
   d. Japan to import both cars and steel.

4. In a two-good, two-country world, international trade can increase
   a. consumer welfare in both countries, but not total output of both goods.
   b. total output of both goods, but not consumer welfare in both countries.
   c. consumer welfare only if output of both goods is increased.
   d. output of both goods and consumer welfare in both countries.

5. In Norway, it takes five labor hours to produce a tonne of wheat and five to produce a tonne of fish; in Greece, it takes three labor hours to produce a tonne of wheat and three to produce a tonne of fish. If these are the only two goods and the only two trading countries, we would expect
   a. Norway to export both products.
   b. Norway to import both products.
   c. Norway to export wheat and import fish.
   d. no trade.

6. The "terms of trade" argument for protectionism
   a. has no economic validity.
   b. may be valid for one country but does not suggest that all countries can gain from protection at the same time.
   c. is the one protectionist argument that is valid for all countries.
   d. is more likely to be valid for small countries than for large countries.

7. In the absence of trade, world production will tend to be
   a. outside the world production possibility frontier.
   b. inside the world production possibility frontier.
   c. on the world production possibility frontier, but too far down along it.
   d. on the world production possibility frontier, but too far up along it.

8. A private Canadian citizen's purchase of long-term bonds issued by a British corporation would be considered
   a. a capital inflow.
   b. a capital outflow.
   c. a current account transaction.
   d. an official reserve transaction.

9. Which of the following is considered a capital inflow?
   a. A sale of Canadian assets to a foreign buyer.
   b. A loan from a Canadian bank to a foreign borrower.
   c. A purchase of foreign assets by a Canadian buyer.
   d. A Canadian citizen's repayment of a loan from a foreign bank.

10. If Canada runs a balance of payments deficit on the current account,
    a. it must run a capital account surplus.
    b. it must run an official reserve account surplus.
    c. it must do at least one of the above.
    d. it must do both a and b.

HANDS ON

Now that you have reviewed the concepts introduced in this chapter, it is time for some hands-on practice with the analytical tools that have been introduced. Work through the problem in this section carefully, and then check your results against those given at the end of the book.

Problem 1. In this problem, assume that the two countries and the two goods are the only ones in existence, that labor is the only factor of production, and that costs per unit are constant.

(a) In Canada, a tractor can be produced with 100 labor hours and shoes require 2 labor hours per pair. In China, 500 labor hours are required to build a tractor and 2.5 labor hours to make a pair of shoes. Which country has a comparative advantage in shoes? In tractors? Which country has an absolute advantage in shoes? In tractors?

(b) Assume that Canada has 1 billion labor hours available for production of the two goods and that China has 5 billion labor hours. On the three graphs of Exhibit S15.1, draw production possibility frontiers for Canada, China, and the world as a whole.

(c) Assume that initially, Canada and China each split their available labor hours evenly between tractor and shoe production. What quantities of the two goods will each country produce? Label the initial production point for Canada P_u; that for China P_c; and that for the world P_w.

(d) Would trade of any kind between the two countries be mutually advantageous? If so, which country should export which product?

What is the range of relative prices within which trade would be mutually advantageous?

(e) Assume that a trading ratio of 1 tractor for 100 pairs of shoes is established. Canada completely specializes in tractors, produces no shoes of its own, and exports 40 tractors in exchange for 400 pairs of shoes. China diverts just enough labor from tractor production to produce the necessary shoe exports. What quantities of each good does each country now produce? Label the new production points Q_u, Q_c, and Q_W, respectively. How much does each country now consume? Label the new post-trade consumption points R_u, R_c, and R_W, respectively.

(f) Is either country better off? Are both? How can you tell? Is world production organized more efficiently than before? How can you tell?

Exhibit S15.1

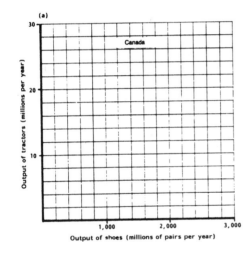

(a)

Canada

Output of tractors (millions per year)

Output of shoes (millions of pairs per year)

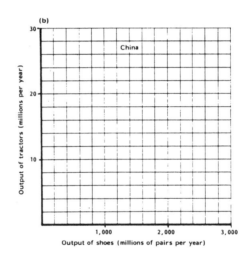

(b)

China

Output of tractors (millions per year)

Output of shoes (millions of pairs per year)

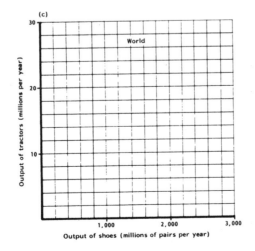

(c)

World

Output of tractors (millions per year)

Output of shoes (millions of pairs per year)

A clamor for protectionism

The clamor for protection from imports is always more shrill in tough times. And governments that move against such pressures deserve all the more credit.

The decision to let the leather footwear quota expire was not a large move towards free trade. The minister balanced it by applying a new global quota to imports of canvas shoes. But the removal of the quota on imported leather shoes, although in keeping with a report by the Anti-Dumping Tribunal, is at least a move in the right direction.

"Protectionism" is, of course, misnamed. It protects nothing. Instead, it has the same effect as barriers to trade between provinces, endangering jobs, prosperity and living standards. In the end, it reduces the market even for the domestic industries that are supposedly protected.

But the short run is always more visible than the long run. And the jobs supposedly at risk as a result of opening trade channels always seem more persuasive to politicians than the large number of jobs that would be created in a more prosperous world.

In this situation, and in times of rising unemployment, we must be thankful for small mercies.

For example, the economic strategy paper tabled with Finance Minister Allan MacEachen's budget was vague enough on most things. But it did contain a section calling for "restructuring" the manufacturing sector by reducing the pressure for support of "less competitive industries" and providing alternative jobs in "higher productivity and higher wage sectors."

The policy paper points out that "when governments are called upon to support uncompetitive industries and firms to protect employment, all Canadians must share these costs.

"Unchecked, these constraints on the economy's productivity growth undermine Canada's trade competitiveness," the paper went on. "When new investment opportunities are realized, when labor is employed more productively and efficiently, the benefits are shared by us all and Canada's trade competitiveness is enhanced."

These words show that the team of cabinet ministers that wrote the policy paper understands the economics involved. But making the political moves to gain these economic benefits is something else.

It is clear that the government will be facing increased calls for protection, not only from the traditional "soft" industries such as footwear but from other sectors, and not only from the private sector but also from its own agencies.

An example was provided by a statement issued by the industrial policies committee of the Science Council of Canada.

The committee called for action to strengthen the competitiveness of the high technology industries. No one can quarrel with such a call in general. But it is clear that the measures preferred are those that would reduce the freedom of trade on grounds that Canada "urgently needs a better regulated system to control its imports."

Economists are not agreed on whether this recession will be short and shallow or long and deep. If we are unlucky enough to have a long, deep recession, the pressures for increased protection can be expected to become intense.

But future prosperity will depend on the government holding steady in the face of such pressure and when possible — as it was in the footwear sector — removing trade restrictions rather than adding new ones.

*From **Financial Times**, November 30, 1981, page 9. Reprinted by permission.*

1. Give at least two reasons why "the clamor for protection from imports is always more shrill in tough times."

2. What do you think the author means when he says protectionism "protects nothing?"

3. Why do you think protectionism always seems more viable in the short run than in the long run?

4. What long-term alternatives are there to protectionist trade policies?

CHAPTER 16
THE INTERACTION OF THE FOREIGN SECTOR AND THE MULTIPLIER

WHERE
YOU'RE GOING
_____

When you have mastered this chapter, you will be able to:

- Use supply and demand analysis to explain determination of the
  current exchange rate in the <u>foreign exchange market</u> when the
  current and capital accounts are considered.

- Explain the <u>purchasing power parity</u> theory of long-term exchange
  rates.

- Explain the meaning and significance of <u>balance of payments</u>
  <u>equilibrium</u> as a condition for general equilibrium.

- Describe the economic conditions necessary for a general equilibrium
  between the money market, the circular flow, and the foreign market.

- Show in general terms the difficulties of achieving general
  equilibrium with monetary policy, fiscal policy, fixed exchange
  rates, and flexible exchange rates.

- Describe the current international monetary system and its evolution
  from the Bretton Woods system.

- Explain the problems Canada faces with its balance of payments
  disequilibrium, and discuss some of the possible solutions.

- Explain the meaning and significance of the following additional
  terms and concepts:

        appreciation of the exchange rate
        depreciation of the exchange rate
        J-curve effect
        par

WALKING TOUR
_____

You have read the chapter at least once and have reviewed the summary
in the text. Now you are going to walk through the material step by
step, filling in the blanks and answering the questions as you go along.
After you have answered each question, check yourself by uncovering
the answer given in the margin. If you do not understand why the answer

given is the right one, refer back to the proper section of the text.

The Theory of Exchange Rate Determination

Current account transactions - those representing payments
for current imports and exports plus the services balance
and net transfers - are only one of a number of kinds of
transactions that take place in foreign exchange markets,
but assuming they are the only kind of international
transaction provides a starting point for learning how
foreign exchange markets work. Consider Exhibit S16.1,
for example. This figure shows hypothetical current
account supply and demand curves in a _____   foreign exchange
market where Canadian dollars are traded for Japanese
yen. As the figure is drawn, the equilibrium exchange
rate is _____ yen per dollar when the supply   280
curve is S₁.

The Supply and Demand for Foreign Exchange

Suppose now that something happens to shift the dollar
supply curve to the position S₂ - say, that there is
a/an [decrease/increase] in Canadian transfer payments   an increase
to Japan or that Canadian buyers develop a/an
[decreased/increased] preference for Japanese goods.   an increased
The immediate result will be an excess [supply/
demand] of dollars, which will cause the dollar to   supply

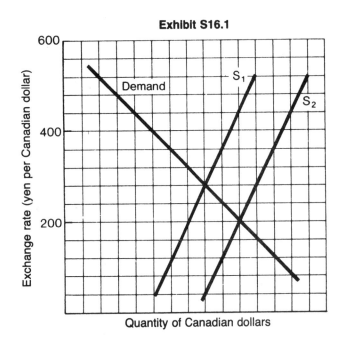

Exhibit S16.1

16-2

[appreciate/depreciate] relative to the yen. As it does so, Japanese consumers will find Canadian goods [more/less] expensive and will [increase/decrease] the quantity of Canadian goods they demand. This means they must [increase/decrease] the quantity of dollars demanded in the foreign exchange market; this increase is represented in Exhibit S16.1 as a [movement along/shift in] the demand curve for dollars. At the same time, the lower exchange rate will cause Canadian buyers to [increase/decrease] the quantities of Japanese goods demanded and thus to [increase/decrease] the quantity of dollars they supply to the foreign exchange market. This is shown as a movement along the supply curve _____ . A new equilibrium exchange rate becomes established at _____ yen per dollar.

depreciate

less; increase

increase

movement along

decrease

decrease

S2

200

The balance of payments capital account records inflows of funds to Canada and outflows of funds from Canada. When both the capital and the current account are considered, imports of goods and services can be paid for either by exports, or by capital [inflows/outflows], or if a country exports more than it imports, capital [inflows/outflows] can be used to balance the accounts.

inflows
outflows

The _____ account in the balance of payments records sales and purchases of foreign _____ reserves held by the Bank of Canada and the corresponding central banks of other countries. These transactions are often made to offset an excess supply or demand of a certain currency, thereby preventing or moderating _____ fluctuations.

official reserve

currency

exchange rate

Upward or downward movements in exchange rates can be initiated by changes affecting either current or capital account transactions. For example, suppose Canadian interest rates increase relative to interest rates abroad, other things being equal. The effect would be to encourage the [purchase/sale] of Canadian assets and to encourage borrowers to borrow [in Canada/abroad] - in other words, the rise in interest rates would encourage a capital [inflow/outflow]. In the foreign exchange market, the capital inflow would add to the [demand for/supply of] dollars and would cause the dollar to [appreciate/depreciate].

purchase

abroad
inflow

demand for
appreciate

Alternatively, suppose the rate of inflation in Canada is expected to increase, other things, including interest rates, being equal. This would make Canadian assets [more/less] attractive relative to assets denominated in more stable foreign currencies and would thus cause a capital [inflow/outflow]. This, in turn, would tend to cause the dollar to [appreciate/depreciate].

less

outflow
depreciate

The Long Run: Purchasing Power Parity

A theory of exchange rate determination, the
_____ parity theory, says that the price   purchasing power
of a unit of Currency A in terms of Currency B will,
in the long run, tend to be equal to the ratio of
the _____ in Country B to the price level   price level
in Country A. If there were no barriers to trade or
no transportation costs, the purchasing power parity
theory would probably hold exactly. In real life,
the theory does not hold exactly. The differences
can be accounted for by the fact that the purchasing
power parities reflect the prices of _____   all

goods and services, while _____ tend to   exchange rates
reflect the values of goods and services involved
in international trade.

The Interaction of Money, National Income, and the Balance of Payments

The balance of payments _____ is a   equilibrium
situation in which there are no changes in reserves
at all. This would happen when the _____   current

account exactly balances the _____ account.   capital

Since Canada consistently runs a _____ on   deficit
its current account, equilibrium in the balance of
payments only results when capital inflows exceed
capital outflows by the amount of the current account
[surplus/deficit].   deficit
   Our model assumes that exports are autonomous,
and that imports [increase/decrease] as nominal   increase
national income [increases/decreases]. Thus, net   increases
exports decline as nominal national income
[increases/decreases] , and the current account balance   increases
becomes negative at [higher/lower] levels of income.   higher
   Since capital inflows and outflows are
influenced by the rates of interest within Canada,
net capital inflows will be [positively/negatively]   positively
related to the rate of interest.
   A particular level of nominal national income
will produce a certain level of net exports, and
will require a certain rate of _____ to   interest
create capital flows that exactly match net exports
if equilibrium is to be reached. Equilibrium in the
foreign market requires a matching of _____   interest

rates and nominal _____ , just as matching   national income
interest rates and nominal national income is required
to create equilibrium between the _____   money

market and the _____ flow. When a certain   circular
rate of interest and a certain level of nominal

national income combine to produce equilibrium in the foreign market, the money market, and the circular flow, the economy is in a state of _____.   general equilibrium

A general equilibrium situation is very difficult for policymakers to achieve, since domestic economic concerns may call for policy measures that remove the foreign sector from an equilibrium with the _____ and the _____ flow.   money market; circular
For instance, if policymakers want to stimulate a sluggish economy, they could suggest the Bank of Canada increase the money supply, causing interest rates to [rise/fall]. Although an equilibrium may   fall
still exist between the money market and the circular flow, at the [higher/lower] rate of interest net   lower
capital [inflows/outflows] will [increase/decrease],   inflows; decrease
and net exports will [increase/decline] at the new   decline
higher level of nominal national income. The current account [deficit/surplus] will grow larger and the   deficit
capital inflow required to pay for the [deficit/ surplus] will have diminished. The balance of   deficit
payments is now in disequilibrium, and foreign currency reserves will have to be drawn down in order to pay for the current account [deficit/surplus].   deficit

If the Bank of Canada policy that was used in the example above occurs at a time when the exchange rate is [fixed/flexible], the monetary policy will   fixed
be completely stymied. However, if the exchange rate is [fixed/flexible], the results will be quite   flexible
different. When the money supply increases, the current account deficit increases, and the net capital inflows diminish, the value of the Canadian dollar will [increase/decline]. This will happen as   decline
Canadians [increase/decrease] the supply of Canadian   increase
dollars in the foreign exchange market to buy goods and services from foreigners, and to invest funds in countries that have higher interest rates. Foreigners will [increase/decrease] their demand for Canadian   decrease
dollars because of low interest rates in Canada. As a result, the value of the Canadian dollar will [decline/increase] relative to foreign currencies.   decline

Capital account transactions will vary with interest rates within each country. For instance, a low interest rate in Canada will cause an [inflow/outflow] of funds. On the foreign exchange   outflow
market, this will cause a reduced [supply/demand]   demand
for Canadian dollars, since a low interest rate will not make investment in Canadian securities attractive to foreigners. A reduced demand for Canadian dollars would show up graphically as a [leftward/rightward] shift in the demand for   leftward
Canadian dollars and would cause the Canadian dollar

to [appreciate/depreciate] in value in terms of   depreciate
foreign currencies. The analysis in this example
would apply to short-run changes in the foreign
exchange rate.

_____ exchange rates are favored   Flexible
by many economists because they eliminate
imbalances in the foreign sector that might
result from domestic monetary and fiscal policies.
Other economists prefer _____ or semifixed   fixed
exchange rates, to make foreign trade arrangement
easier. When a currency _____ relative   appreciates
to other currencies, export industries find it
harder to compete on world markets. When a currency
_____, imports decrease and there is less   depreciates
competition for domestic production.

An argument for fixing exchange rates is that,
when a country's currency first depreciates, it may
_____ rather than _____ its   worsen; improve
balance of payments current account. Eventually,
however, the current account may rise to a surplus.
This is known as the _____-curve effect.   J

Another argument for fixed exchange rates is
that the _____ of a currency caused by   depreciation
domestic inflation may cause [more/less] inflation.   more
This could result in a vicious inflationary cycle
that might be avoided if exchange rate fluctuations
were not allowed.

After World War II, the major trading nations
of the world set up the _____ system and   Bretton Woods
                                                              International
the _____ to administer the system.   Monetary Fund
                                                              pegged
Exchange rates were _____ and allowed to
fluctuate within a narrow range under the influence
of supply and demand. A government faced with an
excess demand for its currency at the limit rate
had to _____ enough of its currency to   sell
soak up excess demand. If there was an excess supply
of the currency, the government had to _____   buy
its currency to remove the excess supply.

Many governments did not cooperate fully when
there was downward pressure on their currency, because
they feared domestic unemployment and [high/low]   high
interest rates. In a severe crisis involving the
U.S. dollar, the German _____, and the   mark

Japanese _____ in 1973, the major trading   yen
nations removed the adjustable pegged rates and
allowed currencies to _____ relative to   float
each other.

Today, Canada uses a _____ float   dirty
to set the exchange rate between the Canadian and
foreign currencies.

Canada's Dilemma in the Foreign Market

Canada's dependence on American investment has resulted in [light/heavy] debt payments that push [up/down] the value of the Canadian dollar, and often cause a	heavy; down
[surplus/deficit] in our current account with the United States. Attempts have been made in the past to keep the values of the Canadian and American	deficit
dollars equal or around _____, but in the early 1980s the Canadian dollar has been stabilized at about $.83 U.S. The Bank of Canada has used interest rate policy and	par
intervention with _____ funds to support the value of the Canadian dollar. This has meant	reserve
keeping the Canadian interest rate [above/below] the United States interest rate, and the Bank	above
purchasing [Canadian/American] dollars in the foreign exchange market. High interest rate policies have	Canadian
been [popular/unpopular] with some economists who feel that this policy [adds to/subtracts from]	unpopular adds to
inflationary pressures and worsens the _____ situation.	unemployment

SELF TEST

These sample test items will help you check how much you have learned. Answers and explanations can be found at the end of this book. Scoring yourself: one or two wrong - on target. Three or four wrong - passing, but you haven't mastered the chapter yet. Five or more wrong - not good enough; start over and restudy the chapter.

Multiple Choice

1. Which of the following would be likely to cause the Canadian dollar to appreciate relative to the French franc?
   a. An increase in French interest rates.
   b. An increase in the Canadian rate of inflation.
   c. A purchase of francs by the French central bank.
   d. None of the above.

2. Which of the following would be likely to cause the Canadian dollar to depreciate relative to the British pound?
   a. Inflation that is more rapid in Britain than in Canada.
   b. Inflation that is more rapid in Canada than in Britain.
   c. Rising Canadian interest rates.
   d. Increased British tourism in Canada.

3. According to the purchasing power parity theory, a country's currency will appreciate if
   a. it is expected to have less inflation than other countries.
   b. it is expected to have more inflation than other countries.
   c. its interest rates are expected to fall.
   d. it does not produce internationally-traded goods.

4. According to advocates of flexible exchange rates,
   a. flexible exchange rates increase imbalances in the foreign sector (balance of payments accounts) that might result from monetary and fiscal policy.
   b. flexible exchange rates eliminate imbalances in the foreign sector (balance of payments accounts) that might result from monetary and fiscal policy.
   c. the J-curve effect never occurs when a currency is devalued.
   d. none of the above.

5. Advocates of fixed exchange rates
   a. are concerned about the so-called J-curve effect.
   b. think fixed rates help insulate the domestic economy from foreign disturbances.
   c. think fixed rates encourage central banks to pursue anti-inflationary monetary policy.
   d. agree with all of the above.

6. According to the J-curve effect, when a country's currency depreciates, its current account balance
   a. first moves toward deficit, then later toward surplus.
   b. first moves toward surplus, then later toward deficit.
   c. moves into deficit and stays there.
   d. moves into surplus and stays there.

7. The Bretton Woods system is best characterized as
   a. a rigid fixed rate system.
   b. an adjustable peg system.
   c. a clean float.
   d. a dirty float.

8. The Bretton Woods system
   a. never really got off the ground.
   b. lasted more than twenty years but proved crisis prone.
   c. is still in effect.
   d. puts more emphasis on floating rates than does the present system.

9. A gasoline shortage in the United States causes an increase in demand for highly efficient Japanese cars; in the yen/dollar foreign exchange markets, the consequences would best be represented by
   a. a rightward shift in the U.S. dollar supply curve.
   b. a leftward shift in the U.S. dollar supply curve.
   c. a rightward shift in the U.S. dollar demand curve.
   d. a leftward shift in the U.S. dollar demand curve.

10. When both the current account and the capital account are considered, equilibrium in the foreign exchange market requires that
    a. every dollar's worth of goods or services imported be paid for by a dollar's worth of goods or services exported.
    b. imports of goods or services be paid for either by exports or by capital inflows.
    c. imports of goods or services be paid for either by exports or by capital outflows.
    d. none of the above.

HANDS ON

Now that you have reviewed the concepts introduced in this chapter, it is time for some hands-on practice with the analytical tools that have been introduced. Work through the problem in this section carefully, and then check your results against those given at the end of the book.

Problem 1. The following questions refer to Exhibit S16.2 that illustrates changes in the equilibrium exchange rate between the Canadian and U.S. dollar as a result of changes in supply and demand for Canadian dollars.

Exhibit S16.2

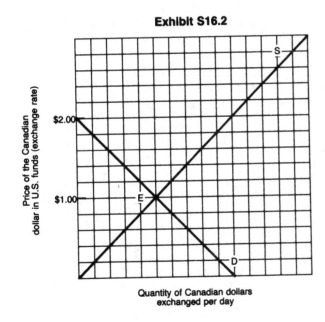

Quantity of Canadian dollars
exchanged per day

(a) What is the equilibrium exchange rate indicated in Exhibit S16.2? Taking only current account transactions into consideration, illustrate the effect on the exchange rate of increased American tourism in Canada. Assume your new equilibrium exchange rate is $1 Cdn. = $1.04 U.S. Mark this equilibrium E_1 on your graph. Does your graph show a change in demand, a change in supply, a change in the quantity demanded and/or a change in the quantity of Canadian dollars supplied? Has the Canadian dollar appreciated or depreciated relative to the United States dollar?

(b) The higher exchange rate at E_1 is likely to encourage Canadians to import more American goods and to take more holidays in the United States. Should this be represented on the graph by a shift of either the demand or supply curves? If so, mark the new equilibrium as E_2. Has there been a change in demand, a change in supply, a change in the quantity demanded, and/or a change in the quantity of Canadian dollars supplied?

DON'T MAKE THIS COMMON MISTAKE!

When using supply and demand graphs to illustrate changes in equilibrium exchange rates, be sure that all labels on your graph are in terms of one currency. For instance, a graph could show the quantity of Canadian dollars exchanged per day on the horizontal axis, and the exchange rate (units of another currency per Canadian dollar) on the vertical axis. The supply curve refers to the supply of Canadian dollars and the demand curve to the demand for Canadian dollars.

Students often confuse themselves by labeling one of the axes or curves in terms of another currency. To reach the correct conclusion, all parts of a foreign exchange graph must be in terms of one currency.

Drop in dollar no answer

By Ken Bell
Province Business Editor

The suggestion by some premiers that the Canadian dollar be allowed to float down to allow a reduction in interest rates is a political solution to an economic problem.

And like most political solutions, the cure is likely to be worse than the condition.

Here's some of the short term effects that would occur if our dollar was devalued from its current level of 83 cents in comparison to the U.S. dollar to 75 cents.

● There would be an immediate 11-per-cent increase in the price of imports. As imports form a considerable portion of our total consumption, the consequences would be sharply inflationary.

● Theoretically Canadian export commodities would look a little better to foreign eyes because they would appear to have gone down in price by about 9.6 per cent.

That's just about where the economic advantages cease. And they would cease very quickly indeed.

Here's why.

Bank of Canada governor Gerald Bouey has been explaining patiently for some time now that our interest rates are high because of inflation and because of the need to support the Canadian dollar.

While Bouey continues as head of the Bank of Canada he will fight inflation with higher interest rates. If inflation goes up because a devalued Canadian dollar makes the price of vital imports (such as food) go up, then the bank's reaction is likely to increase interest rates.

In addition, many Canadian corporations — such as B.C. Hydro — have borrowed extensively in the U.S.

Devaluing the Canadian dollar would increase the cost of paying U.S. dollar interest by 11 per cent, not a happy thought if the interest bill is in the hundreds of millions of dollars.

Then there's the problem of the interest rate spread — the difference between interest rates here and in the U.S.

Last year when that spread widened, hundreds of millions of Canadian dollars sought a refuge in the U.S., putting downward pressure on the Canadian dollar as people bid up the price of the U.S. dollar.

Bill Bennett and the other premiers should not have to be reminded that the Canadian dollar last year reached a 50-year low before the Bank of Canada moved to widen the interest rate gap so that investing in Canada looked a better deal than investing in the U.S.

And it simply may not be true that we might be able to sell more of our goods overseas because they would become cheaper in the eyes of foreign buyers.

Over the past four years the Canadian dollar has dropped from par to as low as 81 cents, and is now trading at 83 cents.

Any competitive advantages we might have had are probably already taken up by that 20-per-cent devaluation.

From the **Vancouver Province**, *February 3, 1982, p. A8.*

1. The article implies that the exchange rate of $1 Cdn. = $.83 U.S. is being maintained artificially, and that if the Canadian dollar were allowed to float freely, the rate would fall to near $.75 U.S. From information given in the chapter, how is the higher exchange rate being maintained?

2. Use a foreign exchange diagram similar to that in Exhibit 16.1 in the text to illustrate what would happen in the foreign exchange market if the Canadian dollar were not artificially maintained at $.83 U.S. The final equilibrium rate in your diagram should be $1 Cdn. = $.75 U.S.

3. A drop in the value of the Canadian dollar to $.75 U.S. would likely reduce imports. Starting with an equilibrium rate of $1 Cdn. = $.75 U.S., illustrate the probable effect of reduced imports on a foreign exchange diagram. The depreciated value of the Canadian dollar is also likely to increase exports. Illustrate the probable effect on your diagram. In what direction is the equilibrium rate likely to move if imports fall by ten percent and exports rise by ten percent?

4. How, if at all, does keeping Canadian interest rates higher than United States interest rates affect the exchange between the two dollars?

CHAPTER 17
UNEMPLOYMENT AND INFLATION: THE MODERN DILEMMA

WHERE
YOU'RE GOING

When you have mastered this chapter, you will be able to:

- Explain the crude Keynesian theory of inflation, using the Keynesian cross diagram.

- Explain the importance of aggregate real demand and how it differs from aggregate nominal demand.

- Explain the importance of the aggregate real supply curve and why it becomes vertical at some level of real output.

- Use aggregate real demand and aggregate real supply curves to analyze an economic recession and recovery.

- Define demand-pull inflation and its causes, and use aggregate real demand and supply analysis to illustrate its effects on the economy.

- Sketch a Phillips curve, and explain why it is not possible to treat the Phillips curve as a fixed policy menu.

- Define cost-push inflation and its causes, and use aggregate real demand and supply analysis to illustrate its effects on the economy.

- Use aggregate real demand and supply analysis to illustrate a situation of inflationary recession.

WALKING TOUR

You have read the chapter at least once and have reviewed the summary in the text. Now you are going to walk through the material step by step, filling in the blanks and answering the questions as you go along. After you have answered each question, check yourself by uncovering the answer given in the margin. If you do not understand why the answer given is the right one, refer back to the proper section of the text.

Unemployment, Inflation, and the Keynesian Cross

The traditional Keynesian cross analysis uses aggregate
[nominal/real] _____ and _____   nominal supply;
analysis to develop a theory of unemployment and   demand
inflation. The early Keynesian theory of inflation

held that inflation is a problem only when the level of nominal national income is [above/below] the full employment level. Below that level, any change in nominal GNP will take the form of a change in [prices/real output]. The major shortcoming of the crude Keynesian theory is that it does not explain how high rates of inflation and unemployment can occur simultaneously.

above

real output

To modify the traditional Keynesian model, nominal values are converted to _____ values. For instance, if the initial equilibrium value of nominal national income is $2,000 and the average selling price of goods produced is $2.00, _____ physical units of the goods are being produced. This situation is represented by AND_1 in Exhibit S17.1a. Similar relationships are represented by AND_2 and AND_3.

real

1,000

Aggregate real _____ values are determined by [multiplying/dividing] equilibrium nominal national income levels by the price level. Using price levels of $1.75, $2.00, and $2.25 per unit of output and a nominal national income level of $2,000, plot three points on grid b in Exhibit S17.1 and connect them to form an aggregate real demand curve (ARD_1). At price levels of $1.75, $2.00, and $2.25 per unit, real output levels indicated by ARD_1 will be approximately _____, _____,

demand
dividing

1,143; 1,000

and _____. ARD_2 and ARD_3 were determined from AND_2 and AND_3 in a similar manner. Note that the equilibrium price level for ARD_1 and ARD_2 is [higher/lower] than that for ARD_3.

889

lower

The aggregate real _____ curve, ARS, in grid b of Exhibit S17.1 shows how much _____ output is produced at different _____ levels. The horizontal portion of the ARS curve shows that _____ increases with [increases/decreases/no change] in the price level. The upward sloping portion of ARS shows that the output level [increases/ decreases] with [increases/decreases/no change] in the price level. At full employment, ARS is [vertical/horizontal] in the textbook model.

supply

real

price
output
no change

increases
increases

vertical

The ARS curve may also shift. A/an [upward to the left/downward to the right] shift could result from a rise in the price of other inputs. A/an [upward to the left/downward to the right] shift of the ARS curve could result from a fall in input prices.

An upward to the left

A downward to the right

Exhibit S17.1a

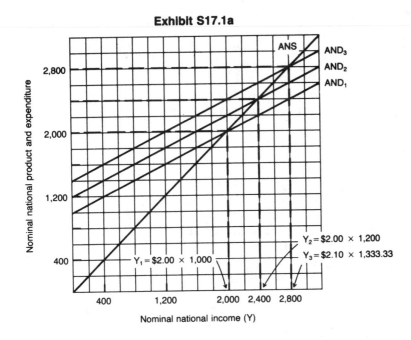

Exhibit S17.1b

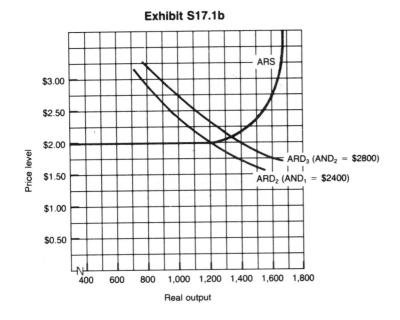

Applications of Aggregate Real Supply and Demand

At the onset of a classic recession, aggregate real
_____ falls and the economy moves [upward/   demand
downward] along the aggregate real _____   downward; supply
curve. In the process, both the level of real
_____ and the _____ level fall.   output; price
    The opposite of a recession is _____   demand-pull
inflation, which is an increase in the price level
caused by a/an [expansion/contraction] of aggregate   an expansion
nominal demand relative to the productive capacity
of the economy.

The Phillips Curve

In 1958, A.W.H. Phillips published the results of an
empirical study, which showed that the rate of increase
of wages tended to [rise/fall] as the unemployment   rise
rate fell. The trade-off appeared to have been stable
over a long time period in Great Britain. At first,
the Phillips curve appeared to offer a policy menu
from which various combinations of inflation and
unemployment could be chosen. However, if inflation-
unemployment combinations for the 1970s are plotted
on a graph along with a Phillips curve from the
1960s, the more recent points lie [above/below] the   above
curve, rather than on it. This suggests that a
more complete theory of inflation must be used to
explain why the position of the Phillips curve
changes over time.

The Cost-Push Theory

The cost-push theory of inflation attempts to explain
why the price level sometimes rises when there is no
apparent pressure from _____. Instead,   aggregate demand
the rise in the price level is touched off by a
spontaneous increase in wage costs, profits, or prices
of basic commodities.
    Cost-push inflation produces an [upward/downward]   an upward
shift in the aggregate real supply curve relative to
the aggregate real demand curve.

SELF TEST

These sample test items will help you check how much you have learned.
Answers and explanations can be found at the end of this book. Scoring
yourself: one or two wrong - on target. Three or four wrong - passing,
but you haven't mastered the chapter yet. Five or more wrong - not
good enough; start over and restudy the chapter.

Multiple Choice

1. According to the crude Keynesian theory of inflation, expansion of aggregate nominal demand will be inflationary only if
    a. the economy is already at full employment.
    b. productivity grows more slowly than its long-term trend.
    c. the expansion of demand arises from monetary policy.
    d. the expansion of demand arises from deficit-financed fiscal policy.

2. Assuming that the target level of national income and the full employment level are the same, the crude Keynesian theory predicts which of the following?
    a. Policies undertaken to fill a deflationary gap will cause only real output to change.
    b. Policies undertaken to fill a deflationary gap will cause only the price level to change.
    c. Policies undertaken to fill a deflationary gap will have results divided about equally between changes in real output and changes in the price level.
    d. The crude Keynesian theory says nothing about these matters.

3. Which of the following does not change as the economy moves along its aggregate real demand curve?
    a. Real output.
    b. Aggregate nominal demand.
    c. The price level.
    d. The unemployment rate.

4. If aggregate nominal demand is $7,200 and the price level is 3.0, the level of aggregate real demand must be
    a. $2,400.
    b. $3,000.
    c. $7,200.
    d. $21,600.

5. The economy's aggregate real supply curve assumes roughly the shape of the letter
    a. U.
    b. L.
    c. V.
    d. J.

6. Which of the following is not likely to cause a downward shift in the aggregate real supply curve?
    a. A fall in money wages.
    b. A fall in input prices.
    c. Productivity increases.
    d. A rise in input prices.

7. A leftward shift in the aggregate real demand curve would produce
   a. a recession.
   b. cost-push inflation.
   c. demand-pull inflation.
   d. an inflationary recession.

8. Which of the following is not true of the Phillips curve?
   a. The curve shows the relationship between the rate of inflation and the level of unemployment.
   b. The curve shows an inverse relationship between inflation and unemployment.
   c. The curve offers a fixed trade-off between inflation and unemployment that provides an excellent policy menu.
   d. The original curves were drawn by A.W.H. Phillips for the British economy.

9. When people blame part of the inflation of the late 1970s on the increase in OPEC oil prices, they are talking about
   a. demand-pull inflation.
   b. cost-push inflation.
   c. wage-push inflation.
   d. the Phillips curve.

10. The result of a negative supply shock, beginning from a point of equilibrium, is likely to include
    a. a drop in real output.
    b. an increase in the price level.
    c. an increase in real output.
    d. a and b.

HANDS ON

Now that you have reviewed the concepts introduced in this chapter, it is time for some hands-on practice with the analytical tools that have been introduced. Work through each problem in this section carefully, and then check your results against those given at the end of the book.

Problem 1. Fill in the blanks in Exhibit S17.2a with the value of aggregate real demand corresponding to each price level (row) and aggregate nominal demand level (column). Use the completed table to graph the three aggregate real demand curves in Exhibit S17.2b.

Exhibit S17.2a

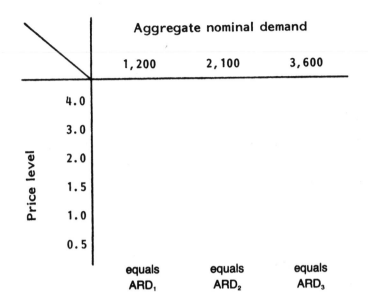

Aggregate nominal demand

| | 1,200 | 2,100 | 3,600 |

Price level

4.0
3.0
2.0
1.5
1.0
0.5

| equals | equals | equals |
| ARD₁ | ARD₂ | ARD₃ |

Exhibit S17.2b

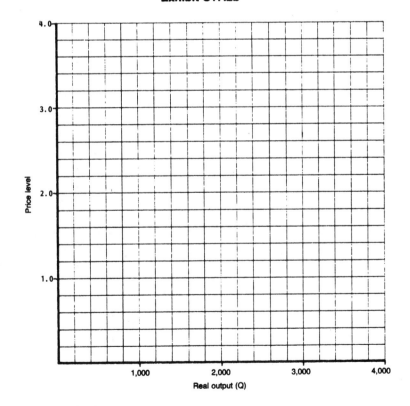

Price level

Real output (Q)

Problem 2. The following questions are based on Exhibit S17.3.

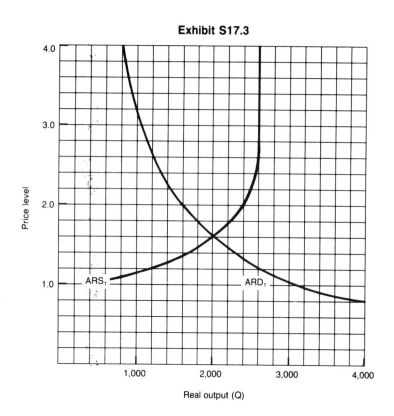

Exhibit S17.3

(a) As the exhibit is drawn, what is the equilibrium level of real output? The level of aggregate nominal demand? The price level at the equilibrium? Label the equilibrium E_1.

(b) Assume now that the government takes fiscal or monetary policy actions having the effect of increasing the level of aggregate nominal demand to $4,800. Draw the new aggregate real demand curve and label it ARD_2.

(c) Describe the results of the expansionary policy that has just been undertaken in terms of real output, the price level at the new equilibrium, and the probable level of unemployment. Where will the new equilibrium be in terms of real output? Label this new equilibrium E_2.

DON'T MAKE THIS COMMON MISTAKE!

Many exam errors result from a failure to learn the simple mechanics of drawing aggregate real demand curves. Master the mechanics of sketching and shifting these curves before you even BEGIN to study the applied material in this chapter. Believe it or not, for once there is a shortcut! Each curve has a KEY REFERENCE POINT that will allow you to sketch in the curve quickly and accurately.

For the aggregate real demand curve, the KEY REFERENCE POINT is a price level of 1.0 and an aggregate real demand equal to aggregate real supply. (Example: You are given AND = $1,800; the key reference point is $1,800 horizontal, 1.0 vertical.) If you are in a panic, just sketch a smooth, downward-sloping curve freehand through the key reference point. Better: For a second reference point, go up to a price level of 2.0 and cut the horizontal distance in half. For a third, go down to a price level of 0.5 and double the horizontal distance. Draw a smooth curve through these three points. Remember: The aggregate real demand curve will shift if, and only if, there is a change in aggregate nominal demand.

Domestic factors

By Russell E. Harrison

Many of our problems have been similar to those experienced by other countries, particularly the United States. Therefore, there is a tendency to blame our own difficulties — hesitant growth, high unemployment, high inflation and a weak balance of payments — on developments outside our own borders. In particular, it has been fashionable to claim that factors beyond our control, such as harvest failures and the sharp raising of oil prices by OPEC, account for our present condition of "stagflation" — that is, slow growth along with high inflation.

It is difficult to understand this line of reasoning. The fact is, although inflationary influences from abroad can be difficult to cope with, inflation is essentially "homemade". By this I mean that for inflation to persist for any length of time in any country it has somehow to be financed; and this, as a rule, can be done only by the national monetary authority — in our case, the Bank of Canada. As soon as it is recognized that inflation is basically a domestic problem, then it is up to government to check it by means of responsible economic policy.

Unfortunately, Canada was late in recognizing this hard and basic truth. This is very evident when we look at policy behaviour, both fiscal and monetary, in the period since the early 1970s. Even a casual glance at the numbers involved shows that the federal government adopted a remarkably relaxed attitude towards the problem of inflation in those years. The preoccupation was with maintenance of economic and employment growth and with income redistribution, both among different income groups and among different regions of the country. Generally, economic thinking was still dominated by the enormous expansion in production and income growth which had typified the two decades following World War II.

There was still very little acknowledgement that international trade had become more competitive. It was not yet realized that an ever-increasing standard of living could no longer be taken for granted but would have to be bought through unceasing efforts on the part of all Canadians to improve productivity. In fact, one of the more disturbing aspects of our performance in recent years has been low productivity growth; since 1973 it has risen at only half the rate prevailing during the 1960s. A slowdown in business investment in manufacturing is undoubtedly a key factor in this trend.

This weakness in investment has been brought about by a variety of factors, including the increased risk caused by inflation. Uncertainty regarding government policy has also had an adverse effect on capital investment. This has stemmed, at least in part, from the feeling that governments did not take the inflation danger seriously enough — as evidenced by rapid increases in money supply and growing budget deficits — and that the economic situation was bound to get worse before it got better.

Until the mid-1970s, our federal government did little to discourage the excessive economic expectations of the Canadian people. It responded instead by expanding its own sphere of operations, thus causing an ever-increasing share of our national production to be channelled through the government sector. Total government expenditures in Canada, which in the mid-1960s had amounted to about 30 per cent of Gross National Product, rose to more than 40 per cent of GNP by the second half of the 1970s. Much of this rise was accounted for by increasingly generous federal transfer programs.

The federal government's own excessive expectations were undoubtedly influenced by rapid growth in revenues. These had helped to hold down its budget deficit and net financing requirements until the mid-1970s, after which there was a very sharp deterioration in the government's fiscal position. It is true that government revenue growth had fluctuated along with the business cycle. However, the tax system, which had been designed to maximize the government's revenue intake during World War II, had continued to provide the public sector with a large cash inflow each year after the war. In fact, this inflow was so large that governments often had to exercise considerable ingenuity to find ways of spending their funds and avoiding embarrassing surpluses.

The preoccupation with economic expansion, as opposed to price stability, can be seen equally clearly on the monetary side. Here the Bank of Canada condoned an extremely rapid escalation in money supply growth after 1970, and it is only in recent years that the central bank has attempted to repair the damage by gradually bringing growth in the total money supply under better control.

From "Change, Choice and Challenge: Canada's Economy in the 1980s," **Spectrum**, *Canadian Imperial Bank of Commerce Newsletter, Vol. I, No. 2, pp. 5–7. Reprinted by permission.*

1. According to the author, how has government policy since the early 1970s influenced aggregate real demand? What policy alternatives did the government have?

2. What kind of inflationary pressures did harvest failures and OPEC oil price increases cause in Canada? What happened to the aggregate real supply curve as a result of these occurrences?

3. How might "excessive economic expectations" on the part of the Canadian people and the federal government "expanding its own sphere of operations" influence aggregate real demand in the Canadian economy?

4. Is there information in this article that would make you think the Phillips curve for Canada has shifted? Explain.

CHAPTER 18
THE DYNAMICS OF INFLATION AND UNEMPLOYMENT

WHERE
YOU'RE GOING

_____

When you have mastered this chapter, you will be able to:

- Define and explain Okun's law.

- List and explain the four major building blocks of the theory of inflation.

- Construct a job search diagram, using reservation and wage offer curves.

- Explain how the effects of an initial dose of expansionary fiscal or monetary policy are split between a change in inflation and a change in unemployment, assuming a standing start.

- Explain the conditions under which an inflationary recession can occur.

- Explain how, during a period of reflation, fiscal and monetary policy can be used to lower the unemployment rate, with little or no penalty in terms of rising inflation.

- Explain the economic and political causes of a stop-go policy cycle.

- Use the simple theory of the dynamics of inflation to interpret recent Canadian macroeconomic experience.

- Explain the meaning and significance of the following additional terms and concepts:

      accelerationist theory of inflation
      adaptive expectations hypothesis
      rational expectations hypothesis

WALKING TOUR

_____

You have read the chapter at least once and have reviewed the summary in the text. Now you are going to walk through the material step by step, filling in the blanks and answering the questions as you go along. After you have answered each question, check yourself by uncovering the

answer given in the margin. If you do not understand why the answer given
is the right one, refer back to the proper section of the text.

The Effects of Accelerating Inflation

The first building block of inflation theory explains
the effects of monetary and _____ policy   fiscal
on nominal income, national income, and
_____. The second block sets the rate   product
of growth of [nominal/real] national product equal   nominal
to the growth rate of [nominal/real] output plus   real
the rate of inflation.

    The third building block of inflation theory,
Okun's law, states the observed relationship between
the rate of growth of _____ output and   real

changes in the _____ rate. The law says   unemployment
that each one percentage point [increase/decrease]   increase
in unemployment results in a _____   three
percent decrease in real economic growth. Canada's
potential output growth has been approximately
_____ percent, based on a "normal"   three
unemployment rate of about five percent. This
potential real growth rate can be expected as a
result of changes in _____, labor   population

force participation, and labor _____.   productivity
    The fourth building block of inflation
theory involves the mark-up policy businesses
use to set prices and the job search theory. Since
labor costs average about _____ percent   seventy-five
of net national income, wages are a major
determinant of production costs. When wages
_____ but labor productivity does not   rise
increase at the same rate, the _____   unit
labor cost of production increases, and usually
with it, the price of the output.

Job Search: A Theory of Labor Market Behavior

It has been observed that when the unemployment
rate rises, the average duration of unemployment
[rises/falls]. For this reason, much recent work   rises
in employment theory has focused on what determines
the average duration of the unemployed worker's
process of job search. Exhibit S18.1 can be used to
illustrate some of the findings of this research.
This exhibit contains two wage offer curves, labeled
W_1 and W_2, and two reservation curves, labeled R_1
and R_2. Assume that if there is no inflation and
none is expected, the curves W_1 and R_1 apply. In
this case, the average duration of unemployment

Exhibit S18.1

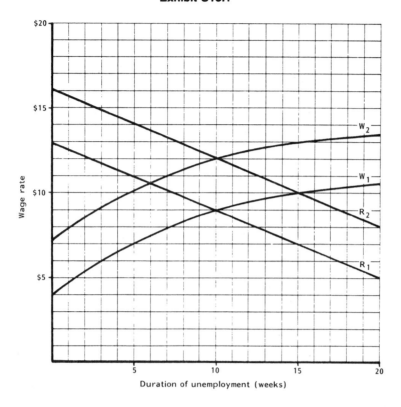

Wage rate

Duration of unemployment (weeks)

would be _____ weeks. Assume now that in Year   ten
1, the actual price level rises, and is reflected in
higher actual wages, but the expected price level
does not change. Of the curves given in Exhibit S18.1,
the pair that would best represent the situation in
Year 1 would be _____. The average R_1 and W_2
duration of unemployment in Year 1 would thus
[rise/fall] to _____ weeks.   fall; six
    Assume instead that workers had fully expected
the Year 1 price increase. Then, of the curves
drawn in the exhibit, the pair best representing
the situation would be _____. The R_2 and W_2
average duration of unemployment would then
[rise to/fall to/remain at] _____   remain at; ten
weeks. Finally, assume that in Year 1, the
actual rate of inflation had been zero but that
workers had expected the price level to rise. Of
the curves shown, those best representing this
situation would be _____. The average R_2 and W_1
duration of unemployment would [rise/fall] to   rise
_____ weeks.   fifteen
    The four building blocks of inflation theory
combine to describe a dynamic inflationary process

18-3

called the _____ theory of inflation.   accelerationist
This theory states that changes in the inflation
rate, rather than the rate itself, influence
_____ output and _____.   real; employment
   Expectations about future rates of inflation
also play an important role in the theory of
inflation. The _____ expectations   adaptive
hypothesis states that people form their
expectations of the future rate of inflation
primarily on the basis of inflationary experience
in the [immediate/distant] past. The   immediate
_____ hypothesis states that people   rational expectations
form their inflationary expectations on the basis
of immediate-past inflationary experiences and on
forward-looking judgments of the probable course
of economic policy and its effects on the economy.
   The effects of expansionary monetary and fiscal
policy on an economy can be illustrated by a
short-run _____ curve and a job search   Phillips
diagram. See Exhibit S18.2. Assume the economy
starts from a point where both the actual and
expected rates of inflation are zero. Expansionary
policy [increases/decreases] aggregate demand,   increases
and firms react by _____ output   increasing
and/or _____. In the labor market,   prices
the increased demand for workers will shift
the wage offer curve [upward/downward], while   upward
the reservation wage curve is likely to [rise/
fall/remain constant]. Sketch the probable new   remain constant
wage offer curve in Exhibit S18.2a, and
label it W_2.
   At this point, the economy will be moving
[up/down] and to the [left/right] along the   up; left
short-run Phillips curve (Ph_1 in Exhibit S18.2b),
showing that the unemployment rate is [rising/
falling/remaining constant] and the inflation   falling
rate is [rising/falling/remaining constant].   rising
   If expansionary policy continues, the
economy will move to a new Phillips curve that
is to the [left/right] of and [below/above]   right; above
the original curve Ph_1, since people will have
come to expect increased _____.   inflation
Sketch a probable new short-run Phillips curve
in Exhibit S18.2b and label it Ph_2. In the
job search diagram, the reservation wage curve
will shift [upward/downward] and the duration of   upward
unemployment will [increase/decrease]. Sketch   increase
the probable new reservation wage curve in
Exhibit S18.2a, and label it R_2.
   Continued expansionary policy could result

Exhibit S18.2

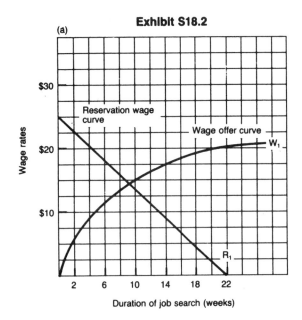

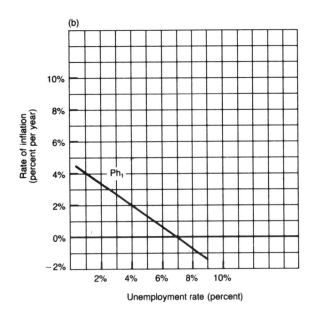

in [continued/sharply decreased] inflation, and no
further decreases in unemployment or growth of real
_____.   Contractionary monetary and fiscal policy
designed to _____ aggregate demand may
lead to an _____ recession, since people
will expect inflation to continue. The duration of
unemployment will probably [increase/decrease], since

continued

output

reduce

inflationary

increase

people's reservation wages remain [high/low] for a   high
period of time. Eventually, the inflation rate
falls, but unemployment may stay high or even
[rise/fall] for a while.   rise
          Pressure on governments to reduce the
unemployment rate may result in a stop-go policy
and _____. This occurs when demand   reflation
management policy becomes more expansionary while
the expected rate of inflation is [rising/falling].   falling

SELF TEST
_____

These sample test items will help you check how much you have learned.
Answers and explanations can be found at the end of this book. Scoring
yourself: one or two wrong - on target. Three or four wrong - passing,
but you haven't mastered the chapter yet. Five or more wrong - not
good enough; start over and restudy the chapter.

Multiple Choice

1. Okun's law states that
    a. each 1 percent increase in unemployment results in a 3 percent
        decrease in real economic growth.
    b. each 3 percent decrease in real economic growth results in a
        1 percent increase in unemployment.
    c. each 1 percent increase in unemployment results in a 3 percent
        increase in real economic growth.
    d. both a and b.

2. If a company was paying an hourly wage rate of $6 and the output
    of each unit of labor was 6 units per hour, an increase in the
    wage rate to $7 per hour and in output to 6.5 units per hour
    would represent
    a. an increase in the unit labor cost.
    b. a decrease in the unit labor cost.
    c. no change in the unit labor cost.
    d. There is not enough information to calculate an answer.

3. According to the job search theory of unemployment, the longer a
    person is out of work,
    a. the higher that person's reservation wage.
    b. the lower that person's reservation wage.
    c. the lower that person's expected rate of inflation.
    d. the lower that person's chance of ever finding work.

4. According to the job search theory of unemployment, an increase in
    the expected rate of inflation, other things being equal, will
    shift
    a. the reservation wage curve.
    b. the wage offer curve.

c. both of the above.
d. neither of the above.

5. The adaptive expectations hypothesis of inflation states that
   a. people adapt to whatever rate of inflation occurs.
   b. people form their expectations of the future rate of inflation primarily on the inflationary experience of the immediate past.
   c. people form their expectations of the future inflation rate by evaluating the probable course of current monetary and fiscal policy.
   d. both b and c.

6. During accelerating inflation,
   a. workers have lower reservation wages than they would have if their inflationary expectations were accurate.
   b. workers have higher reservation wages than they would have if their inflationary expectations were accurate.
   c. workers' inflationary expectations are accurate.
   d. none of the above is true.

7. According to the theory of inflationary dynamics given in this chapter, unemployment can be kept below the previous equilibrium rate for a sustained period under which of the following conditions?
   a. Only at the cost of a constantly high rate of inflation.
   b. Only at the cost of continuously accelerating inflation.
   c. Only at the cost of declining growth of potential GNP.
   d. None of the above; unemployment can fall below the equilibrium rate only temporarily.

8. If, during an inflationary recession, the unemployment rate rises from 4 percent in one year to 6 percent in the next, and if the growth rate of potential real GNP is assumed to be 3 percent, what will be the growth rate of actual real GNP?
   a. -6 percent.
   b. -3 percent.
   c. 0 percent.
   d. 3 percent.

9. Beginning from a standing start position, suppose the rate of growth of nominal GNP accelerates to 7 percent in the next year. Assuming the trend growth rate of potential real GNP to be 3 percent and the equilibrium rate of unemployment to be 5 percent, which of the following is a possible inflation-unemployment combination for that year?
   a. 4 percent unemployment and 1 percent inflation.
   b. 3 percent unemployment and 1 percent inflation.
   c. 4 percent unemployment and 3 percent inflation.
   d. Insufficient information is given for an answer to be reached.

10. Stop-go cycles occur because
    a. policymakers don't really understand how monetary and fiscal policy tools work.
    b. governments are often under pressure to implement expansionary policy during periods of high unemployment.
    c. governments are often under pressure to implement contractionary policy during periods of high inflation.
    d. both b and c.

HANDS ON

Now that you have reviewed the concepts introduced in this chapter, it is time for some hands-on practice with the analytical tools that have been introduced. Work through the problem in this section carefully, and then check your results against those given at the end of the book.

Problem 1. Use the short-run Phillips curve in Exhibit S18.3 to answer the following questions.

Exhibit S18.3

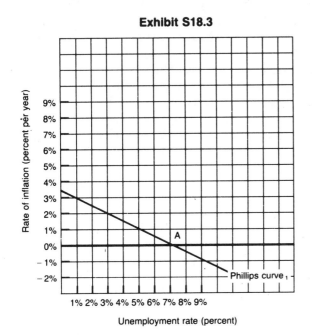

(a) Assume that in year 0 the economy is at a standing start with expected and actual rates of inflation at zero; unemployment is at an equilibrium rate of 7 percent; the growth rate of actual real GNP is equal to the growth rate of potential real GNP, which is zero in this special case. The economy is at point A in Exhibit S18.3. The government now decides to stimulate the economy to reduce unemployment and achieve some economic growth. The expansionary policy raises the growth rate of nominal GNP from zero to 7 percent by the start of year 1. What is likely to happen to the wage offer curve in a job search diagram? To the reservation wage curve? To the duration of unemployment? To the unemployment rate?

(b) By the start of year 1, nominal GNP has grown by 7 percent. Knowing from the building block theory of inflation that the inflation rate plus the growth rate of real output must equal the growth of nominal GNP, and that according to Okun's law, each 1 percent decrease in unemployment results in a 3 percent increase in real economic growth, mark the point on the Phillips curve in Exhibit S18.3 that shows the position of the economy at the start of year 1. Label this point B.

(c) Assume that the expansionary policy continues and nominal GNP has increased by another 7 percent by the start of year 2. Remembering the adaptive expectations hypothesis, illustrate in Exhibit S18.3 the shift of the short-run Phillips curve.

(d) If there had been no inflation between year 0 and year 1, what would have happened to the economy as a result of the expansionary policy? Explain your answer in terms of the short-run Phillips curve.

(e) If the government introduces contractionary policy at the end of year 2, causing nominal GNP to increase by only 4 percent, what is likely to happen to inflation? Assume that real output rises by 1 percent during this year. Is this contractionary policy a quick cure for inflation? What name does the text use to describe the events that are likely to occur as a result of this contractionary policy?

Key inflation lessons for policymakers

By Richard Lipsey and Douglas Purvis

INFLATION has not always been a prominent feature of the Canadian economic landscape. But it has recently become one.

Inflation is perceived by Ottawa to be "public enemy number one," and policymakers currently find themselves in the uncomfortable position of pursuing restrictive policies at a time when unemployment is at postwar record levels. (The apparent anomaly of this last situation is resolved when one recognizes that the current high unemployment is in large part a result of the recession *created* by government in order to combat inflation.)

Let us set the current inflation in perspective and draw out the lessons for public policy that can be learned from our experience. One basic lesson is simple enough to be stated at the outset:

Lesson 1: It took a long time to build inflation to its current level, and we should not be surprised if it takes a long time to reduce inflation.

Those who offer "quick and simple" cures would, if their advice were acted on, prove to be false prophets. Similarly, those who condemn current policies as a failure may prove to be premature in their judgment.

High and accelerating inflation is not inevitable. Inflation actually fell during the period 1957–65. Much of this fall was the result of contractionary policies pursued over the 1958–61 period by the Diefenbaker government and supported by James Coyne, then the governor of the Bank of Canada. Those contractionary policies also led to a serious recession; over the period 1958–61 the economy experienced no real growth, and unemployment averaged 7%.

Lesson 2: Reductions in inflation do not come easily; disinflation is usually accompanied by temporary increases in unemployment.

Costs are an unfortunate but necessary part of any disinflation program, and any honest policy which aims at reducing inflation must explicitly recognize that these costs will arise.

In 1961, expansionary policies were initiated by the Diefenbaker government; these were reinforced by the new governor of the Bank of Canada, Louis Rasminsky, and continued by the Pearson government (1963–68). This stimulus caused the inflation rate to more than double in the second half of the decade.

Even if one believes the contractionary policies of the Coyne-Diefenbaker period were excessive, it must be admitted that they did reduce inflation. By 1961, the costs of reducing inflation, measured in terms of high unemployment, had largely been paid and the economy was on the road to recovery at a lower inflation rate. However, the excessive expansion undertaken in the early 1960s ultimately led to the increased inflation of the latter part of the decade.

A similar episode occurred at the turn of the next decade, when a deliberately engineered recession led to reduced inflation and a record balance of payments surplus culminating with the appreciation of the Canadian dollar in June 1970. Again, the costs of reducing inflation were paid, and again the benefits were quickly dissipated following the adoption of excessively expansionary policies in 1970–71.

Inflation rose steadily from 2.9% in 1971 to 4.8%, 7.5% and 10.9% in successive years. The Opec crisis in 1973 combined with raw material and food shortages contributed to this acceleration, but the seeds of increased inflation appear to us to have been sown by domestic monetary policies well in advance of those external events.

Lesson 3: The costs of disinflation are large, but the benefits are quickly dissipated if policy is reversed too quickly.

Much of the increase in world inflation over the period 1973–74 could have been avoided in Canada had monetary growth been curtailed and the Canadian dollar allowed to appreciate. However, in a vain attempt to overly protect the competitive position of our export industries, the exchange rate was stabilized. This led to increased monetary expansion and domestic inflationary pressures. In the end, the competitive position of the export industries was not protected since the inflation caused their costs to rise.

*From **The Financial Post**, May 29, 1982, p. 10. Reprinted by permission.*

1. Given the theory developed in this chapter, why would it take a "long time to build inflation to its current level" and take a "long time to reduce inflation?"

2. What probably happened to the reservation wage curve, the wage offer curve, the duration of unemployment, and the short-run Phillips curve during the 1958 to 1961 period? Explain.

3. What probably happened to the reservation wage curve, the wage offer curve, the duration of unemployment, and the short-run Phillips curve during the 1961 to 1968 period? Explain.

4. Cite passages from the article to show that the Canadian government has used stop-go policies in the past. Why would such policies have been used?

CHAPTER 19
COMBATING INFLATION AND UNEMPLOYMENT

WHERE
YOU'RE GOING

_____

When you have mastered this chapter, you will be able to:

- Give a brief recap of the tools and effects of economic
  stabilization policy.

- Explain how recession can curb inflation.

- Describe how actions by both business and labor have fueled
  inflation in Canada.

- Identify the circumstances under which incomes policies are most
  likely to work.

- Define industrial democracy and explain how this concept might be
  used to help control inflation and unemployment.

WALKING TOUR

_____

You have read the chapter at least once and have reviewed the summary in
the text. Now you are going to walk through the material step by step,
filling in the blanks and answering the questions as you go along. After
you have answered each question, check yourself by uncovering the answer
given in the margin. If you do not understand why the answer given is
the right one, refer back to the proper section of the text.

Recap of Inflation and Unemployment Theory

According to previous chapters of this book, the
government can, within limits, control the level of
[real/nominal] national income but is able to control   nominal
employment, inflation, and real growth only indirectly.
Expansion of aggregate demand can reduce unemployment
if it causes the actual rate of inflation to [exceed/
fall short of] the expected rate of inflation.   exceed
However, unemployment can be kept below the
equilibrium rate for a sustained period only if
inflation steadily _____. When inflation   accelerates
unexpectedly slows after a period of acceleration,
[inflation/unemployment/both inflation and
unemployment] are likely to increase; this is called   both inflation and
a/an _____. Continued contractionary   unemployment
                                                                       an inflationary
                                                                         recession

policy by government can eventually end inflation, but only slowly. As long as inflation continues to fall, with the actual rate of inflation less than the expected rate, unemployment will remain [above/below] the equilibrium rate.   above

Going Beyond Demand Management

Demand management implicitly relies on the creation of a _____ to curb inflation. This   recession
kind of cure for inflation has high human costs
as a result of increased _____ and   unemployment
_____ rates.   bankruptcy
     Business and labor contribute to
inflationary pressures through increased
_____ and _____ demands.   prices; wage
However, according to evidence in the text,
their efforts [were/were not] able to keep real   were not
wages and after-tax returns on equity rising as
fast as inflation in the early 1980s.
     Canada's current inflation and unemployment
problems have many causes, some of which are:
[large/small] increases in the labor force, sharp   large
[increases/decreases] in commodity prices, interest   increases
rate pressure from other nations, increasing
protectionism, [drops/increases] in productivity,   drops
and technological breakthroughs that leave many
people untrained for current job openings.

Some New Alternatives

Because past demand management policies have not
resulted in the achievement of all the goals of
economic stabilization, economists have looked
for additional policy alternatives. One is to try
to control prices and wages directly by use of
_____ policies. Incomes policies are   incomes
theoretically strongest as [temporary/long-term]   temporary
measures to fight inflationary recessions. Controls
have been tried several times in Canada with
[varying degrees of/great/no] success. Economists   varying degrees of
are [in agreement/divided] about the wisdom of   divided
future uses of controls.
     _____ arrangements which allow   Industrial
workers to participate more fully in economic   democracy
decision making have been proposed as a method
of increasing cooperation between workers and
management. A number of countries who use forms
of industrial democracy have experienced [lower/
higher] rates of unemployment and _____   lower; inflation
than countries who do not use many such
arrangements. Canada falls into the group of countries
who use [few/many] forms of industrial democracy.   few

_____

These sample test items will help you check how much you have learned.
Answers and explanations can be found at the end of this book. Scoring
yourself: one or two wrong - on target. Three or four wrong - passing,
but you haven't mastered the chapter yet. Five or more wrong - not
good enough; start over and restudy the chapter.

Multiple Choice

1. The goal of stabilization policy is
    a. full employment.
    b. price stability.
    c. real economic growth.
    d. all of the above.

2. Inflation can occur when
    a. aggregate nominal demand grows faster than the economy's real
        productive capacity for a sustained period.
    b. firms and workers expect prices to rise and therefore, they
        raise their prices and wage demands accordingly.
    c. aggregate nominal demand grows slower than the economy's real
        productive capacity for a sustained period.
    d. both a and b.

3. If real output is held below its equilibrium level and unemployment
    above its equilibrium level for a sustained period of time
    a. inflationary expectations will rise.
    b. inflationary expectations will continue to be revised downward
        until they approach zero.
    c. inflationary expectations will remain unchanged.
    d. none of the above.

4. A restrictive demand management policy
    a. implicitly relies on the creation of a recession to curb inflation.
    b. usually causes unemployment to fall.
    c. often increases small business investment.
    d. rarely affects the rate of inflation.

5. Business firms and labor unions
    a. behave totally differently when faced with inflation.
    b. behave in similar ways when faced with inflation.
    c. are always hurt by inflation.
    d. none of the above.

6. Which of the following have not contributed to inflation and
    unemployment problems in Canada?
    a. Sharp increases in commodity prices.
    b. Applications of new computer technology.
    c. Low interest rates in the United States.
    d. Protectionism in the foreign sector.

7. According to the accelerationist theory of inflation, the mechanism through which incomes policies potentially could operate most effectively is
   a. slowing the growth of aggregate nominal demand.
   b. slowing the growth of real GNP.
   c. raising the unemployment rate.
   d. reducing inflationary expectations.

8. According to the theory of inflation presented in this book, an incomes policy would most likely be effective against which type of inflation?
   a. Demand-pull inflation.
   b. Accelerating inflation.
   c. Commodity inflation.
   d. Inflation already beginning to slow.

9. Industrial democracy agreements now in place in many countries usually grant workers more rights
   a. in decisions involving working conditions.
   b. in executive decisions on plant relocations and new investments.
   c. in rules for dismissals and layoffs.
   d. all of the above.

10. Business or labor leaders may be apprehensive about industrial democracy agreements for the following reasons:
   a. Management may fear that workers will use their increased power irresponsibly.
   b. Union leaders may fear that they will be forced to serve management goals.
   c. Both a and b.
   d. Industrial democracy agreements have proved to be unworkable in most countries where they have been tried.

Controls don't work

The problem with any new version of wage and price controls is that controls have already lost their value as a quick-fix solution. If they were introduced now to help deal with inflation, as some sources indicate they may be, it would mean the 1975–78 controls failed.

A new incomes policy would probably have to remain in place much longer than before to make sure there would be no second failure. Some form of control might even have to become permanent or, alternatively, remain in the government's arsenal to be trotted out quickly whenever Ottawa thinks they're necessary. In that case, the economy could find itself in a government strait-jacket.

Such controls would represent a fundamental change in Canada's free enterprise market system and in the long run that would be very damaging indeed. They would interfere with industry's ability to react to market conditions that, for Canada, are largely set outside the country. And they would deprive business of the essential drive in any successful economy — to make as much profit as the market can reasonably bear.

Speculation is intensifying in Ottawa that the government will return to controls. Treasury Board president Don Johnston says he has no plans for controls on federal civil service wages. But the Finance Minister is less convincing. He says he is not considering general controls *now*. It would be better, he says, for business and unions to trim their demands so that controls will not be necessary. The impression is clear that, if they don't, controls will be brought back.

Public sector unions in federal and provincial jurisdictions are readying hefty catch-up demands. The Conference Board of Canada says 1982 wages are likely to get ahead of inflation for the first time in five years and public sector unions will lead the way.

Wage increases this year are predicted to be a full four or five percentage points higher than in the U.S. where massive layoffs in key industries are forcing down expectations. Canada's recovery will be hurt if our payroll costs get too far ahead of those in our biggest market and we can't sell our goods there. Controls might be seen as a quick solution.

But if Canadian wages have been lagging behind inflation, they are clearly less to blame for inflation than other factors. Rapidly rising energy prices resulting from government policies are clearly more important. So are Ottawa's rather expensive plans to buy much of the energy industry back from its American owners. These government interventions, justified as they may be, have changed the conditions under which recent labor contracts were negotiated.

Wage negotiations seldom keep pace with what is happening in the economy. Too often unions try to recover on the down side of the cycle, having failed to keep up with the rising side. A declining economy can't afford their demands.

Incomes control doesn't take care of this problem, unless it is permanently in place and some government body can respond quickly to economic performance by mandating wage rates. To be equitable, controls would have to cover prices and profits, thus business would be unable to operate effectively in the marketplace.

It might be better in the long run to look for some way of tuning income more directly to living costs. Perhaps wages should be less locked into precise union contract periods. Or maybe cost-of-living adjustment clauses could be adapted so unions would not have to seek big catch-up settlements.

There may be problems with such new approaches. But they may be less severe than income controls.

*From the **Vancouver Province**, February 1, 1982, Editorial, p. B1.*

1. Why would the introduction of wage and price controls in 1982 have meant that the 1975-78 controls failed? Why would the author feel that controls introduced in 1982 would "probably have to remain in place much longer" than three years?

2. Look at Exhibit 19.1 and Case Study 19.1 in the text. What influence did the 1975-78 controls have on weekly wages and salaries and business after-tax rates of return on equity while they were in effect? What happened to these two measures when controls were removed?

3. In what way, if any, could controls help Canada's export sector?

4. "Wage negotiations seldom keep pace with what is happening in the economy. Too often unions try to recover on the down side of the cycle, having failed to keep up with the rising side." Does the evidence in Exhibit 19.1 support these statements by the author?

CHAPTER 20
SUPPLY AND DEMAND: BUILDING ON THE BASICS

WHERE
YOU'RE GOING
_____

When you have mastered this chapter, you will be able to:

- Use supply and demand curves to show how changes in economic
  conditions affect equilibrium price and quantity in the market
  in question.

- Define price elasticity of demand and explain why knowing elasticity
  of demand is important in economic decision making.

- Calculate price elasticity of demand for any specified range of
  price along a demand curve.

- Define price elasticity of supply and calculate price elasticity of
  supply for any specified range of price along a supply curve.

- Define income elasticity of demand and calculate income elasticity
  of demand, given data on income and quantity changes.

- Explain the meaning and significance of the following additional
  terms and concepts:

        elastic demand
        inelastic demand
        unit elastic demand
        perfectly inelastic demand

WALKING TOUR
_____

You have read the chapter at least once and have reviewed the summary
in the text. Now you are going to walk through the material step by
step, filling in the blanks and answering the questions as you go along.
After you have answered each question, check yourself by uncovering
the answer given in the margin. If you do not understand why the answer
given is the right one, refer back to the proper section of the text.

A Review of the Basics

Exhibit S20.1 shows hypothetical supply and demand
curves for soybeans. As the graph is drawn, the
equilibrium price for soybeans is _____ $350
per tonne, and the equilibrium quantity produced

These sample test items will help you check how much you have learned. Answers and explanations can be found at the end of this book. Scoring yourself: one or two wrong - on target. Three or four wrong - passing, but you haven't mastered the chapter yet. Five or more wrong - not good enough; start over and restudy the chapter.

Multiple Choice

1. An increase in consumer income, other things being equal, would be likely to have which of the following effects on the market for cars?
   a. First a shift in the demand curve, then a shift in the supply curve.
   b. First a shift in the supply curve, then a shift in the demand curve.
   c. First a shift in the demand curve, then a movement along the supply curve.
   d. First a movement along the demand curve, then a shift in the supply curve.

2. If good X is an inferior good, an increase in consumer income will
   a. shift the demand curve to the left.
   b. shift the demand curve to the right.
   c. cause an upward movement along the demand curve without shifting it.
   d. cause a downward movement along the demand curve without shifting it.

3. Which of the following would cause a movement along the supply curve for lawnmowers, without shifting the curve?
   a. A change in the wage rate of lawnmower workers.
   b. A change in the technology of lawnmower production.
   c. A change in the price of hired lawn care services.
   d. None of the above.

4. Assuming beef to be a normal good, which of the following would not happen on the way to a new equilibrium if, other things being equal, consumer income increased?
   a. Depletion of inventories.
   b. A shortage.
   c. An upward movement of prices.
   d. An upward shift of the supply curve.

5. In July 1979, Moore's Grocery sold thirty-two jars of pickles, earning a total revenue of $31.36. In July 1980, the same store sold thirty-two jars of pickles, earning a total revenue of $38.08. From this data, it can be concluded that
   a. the supply of pickles is perfectly inelastic.
   b. the demand for pickles is elastic.
   c. the supply curve for pickles shifted upward.
   d. none of the above is necessarily true.

6. If the excess quantity of wheat supplied is 300 tonnes per year when the price is $200 per tonne and 600 tonnes per year when the price is $210 per tonne, which of the following can be concluded?
   a. The demand for wheat is elastic.
   b. The supply of wheat is elastic.
   c. At least one of the above is true.
   d. None of the above can be concluded from the information given.

7. If the number of movie tickets sold increases by 10 percent when the price is cut by 20 percent, other things being equal, it can be concluded that
   a. demand is price elastic.
   b. demand is price inelastic.
   c. demand is income elastic.
   d. demand is income inelastic.

8. If raising the cigarette tax from $.10 per pack to $.20 per pack left cigarette tax revenues unchanged, it could be concluded that the price elasticity of demand for cigarettes was which of the following? (Hint: Assume tax revenues are $1.00; then work out quantities necessary to keep tax revenues at $1.00 with the per pack tax increase.)
   a. Elastic.
   b. Inelastic.
   c. Unit elastic.
   d. Impossible to calculate from the information given.

9. If the quantity of apples sold at a certain fruit stand increases from 20 kg per day to 30 kg per day when the price is lowered from $.40 per kilogram to $.30 per kilogram, the elasticity of demand is closest to which of the following?
   a. 0.2.
   b. 0.7.
   c. 1.4.
   d. 4.1.

10. If the income elasticity of demand for intercity bus travel is -0.5, we would expect, other things being equal, that
   a. bus company revenues will rise when incomes fall.
   b. bus company revenues will fall when incomes fall.
   c. a is true, but only if demand is also price elastic.
   d. a is true, but only if demand is also price inelastic.

HANDS ON

Now that you have reviewed the concepts introduced in this chapter, it is time for some hands-on practice with the analytical tools that have been introduced. Work through each problem in this section carefully, and then check your results against those given at the end of the book.

Exhibit S20.2

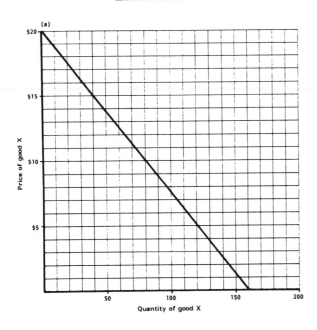

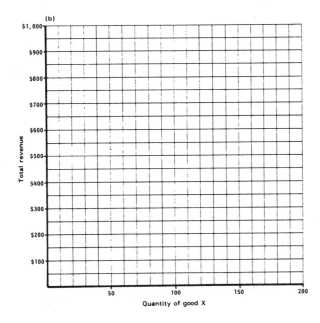

Problem 1.

(a) Using the demand curve in Exhibit S20.2a as your source of information, draw a graph in grid b, showing the total revenue associated with each quantity demanded of good X.

(b) Using your total revenue graph as a guide, identify and label elastic, inelastic, and unit elastic points or segments on the demand curve.

Problem 2.

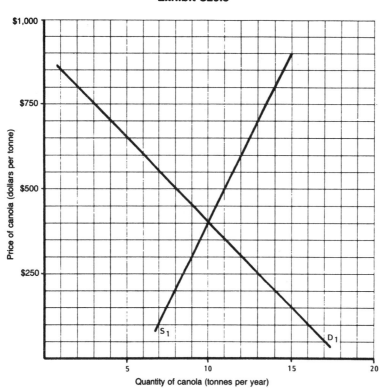

Exhibit S20.3

(a) Find the equilibrium price and quantity for the canola market as Exhibit S20.3 is drawn. Label the equilibrium E_1.

(b) Suppose an improved seed variety reduces the cost of growing canola, so that farmers are willing to supply any given quantity at a price $300 lower than previously. Indicate any shifts in the supply or demand curves on the diagram. Find the new equilibrium point and label it E_2.

(c) In the range between E_1 and E_2, what is the price elasticity of demand for canola?

(d) With the cost reduction still in effect, suppose an increase in the prices of substitute grains increases the amount of canola consumers are willing to buy at any given price by 6 tonnes per year. Indicate any shifts in the supply or demand curves on the diagram. Find the new equilibrium and label it E_3.

(e) In the range between E$_2$ and E$_3$, what is the price elasticity of supply for canola?

APPLICATION

Mail volume up despite cost

TORONTO (CP) — If postal users don't like the higher prices they are paying to move the mail, postal officials say they aren't indicating it by cutting down on use of the system.

"We haven't seen anything that would indicate a flood tide of protest," against new postal rates that went into effect Jan. 1, said Ed Roworth, director of public affairs of the Ontario postal region.

"On the contrary, it appears volume has gone up," Roworth said yesterday.

Some post offices in the province have reported shortages of stamps, especially denominations used to supplement the old 17-cent stamps.

Domestic first class letter rates rose to 30 cents from 17 cents, while letters bound for the U.S. now are 35 cents.

There were also increases for other categories of mail.

Roworth said volume in street letter boxes has been down about five or 10 per cent, but says it is "nothing drastic."

"A drop is usual after Christmas, and this is a little less than we might have expected considering the size of the price increase."

Close to 90 per cent of the post office's volume is business mail, and Roworth says volume in that category has gone up between 10 and 20 per cent since the new rates went into effect.

Billings for goods bought at Christmas have increased the volume, Roworth said.

The post office is also dealing with an increase of third-class mail, most of it posted before Jan. 1.

From Winnipeg Free Press, January 9, 1982, p. 15. Reprinted by permission of Canadian Press.

1. Using the figures given by Mr. Roworth for street letter box volumes, calculate the price elasticity of demand for domestic first-class letters. Since Mr. Roworth gives two figures, calculate both elasticity coefficients.

2. Is the price elasticity of demand for domestic first-class mail elastic, inelastic, or unitary? What facts about domestic first-class mail service would have led you to expect this elasticity?

3. From what Mr. Roworth said, did he expect the price elasticity of demand to be greater or less than what you calculated in Question 1? Cite a passage from the article to support your answer.

4. The article says that the volume of business mail increased when the postage rates went up. Does this mean that the demand curve for mail service by businesses is upward sloping? Explain your answer.

CHAPTER 21
THE LOGIC OF CONSUMER CHOICE

WHERE
YOU'RE GOING

When you have mastered this chapter, you will be able to:

- Explain what economists mean by utility and why economists approach the question of satisfying human needs from a point of view that differs from that of psychologists.

- Define marginal utility, and explain what is meant by the principle of diminishing marginal utility.

- Explain the state of consumer equilibrium as the solution to a problem of pure economizing.

- Discuss the law of demand in terms of the income effect and the substitution effect.

In addition, when you have mastered the appendix to this chapter, you will be able to:

- Analyze patterns of consumer preference in terms of indifference curves.

- Use indifference curves to solve problems in consumer equilibrium.

- Use indifference curves to derive demand curves.

- Discuss the meaning and significance of the following additional terms and concepts:

     indifference set
     marginal rate of substitution
     indifference map
     transitivity
     budget line

WALKING TOUR

You have read the chapter at least once and have reviewed the summary in the text. Now you are going to walk through the material step by step, filling in the blanks and answering the questions as you go along. After you have answered each question, check yourself by uncovering the answer given in the margin. If you do not understand why the answer given is the right one, refer back to the proper section of the text.

Consumption and Utility

Economists refer to the pleasure and satisfaction that people derive from the consumption of goods and services as _____. The utility one gets   utility
from the consumption of one additional unit of a good is known as the _____ of that good.   marginal utility
The important principle of diminishing marginal utility says that, as consumption increases, the additional satisfaction received from a one-unit increase in consumption [rises/falls]. In practice,   falls
utility cannot be directly measured, but if there were such a thing as a utility meter, it might give a set of readings like those shown in the table below. Use the data given in the total utility column to fill in the marginal utility column.

Number of Units of Goods Consumed	Total Utility	Marginal Utility	
1	100		
		_____	20
2	120		
		_____	15
3	135		
		_____	10
4	145		
		_____	8
5	153		

The concept of diminishing marginal utility is useful in analyzing the problem in pure economizing that all consumers face. In this problem, the various goods and services available represent
_____. The prices of the goods,   alternative activities
together with the consumer's budget, provide the _____ of the problem.   constraints
Maximizing utility is the _____.   objective
The problem is solved by choosing a selection of goods that makes the [marginal/total] utility   marginal
per dollar's worth of each good just equal to the marginal utility per dollar's worth of each other good. An equivalent way to express this rule is to say that in consumer equilibrium, the ratio of the marginal utility of each good to its
_____ must be the same for all goods   price
consumed.

Substitution and Income Effects and the Law of Demand

The change in quantity consumed of a good whose

21-2

price has fallen can be divided into two parts. The
part of the increase in consumption resulting from
substituting more of the relatively cheap good is
known as the _____ effect. The part   substitution
resulting from the effective increase in real income
is known as the _____ effect. The   income
substitution effect leads to an increase in quantity
demanded when price falls for [normal/inferior/all]   all
goods. The income effect leads to an increase in
quantity demanded when price falls for [normal/
inferior/all] goods and to a decrease in quantity   normal
demanded when price falls for [normal/inferior/all]   inferior
goods. Even for inferior goods, the [income/
substitution] effect is normally the stronger of the   substitution
two, so that in all or virtually all cases, quantity
demanded increases when the price [falls/rises].   falls

Appendix to Chapter 21: An Introduction to Indifference Curves

An indifference curve is the graphical representation
of a set of baskets of goods, none of which is
preferred to any other basket in the set. Such
curves have certain standard properties, including
the following: they all have [positive/negative]   negative
slopes. The slope of an indifference curve at
any point is equal to the ratio of the marginal
utility of the good on the [horizontal/vertical]   horizontal
axis to the marginal utility of the good on the
[horizontal/vertical] axis. The slope of an   vertical
indifference curve [increases/decreases] as one   decreases
moves down and to the right along the curve. An
indifference curve can be drawn through any point
between the axes. Indifference curves do not
cross because of the property of _____   transitivity
of preferences.
    Exhibit S21.1 will give you some practice in
using indifference curves. The indifference map
drawn there represents (hypothetically) my
preferences for books versus movies. You have to
figure out how many books and how many movies I
will consume under various price conditions.
Assume throughout the exercise that the price of
movies is $3 per movie and that my entertainment
budget (spent entirely on these two items) is
$120 per year.
    Begin by assuming that the price of books
is $3 per book. Given this book price, together
with the movie price and my budget, construct
my budget line as follows: if I spend all my
money on movies, I will be able to see
_____ movies per year. Mark a point   forty
at 40 on the vertical axis. If I spend all my
money on books, I will be able to buy

_____ books per year. Mark a point at   forty
40 on the horizontal axis. Connecting these two
points gives you my budget line under the assumed
prices. The point I will choose, given this budget
line, is the point where the indifference curve
_____ is _____ to the budget   14; tangent
line. This will mean consuming approximately
_____ books and _____ movies   thirty-two; eight
per year.

Exhibit S21.1

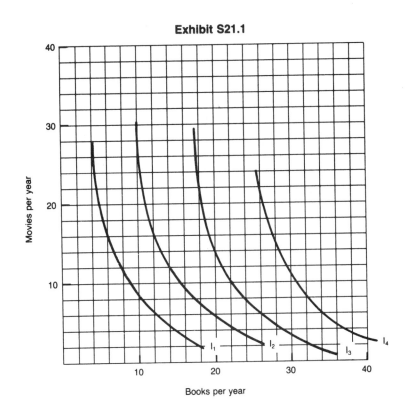

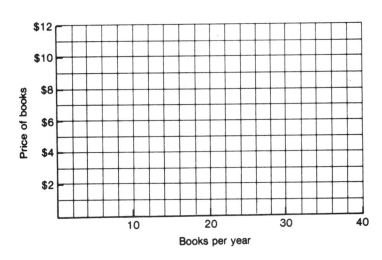

Assume now that the price of a book rises to $4. If I spend all my money on movies, I can still see forty movies, but if I spend it all on books, I can buy only _____ books. Therefore, the new budget line runs from _____ on the vertical axis to _____ on the horizontal axis. The point I will choose on this new budget line will be at the tangency of indifference curve _____. This will mean consuming approximately _____ movies and _____ books. (Note that this would leave $2 unspent.)

thirty
40

30

13

ten

twenty-two

Proceed in a similar fashion to discover what I will consume if the price of a book rises to $6 while my budget and the price of movies remains the same. You will discover that at $6 per book I would buy approximately _____ books and see _____ movies. Finally, perform the same exercise for a book price of $12. At that price, I would consume approximately _____ books and _____ movies. Now, use the data from your figure to fill in the following table:

thirteen

fourteen

six

sixteen

Price of Books	Quantity of Books	
$12	_____	6
6	_____	13
4	_____	22
3	_____	32

Finally, use the table you have just constructed to fill in my demand curve for books in the lower part of Exhibit S21.1. Your completed diagram should look like the one shown in the answers section at the end of this book.

SELF TEST

These sample test items will help you check how much you have learned. Answers and explanations can be found at the end of this book. Scoring yourself: one or two wrong - on target. Three or four wrong - passing, but you haven't mastered the chapter yet. Five or more wrong - not good enough; start over and restudy the chapter.

Multiple Choice

1. According to the principle of diminishing marginal utility, if consumption of a third slice of bread with a meal yields 10 utils, consumption of a sixth slice of bread must give
   a. more than 10 utils.
   b. less than 10 utils.
   c. between 5 and 10 utils.
   d. between 0 and 5 utils.

2. If the consumer choice problem is thought of as a problem in pure economizing, the role of constraint is best represented by
   a. the range of alternative goods available.
   b. the consumer's budget.
   c. the consumer's total capacity for enjoyment.
   d. the consumer's previous patterns of consumption.

3. Assume for a moment that utility is measurable. Then, if a loaf of bread at 20 cents per loaf gives 10 utils, a carton of milk costing 50 cents must give how many utils in consumer equilibrium?
   a. 5 utils.
   b. 12.5 utils.
   c. 25 utils.
   d. 50 utils.

4. Let MU_a represent the marginal utility of good A, MU_b the marginal utility of good B, P_a the price of good A, and P_b the price of good B. Then, in consumer equilibrium, which of the following must hold?
   a. $MU_a = MU_b$.
   b. $P_a = P_b$.
   c. $MU_a/MU_b = P_a/P_b$.
   d. $MU_a/MU_b = P_b/P_a$.

5. In equilibrium, a certain person consumes two units of good X, which costs $.30 per unit, and four units of good Y, which costs $.50 per unit. It can be concluded that for that person, in equilibrium, the ratio of the marginal utility of good X to the marginal utility of good Y is
   a. 2/4.
   b. 4/2.
   c. 3/5.
   d. 5/3.

6. The change in consumption of a good that occurs when its price falls is the result of
   a. the substitution effect.
   b. the income effect.
   c. both of the above effects in combination.
   d. the complementarity of normal and inferior goods.

7. Martha Smith is observed to consume ten cartons of milk per week at $.50 per carton. One week, the price of milk drops to $.40 per carton; but in the same week, a thief steals $1 from her purse, reducing her weekly budget by that amount. On the basis of the theory of consumer behavior, which of the following quantities of milk would she be most likely to consume that week?
   a. Less than 10 cartons.
   b. Ten cartons.
   c. More than ten cartons.
   d. More than ten cartons, but only if milk is assumed to be a normal good.

8. In July 1979, Ed Schwartz ate six ice cream cones at a price of $.50 per cone. In July 1980, he ate seven ice cream cones at a price of $.60 per cone. Which of the following is the most likely explanation of his behavior?
   a. His demand curve for ice cream cones slopes upward.
   b. Ice cream is an inferior good for him; he prefers cake if he can afford it.
   c. The marginal utility of ice cream increases, rather than decreases, as his consumption goes up, other things being equal.
   d. His income and the prices of other goods went up from 1979 to 1980.

Note: The remaining questions are based on the appendix to Chapter 21.

9. Which of the following baskets of goods cannot be a member of an indifference set to which the other three belong?
   a. Four kilograms of meat, four kilograms of cheese.
   b. Three kilograms of meat, ten kilograms of cheese.
   c. Five kilograms of meat, three kilograms of cheese.
   d. Four kilograms of meat, three kilograms of cheese.

10. Given an indifference map, a fixed budget, and a fixed price for the good represented on the vertical axis, an increase in the price of the good represented on the horizontal axis is likely to move the consumption point
    a. up and to the right.
    b. up and to the left along the same indifference curve.
    c. to the left, although either upward or downward, so long as the good is a normal good.
    d. to the left and downward so long as the two goods are substitutes.

HANDS ON

Now that you have reviewed the concepts introduced in this chapter, it is time for some hands-on practice with the analytical tools that have been introduced. Work through each problem in this section carefully, and then check your results against those given at the end of the book.

Note: All problems in this section are based on the appendix to this chapter.

Problem 1. Refer to Exhibit S21.2 in answering the following questions.

(a) Can an indifference curve pass through Points A, D, and H? Through Points A, D, and I? Explain why or why not in each case.

(b) Can an indifference curve pass through Points C, F, and I? Through Points B, E, and H? Through Points A, D, and G? Explain why or why not in each case.

(c) Can an indifference curve pass through Points A, E, and I? Through Points C, D, and G? If one member of a set of indifference curves passes through C, D, and G, can another member of the same indifference set pass through Points A, E, and I? Explain why or why not.

Exhibit S21.2

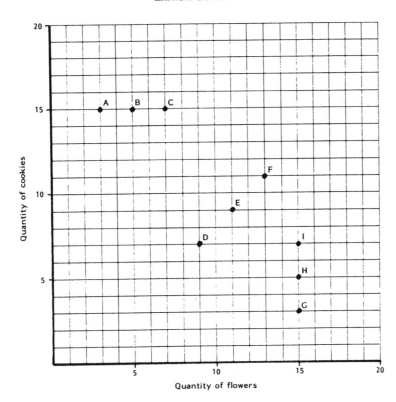

Problem 2. The following questions are based on Exhibit S21.3.

Exhibit S21.3

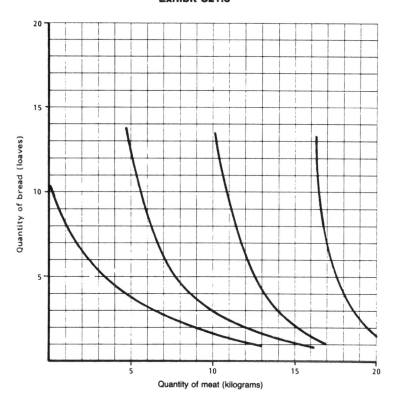

Quantity of meat (kilograms)

(a) Suppose that the indifference curves shown represent your preferences regarding meat and bread, and that these are the only two foods available to you. Bread costs $1 per loaf and meat costs $2 per kilogram. Given these prices, construct budget lines corresponding to food budgets of $10, $20, $30, and $40. Show your consumption equilibrium points for each budget.

(b) In the context of the assumptions made here, is meat a normal or an inferior good? Is bread a normal or an inferior good? How can you tell?

Problem 3. Case 21.1 in Basic Economics, 2/e (Case 5.1 in the paperback Basic Microeconomics) describes an experiment studying the consumption behavior of white rats. The rats are put in cages where root beer and Collins mix are available in response to pushes on different levers. Use the space provided in Exhibit S21.4 to make a graphical analysis of the experiment.

Exhibit S21.4

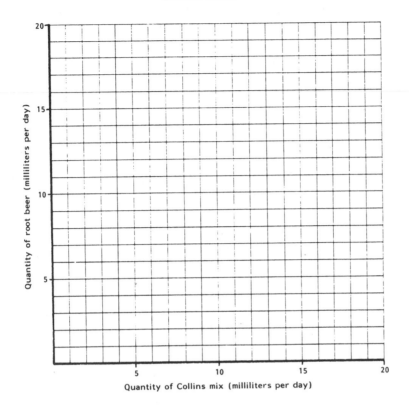

Quantity of Collins mix (milliliters per day)

(a) Initially, one of the rats is given a "budget" of 300 lever pushes per day, and the "prices" of root beer and Collins mix are set at 20 lever pushes per milliliter for each beverage. Draw the rat's budget line under these circumstances and label it B_1.

(b) Under these circumstances, the rat settled down to a regular pattern of drinking about 11 milliliters of root beer per day and about 4 milliliters of Collins mix. Label this point E_1. What does this suggest to you regarding the shape of the rat's indifference curves? Explain your reasoning.

(c) In a second phase of the experiment, the price of root beer was doubled to 40 pushes per milliliter and the price of Collins mix was cut in half to 10 pushes per milliliter. At the same time, the rat's budget of pushes was adjusted to permit it to attain exactly the same consumption pattern as before, if it so chose. Draw the new budget line and label it B_2. How many pushes per day must the rat be given to attain this budget line?

(d) Given budget line B_2, the rat settled down to a new consumption pattern of about 8 milliliters of root beer and about 16 milliliters of Collins mix per day. Find this point on the diagram and label it E_2.

(e) Sketch a possible pair of indifference curves for the rat. You don't have enough information to sketch the whole length of each curve exactly, but make use of all the information you do have.

(f) The experimenters concluded that this rat was subject to a substitution effect of the normal type when the relative price of Collins mix was cut. What makes them think the increase in Collins mix consumption was the result of the substitution effect rather than the income effect?

APPLICATION

Fans gobble up star's dressing

HARTFORD, Conn. (AP) — Paul Newman fans who may never have the chance to join the actor for dinner will soon be able to taste one of his homemade recipes.

For years, the blue-eyed movie star and race car aficionado has combined his favorite ingredients into a salad dressing that he served to his family and gave to friends as holiday gifts. For years, his friends told him the tasty concoction was good enough to sell.

He has taken their advice.

On the shelves of at least two stores in southwestern Connecticut, customers find clear glass bottles bearing labels with portraits of Newman's smiling face wreathed in herbs and vegetables.

Inside each bottle is Newman's own recipe — a vinaigrette dressing made of olive oil, soybean oil, red wine vinegar, water, lemon juice, spices, salt, dehydrated onion and garlic.

It's called Newman's Own, and customers are gobbling it up.

"We've had it about three weeks and we've already sold 10,000 bottles," said Stew Leonard, who works at Stew Leonard's Dairy in Norwalk, a family-run store near Newman's home in Westport.

Even though Newman's Own costs as much as 30 cents more than the store's other popular brands, it's selling like crazy, Leonard said.

"We've sold more bottles of it than all the others combined," he said. "We love to sell things like the Paul Newman salad dressing because it gets the customers excited."

From Winnipeg Free Press, August 27, 1982, p. 17. Reprinted by permission of Associated Press.

1. Why would a customer pay up to 30¢ more for equal-sized bottles of Newman's Own dressing than for regular salad dressings?

2. What is the consumer equilibrium position expressed in terms of marginal utility? Is it possible that buyers of Newman's Own are maximizing satisfaction, given their incomes and salad dressing prices, by buying Newman's Own at $1.30 a bottle when they could be buying the same size bottle of another dressing at $1.00? Explain your answer.

3. Assuming even Paul Newman fans prefer some variety in salad dressings, draw a set of indifference curves to illustrate their preferences. Label the horizontal axis "Quantity of Newman's Own dressing" and the vertical axis "All other salad dressings." Assuming that the consumer has $13 to spend on salad dressings, that regular dressings cost $1 per bottle and Newman's Own $1.30 a bottle, draw a budget line for the consumer. Indicate clearly on your diagram

the maximum satisfaction position for the consumer.

4. Would you say that consumer demand is more or less price elastic for Newman's Own dressing than for salad dressings in general? Cite information in the article to support your answer. (You may want to refer back to Chapter 20 before you answer this question.)

CHAPTER 22
THE THEORY OF COST

When you have mastered this chapter, you will be able to:

- Explain what economists mean by cost, distinguishing between explicit and implicit cost.

- Explain what economists mean by profit, distinguishing between pure economic profit and accounting profit.

- Define total and normal rates of return to capital, explaining the relationship between the two in terms of pure economic profit.

- State the law of diminishing returns and give examples of its operation.

- Explain what is meant by the short run and the long run in economic analysis.

- Draw an illustrative set of short-run and long-run cost curves for a hypothetical typical firm.

- Explain why, according to the marginal average rule, the marginal cost curve must always intersect the average total and variable cost curves at their lowest points.

- Use representative long-run average total cost curves to define and illustrate the concepts of economies of scale, diseconomies of scale, and constant returns to scale.

- Discuss the sources of economies of scale at the plant level and in multiplant firms.

- Explain the meaning and significance of the following additional terms and concepts:

    fixed inputs
    variable inputs
    marginal physical product (of an input)
    marginal cost
    minimum efficient scale

You have read the chapter at least once and have reviewed the summary in the text. Now you are going to walk through the material step by step, filling in the blanks and answering the questions as you go along. After you have answered each question, check yourself by uncovering the answer given in the margin. If you do not understand why the answer given is the right one, refer back to the proper section of the text.

The Nature of Costs

The Acme Photo Company is a small firm that sells darkroom supplies to professional photographers. You have the following information about the firm's operations during 1980:

Fuel bills	$ 15,000
Foregone salary of owner/manager	35,000
Materials purchased	10,000
Capital invested by owner	100,000
Total revenue	100,000
Wages paid	30,000
Opportunity cost of capital	15 percent per year

From this information, you conclude that the firm had explicit costs of _____ during 1980, leaving it with an accounting profit of _____.   In addition, the firm had certain implicit costs, including the owner's foregone salary plus _____, representing the 15 percent return the owner could have realized on the $100,000 of capital had it been invested elsewhere. Total implicit costs thus come to _____ for the year, leaving a pure economic profit of _____ - that is, a pure economic loss. The total return to capital for the firm can thus be calculated as the opportunity cost of capital, which is _____ plus pure economic profit

of _____ expressed as a percentage of

total capital, which comes to _____ percent per year. As always, when a firm experiences a pure economic loss, this percentage is [above/below] the normal rate of return on capital for the economy.

$55,000

$45,000

$15,000

$50,000

-$5,000

$15,000

-$5,000

10

below

Production and Costs in the Short Run

The following table gives you some production data for another firm, the Bravo Company. Use the data given to fill in the marginal product column of the table.

Labor Hours Input	Total Physical Product	Marginal Physical Product	
0	0		
1	2	_____	2
2	7	_____	5
3	17	_____	10
4	30	_____	13
5	38	_____	8
6	42	_____	4
7	45	_____	3

When you have completed the table, draw a graph of the marginal product curve in Exhibit S22.1. First put in points for each entry in the marginal physical product column of the table. (Plot them between the points shown on the labor hours axis - for example, at ½, 1½, 2½, and so on.) Your completed graph should look like the one shown in the answers and solutions section at the end of the book. It shows diminishing returns, beginning with the

_____ unit of labor input.   third

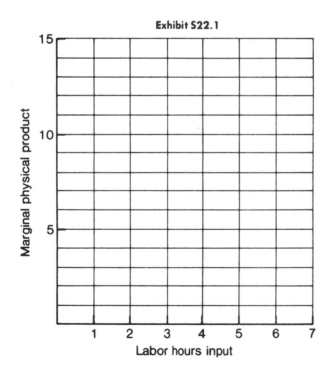

Exhibit S22.1

The next exercise will help you understand the
relationships among the various members of the family
of short-run cost curves for a typical firm. Exhibit S22.2a
gives a total cost curve for the Campbell Company.
This total cost curve provides all the information
needed to sketch the complete family of cost curves in
Exhibits S22.2a and S22.2b. Get a pencil, an eraser,
and a ruler, and proceed as follows.

Exhibit S22.2

(a)

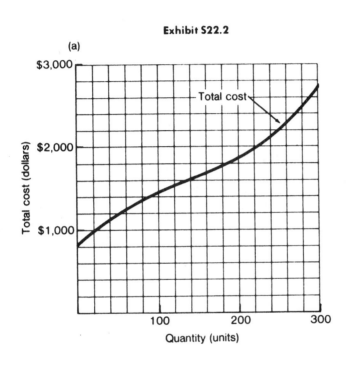

(b)

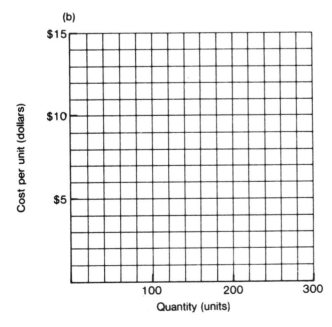

First, sketch in the total variable cost curve in Part a of the exhibit. Because total variable cost is equal to total cost minus fixed cost, the total variable cost curve will be below the total cost curve by a distance equal to total fixed cost, which in this case is _____ . (The $800 value of total fixed cost can be found by looking at the vertical intercept of the total cost curve.) Measure carefully at several points to keep the vertical distance between the two curves constant at $800.

Next, sketch in the marginal cost curve in Part b of the exhibit. The height of the marginal cost curve at any point is equal to the slope of the total cost curve for that level of output. You can start by finding the minimum of the marginal cost curve. Do this by sliding a ruler along the total cost curve and tangent to it until you find the "inflection point" - the point where the curve stops getting flatter and starts getting steeper. That happens at about _____ units of   130 output. The slope of the curve at that point indicates about a _____ increase in $3.50 cost for each unit of output. So put in a point at 130 units and $3.50 on the lower graph, labeling it "Min MC."

According to the marginal average rule, the marginal cost curve must pass through the minimum points on the average cost curves, so find these points next. The average total cost at any quantity of output can be found in Part a as the slope of a straight line from the origin to the total cost curve. The slope of such a line (and hence average total cost) is at a minimum where the line is just tangent to the total cost curve from below. This happens at about _____   260 units of output. The slope of the tangent line at that point indicates about a _____ $9 increase in total cost for each unit increase in output. So plot a point in Part b of the figure at 260 units and $9, labeling it "Min ATC." Proceed to find the minimum point of the average variable cost curve in the same way. If you have drawn the total variable cost curve carefully, "Min AVC" should come out at about _____   200

units of output and _____ in the lower $5.50 diagram.

Once you have these three important reference points, you can sketch in the three curves freehand. Draw a U-shaped marginal cost curve with its minimum point at Min MC and passing through Min AVC

and Min ATC. Draw somewhat more shallow U's for the
two average cost curves, using their minimum points
as reference. Your completed figure should look like
the one given in the answers and solutions section
at the end of the book.

Long-Run Costs and Economies of Scale

Exhibit S22.3 gives you one more exercise - an easier
one - this time concerning long-run costs and economies
of scale. The exhibit shows a number of possible
short-run average total cost curves, each corresponding
to a different plant size for the Davidson Corporation.
If Davidson planned to produce 1,200 units of output
per day in the long run, it would choose the plant
represented by curve _____; if it planned C_2
to produce 3,000 units per day, it would choose the
larger plant represented by _____; and C_6
so on.

   Use these curves now to sketch in the long-run
average total cost curve for the Davidson Corporation.
It should be drawn as the "envelope" of the short-run
curves - that is, it should just be tangent to each of
them in turn.

   Looking now at your new long-run average total
cost curve, you can see that Davidson experiences
economies of scale up to _____ units of   2,400

output and _____ scale beyond that point.   constant returns to
The minimum efficient scale for the firm is thus
_____ units of output.   2,400

Exhibit S22.3

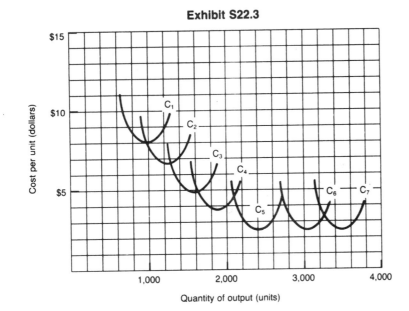

These sample test items will help you check how much you have learned. Answers and explanations can be found at the end of this book. Scoring yourself: one or two wrong - on target. Three or four wrong - passing, but you haven't mastered the chapter yet. Five or more wrong - not good enough; start over and restudy the chapter.

Multiple Choice

1. If a firm has revenues of $100 million, explicit costs of $90 million, and implicit costs of $20 million, its pure economic profit is
   a. $80 million.
   b. $70 million.
   c. $10 million.
   d. -$10 million.

2. Let A stand for accounting profit, P for pure economic profit, E for explicit costs, and I for implicit costs. Then
   a. P = A - E.
   b. P = A - I.
   c. A = P - I.
   d. A = P - E.

3. A firm has total capital of $500 million. The opportunity cost of capital is 12 percent per year. The firm earns a pure economic profit of $15 million. Its total rate of return on capital is thus
   a. 3 percent.
   b. 9 percent.
   c. 12 percent.
   d. 15 percent.

4. If a firm decided it could save on total cost by unplugging itself from the local electric utility and buying its own generating equipment, we could assume that
   a. both its fixed and variable costs would fall.
   b. both its fixed and variable costs would rise.
   c. its fixed costs would rise and its variable costs would fall.
   d. its fixed costs would fall and its variable costs would rise.

5. The law of diminishing returns implies that the marginal physical product curve
   a. must be U-shaped.
   b. must be shaped like an upside-down U.
   c. must have a negative slope throughout its length.
   d. must have a negative slope for at least part of its length.

6. If a marginal physical product curve and an average physical product curve were both drawn on a single diagram,
   a. the marginal curve would cut the average curve at the minimum point of the latter.
   b. the marginal curve would cut the average curve at the minimum

point of the former.

c. the marginal curve would cut the average curve at the maximum point of the latter.

d. the marginal curve would cut the average curve at the maximum point of the former.

7. Suppose that for a certain firm, average variable cost is $10 per unit at twenty units of output and $11 per unit at twenty-one units of output. It follows that marginal cost for that range of output must be
   a. about $1.
   b. about $11.
   c. about $31.
   d. impossible to calculate from the information given.

8. Short-run average total cost is equal to long-run average cost
   a. for all levels of output with a plant of given size.
   b. whenever short-run average total cost is at its minimum.
   c. when long-run average cost is at its minimum.
   d. none of the above.

9. The long-run average cost curve
   a. passes through the minimum points of all short-run average total cost curves.
   b. passes through the minimum points of all short-run average variable cost curves.
   c. is the envelope of all short-run average total cost curves.
   d. is the envelope of all short-run average variable cost curves.

10. The minimum efficient scale for a firm is the level of output at which
    a. economies of scale cease.
    b. diseconomies of scale begin.
    c. short-run average variable cost first exceeds long-run average cost.
    d. none of the above.

HANDS ON

Now that you have reviewed the concepts introduced in this chapter, it is time for some hands-on practice with the analytical tools that have been introduced. Work through each problem in this section carefully, and then check your results against those given at the end of the book.

Problem 1. The following questions refer to the total cost curve for a typical firm shown in Exhibit S22.4. In each case, explain how you obtain your answer.

Exhibit S22.4

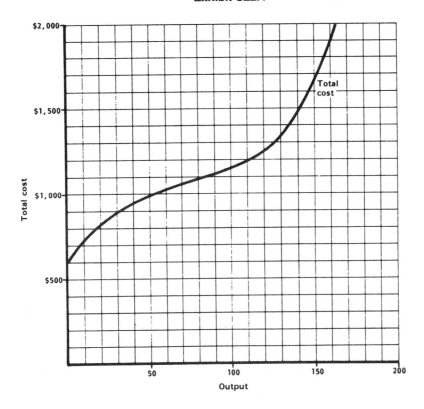

(a) What is total fixed cost for this firm?

(b) What is average total cost for the firm at 50 units of output? At 100 units? At what level of output does average total cost reach a minimum?

(c) What is marginal cost for this firm at 40 units of output? At what level of output is marginal cost a minimum? At what level of output is marginal cost equal to average total cost?

Problem 2. The following questions are based on the average total cost and average variable cost for a typical firm that is shown in Exhibit S22.5. In each case, explain how you obtain your answer.

(a) What is average fixed cost for this firm at 40 units of output? At 80 units? What is total fixed cost for the firm?

(b) What is the firm's marginal cost at an output of 70 units? An output of 100 units?

(c) Sketch the section of the firm's marginal cost curve lying between

22-9

about 60 units of output and about 120 units of output.

Exhibit S22.5

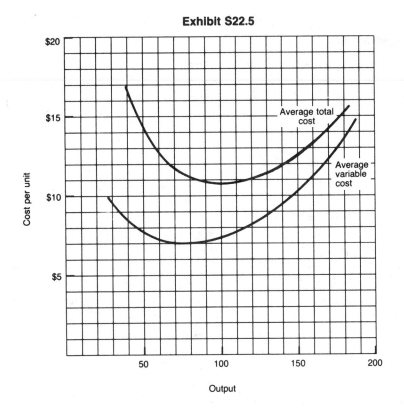

(d) Part c asked you to sketch part of the marginal cost curve. Now, calculate the value of the marginal cost curve at approximately 50, 110, and 130 units of output. Connect these points to the part of the marginal cost curve you sketched in Part c. (It is very difficult to obtain exact figures from this graph, but estimate as best you can.)

Problem 3. The following questions refer to Exhibit S22.6, which shows a long-run average cost curve and two short-run average total cost curves, labeled A and B.

(a) If the firm's plant size is such that short-run average total cost curve A applies, what level of output will minimize short-run average total cost? For what long-run level of output would a plant of size A be the cost-minimizing plant?

(b) One of the two short-run cost curves is not drawn correctly. Which one? What is wrong with it?

(c) Over what range of output does this firm experience economies of scale? Diseconomies of scale?

Exhibit S22.6

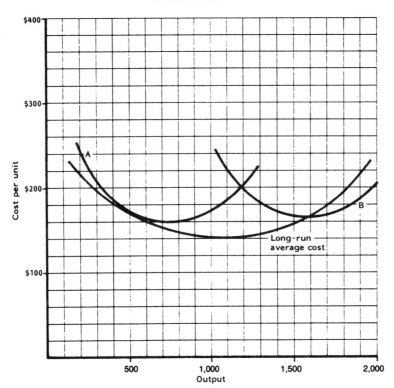

Eaton's eliminates 500 jobs in effort to cut fixed costs

By Paul Goldstein

About 500 employees across Canada of Toronto-based T. Eaton Co. Ltd. will lose their jobs in two weeks as yet another department store chain scurries to slash fixed costs.

In an interview, Fredrik Eaton, chairman and president of the privately owned retailer, said the rationalization "will not affect sales and service."

The staff cuts will result from centralizing and reorganizing departments, including buying, accounting, distribution and personnel. Two of the hardest-hit cities will be Vancouver and Montreal as Eaton's pulls its buyers out to centralize purchasing in Toronto. Hudson's Bay Co. of Winnipeg did the same recently.

Mr. Eaton denied reports that up to 700 employees in Montreal would be cut. The national total will be about 500, he said. Some people will be moved to Toronto, but there will be job losses in Toronto and other cities as well. He hopes the reorganization will be completed "in a couple of weeks."

Although each store has been watching its costs, cutting staff when necessary, "no sweeping, Draconian" move will be made similar to that of Simpsons-Sears Ltd. of Toronto, which has 3,000 fewer part-time employees than a year earlier.

Eaton's sales rose about 10 per cent last year to about $2.5-billion, Mr. Eaton said. "Inventories are in good shape" as buyers slashed the fringe areas — "the top of any line" — and paid more attention to basic merchandise. "There were too many chancy bits."

He sees no quick upturn in slow-moving, big-ticket items such as appliances and furniture. "Fashion is doing very well."

Mr. Eaton joined other major retailers in lamenting the steep slide in sales in once-booming British Columbia and Alberta, "the worst" in the chain. He noted that 40 per cent of British Columbia's gross provincial product is related to the forest products industry, which is in a sad state.

*From **The Globe and Mail**, April 7, 1982, p. B1. Reprinted by permission.*

1. Give three examples of explicit costs and three examples of implicit costs faced by Eaton's. Were the wages of the 500 employees dismissed from Eaton's explicit or implicit costs of the firm?

2. What is an accounting profit, and how does it differ from pure economic profit? How, if at all, will the reduction of staff by 500 affect Eaton's accounting profit? Its pure economic profit?

3. Is Eaton's attempting to change its quantity of fixed inputs by dismissing 500 employees? Can you necessarily assume that Eaton's is operating with a long-run time perspective, when it starts laying off employees? Were these 500 people really part of Eaton's fixed costs?

4. What does the marginal physical product of labor curve for Eaton's look like over the range of the 500 dismissed employees, if this dismissal "will not affect sales and service?"

CHAPTER 23
SUPPLY UNDER PERFECT COMPETITION

WHERE
YOU'RE GOING

When you have mastered this chapter, you will be able to:

- Give the defining characteristics of the <u>market structure</u> known as <u>perfect competition</u>.

- Explain what is meant when it is said that a firm in a perfectly competitive market is a <u>price taker</u>.

- Show how a perfectly competitive firm maximizes short-run profits (or minimizes short-run losses) by producing the quantity of output for which marginal cost is equal to <u>marginal revenue</u>.

- Show how a supply curve for a perfectly competitive firm can be derived from its cost curves.

- Show how a short-run supply curve for an industry can be derived from the short-run supply curves of the individual firms in that industry.

- List the characteristics of long-run equilibrium in a perfectly competitive industry and show how such an industry adjusts in the long run to an increase or a decrease in demand.

- Explain what is "perfect" about perfect competition.

WALKING TOUR

You have read the chapter at least once and have reviewed the summary in the text. Now you are going to walk through the material step by step, filling in the blanks and answering the questions as you go along. After you have answered each question, check yourself by uncovering the answer given in the margin. If you do not understand why the answer given is the right one, refer back to the proper section of the text.

The Structure of Perfect Competition

The market structure known as perfect competition has four defining characteristics, which are, in brief, as follows:

1. _____

2. _____

many small sellers
homogeneous
product

3. _____ good information

4. _____ free entry and exit

A firm operating in such a market has no control
over the price at which it sells its product; that
is to say, the firm is a _____. Another   price taker
way to put it is to say that the perfectly
competitive firm faces a/an _____ demand   a perfectly
curve for its product.   elastic

Short-run Supply Under Perfect Competition

A perfectly competitive firm maximizes profit by
choosing the output for which total revenue exceeds
total cost by the greatest amount. The profit-
maximizing output can also be found by using a
diagram like that in Exhibit S23.1, which is based
on a marginal approach. For example, suppose the
product of the firm in question sells at a market
price of $150 per unit. To find the profit-
maximizing level of output, first draw in the
appropriate marginal revenue curve, which will have
the form of a _____ line at a height of   horizontal

_____. Given this marginal revenue $150
curve, the firm will find it profitable to expand
production as long as the _____ cost   marginal

is less than _____; that is, up to an $150

output of _____ units. Mark this as   260
Point A on the exhibit. Profit per unit at this
point on the marginal cost curve is equal to the
price of $150 minus [marginal/average total/   average total
average variable] cost, which at 260 units of
output is about _____. Profit per unit $102

is thus _____, giving the firm a total $48

profit of _____. Indicate the total $12,480
profit for the firm in Exhibit S23.1 by shading in
the area between the demand or marginal
_____ curve and the average total cost   revenue
of $102 for producing each of the _____   260
units.
      If the product's price falls, the firm will
adjust by moving down along its _____   marginal
cost curve, keeping marginal cost equal to marginal
revenue. For example, at a price of $100, the firm
will produce _____ units of output. Mark   240
this as Point B. Pure economic profit at Point B is
_____. This means that the firm is earning $0
[nothing/a normal return] on its invested capital.   a normal return
      Suppose now that the price drops still further,
say to $70. At this price, the firm will produce

Exhibit S23.1

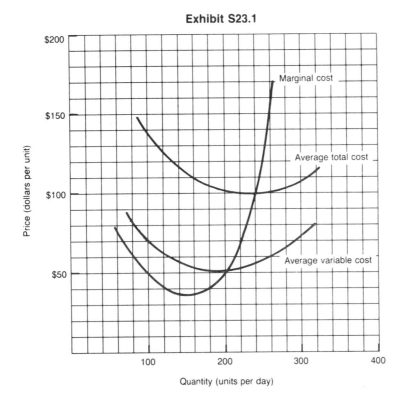

Quantity (units per day)

_____ units. Mark this as Point C. The   220
firm's average total cost at this point is about
_____ per unit, giving it a total cost of $101

_____ in all. Average variable cost is $22,220

about _____ per unit at Point C, or $51

_____ in all. That leaves a total fixed $11,220

cost of _____. It can be seen that the $11,000

firm's total revenue of _____ is enough $15,400
to cover all of the firm's variable cost, plus

_____ of the fixed cost. The firm is $4,180

left with a loss of _____, but this is $6,820

less than the loss of _____ that it would $11,000
sustain if it shut down. In the short run, then, the
firm stays in production, even at a loss.
    Now, suppose that the price falls all the way to
$50. If the firm continues to operate at the point
where marginal cost and marginal revenue are equal,
it will produce _____ units per day. Mark   200

this as Point D. At Point D it will have total
revenues of _____, total costs of $10,000

_____, and it will run a total loss of $21,000

_____, just equal to total fixed cost. $11,000

      Alternatively, the firm can shut down. Mark
the shutdown point ($50 and zero units) as Point
D'. At D' the firm will have total revenues of
_____, total costs of _____ $0; $11,000
because of short-run fixed costs, and a loss of
_____. This is the same as the loss $11,000
at D. It follows that at a price of $50, the firm
will be indifferent between shutting down and staying
in production.

      Finally, suppose the price drops all the way
to $40. In this case, setting marginal cost equal
to marginal revenue will give an output of
_____ units. Mark this as Point E.   180
At Point E, average variable cost will be
_____ per unit, for a total variable $51

cost of _____. The total revenue of $9,180

_____ will not even be enough to $7,200
cover variable cost, let alone the _____ $19,800

total cost. The firm will run a loss of
_____. In comparison, by shutting down $12,600

it will run a loss of just _____, equal $11,000
to total fixed cost. Clearly, then, at a price of
$40, the firm is better off shutting down. Mark
this shutdown point ($40, 0 units) as Point E'.
Now, connect points A, B, C, D, D', and E', and you
have traced out the firm's entire short-run supply
curve.

Long-run Equilibrium Under Perfect Competition

In the long run, the free entry and exit property
of perfect competition becomes important. The
conditions for long-run competitive equilibrium
can be characterized in terms of three equalities.
In order that each individual firm have no incentive
to increase or decrease output, _____   price

must be equal to _____ for each firm.   marginal cost
In order that each firm have no incentive to change
the size of plant in which it operates,   short-run
_____ cost must equal the   average total
                                                          long-run average
_____ cost. And in order that firms
have no incentive either to enter or leave the
industry, _____ cost for each firm must   long-run average

be equal to _____. Only when these   price
conditions hold - that is, when the marginal cost
curve, marginal revenue (price) curve, short-run
average total cost curve, and long-run average
cost curve all pass through a single point - can
the competitive market be in long-run equilibrium.

What Is Perfect About Perfect Competition?

A perfectly competitive market is considered to be
perfect in that when it is in _____,   equilibrium
all potential mutually beneficial transactions
have been carried out. In the long run, perfectly
competitive equilibrium firms are producing at the
_____ possible average total cost, and   minimum
the market has done as well as it can in satisfying
the needs of the _____.   consumer

SELF TEST
_____

These sample test items will help you check how much you have learned.
Answers and explanations can be found at the end of this book. Scoring
yourself: one or two wrong - on target. Three or four wrong - passing,
but you haven't mastered the chapter yet. Five or more wrong - not
good enough; start over and restudy the chapter.

Multiple Choice

1. Which of the following is not a characteristic of perfect competition?
    a. Many firms, each of which is small.
    b. A homogeneous product.
    c. An intense climate of secrecy and business rivalry.
    d. Free entry and exit.

2. A perfectly competitive firm sells its output for $50 a unit. At
    1,000 units of output, marginal cost is $40 and is increasing,
    average variable cost is $35, and average total cost is $60. To
    maximize short-run profit, what should the firm do?
    a. Increase output.
    b. Decrease output but not shut down.
    c. Maintain its current rate of output.
    d. Shut down.

3. A perfectly competitive firm sells its output for $50 a unit. At
    500 units of output, its marginal cost is $50 and is decreasing,
    average variable cost is $55 per unit, and average total cost is
    $65 per unit. To maximize profit, what should the firm do?
    a. Increase output.
    b. Decrease output or shut down temporarily.
    c. Retain its present rate of output.
    d. Insufficient information given for an answer to be reached.

4. A perfectly competitive firm's short-run supply curve is best described as
   a. its marginal cost curve.
   b. the upward-sloping portion of its marginal cost curve.
   c. the upward-sloping part of its marginal cost curve lying above average variable cost.
   d. the upward-sloping portion of its marginal cost curve lying above average total cost.

5. If a perfectly competitive firm is operating at a point where marginal cost and product price are between average variable cost and average total cost, its accounting profit must be
   a. positive.
   b. zero.
   c. negative.
   d. impossible to determine from the information given.

6. If, in the short run, input prices rise as the output of a perfectly competitive industry expands, then the short-run industry supply curve will
   a. be somewhat steeper than the sum of the individual firms' supply curves.
   b. be somewhat flatter than the sum of the individual firms' supply curves.
   c. be the same as the sum of the individual firms' supply curves.
   d. have a negative slope.

7. Which of the following is not equal to the others for a perfectly competitive firm in long-run equilibrium?
   a. Average variable cost.
   b. Long-run average cost.
   c. Short-run marginal cost.
   d. Marginal revenue.

8. A firm will have no incentive to change the size of its plant in the long run if
   a. price is equal to marginal cost.
   b. short-run average total cost equals long-run average cost.
   c. price is equal to long-run average total cost.
   d. marginal revenue is equal to marginal cost.

9. If there is an increase in demand for the product of a perfectly competitive industry, then
   a. firms already in the industry will, for a time, earn pure economic profits.
   b. new firms will be attracted to the industry.
   c. price will rise more in the short run than in the long run, assuming the change in demand to be permanent.
   d. all of the above will occur.

10. If input prices for a perfectly competitive industry decline as the output of the industry expands in the long run, the long-run industry supply curve
   a. will have a positive slope.
   b. will have a negative slope.
   c. will be perfectly elastic.
   d. will be vertical.

HANDS ON

Now that you have reviewed the concepts introduced in this chapter, it is time for some hands-on practice with the analytical tools that have been introduced. Work through each problem in this section carefully, and then check your results against those given at the end of the book.

Problem 1. The following questions are based on Exhibit S23.2a, which shows total cost and total variable cost curves, together with four alternative total revenue curves, for a typical perfectly competitive firm.

Exhibit S23.2a

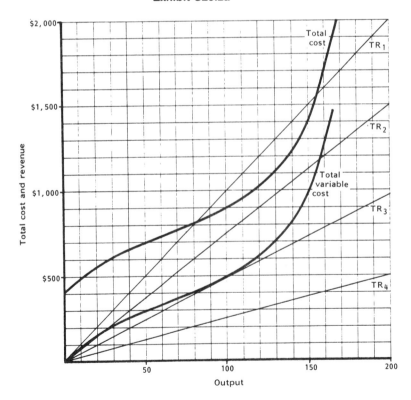

Exhibit S23.2b

Price / Output	Total Revenue				Total Cost	Profit (or Loss)			
	$2.50	$5.00	$7.50	$10.00	same for all prices	$2.50	$5.00	$7.50	$10.00
0	$	$	$	$	$	$	$	$	$
70									
80									
90									
100									
110									
120									
130									
140									
150									

(a) Each of the four total revenue curves shown corresponds to a
    different product price. What is the price for each curve?
    Explain how you obtain your answer.

(b) Working from the figure, fill in the blanks in Exhibit S23.2b.
    What happens to the profit-maximizing level of output as the price
    rises? Does this correspond with your expectations regarding the
    shape of such a firm's supply curve?

(c) Instead of filling in the table, you could find the profit-maximizing
    level of output for each price directly from the graph. Explain
    how you would proceed. Do the profit maximization points you
    obtain by this method correspond to points where marginal cost and
    marginal revenue are equal? Explain how you can tell.

Problem 2. Working from the cost curves in Exhibit S23.3a, complete the
tables in Exhibit S23.3b and S23.3c. Using a colored pen or pencil, show
where this firm's short-run supply curve lies.

Exhibit S23.3a

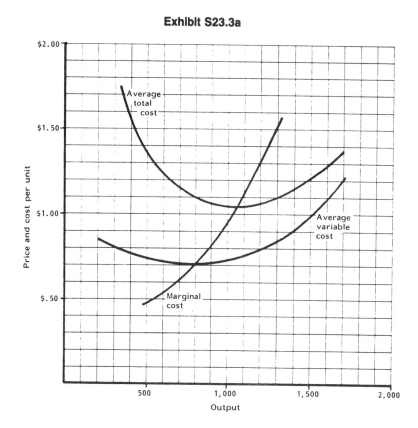

(a) Using Exhibit S23.3a, calculate total fixed costs for this firm
    by examining the average total cost and average variable cost
    curves at 800 units of output.

23-9

Exhibit S23.3b

Find the Profit-Maximizing Output for Each Price

Price	Profit-Maximizing Output	Total Revenue	Total Cost	Profit (or Loss)
$ .60	$_____	$_____	$_____	$_____
.70	_____	_____	_____	_____
.80	_____	_____	_____	_____
.90	_____	_____	_____	_____
1.00	_____	_____	_____	_____
1.10	_____	_____	_____	_____
1.20	_____	_____	_____	_____
1.30	_____	_____	_____	_____

Exhibit S23.3c

Fill in the Data for Each Level of Output--Given a Price of $1.30

Output	Total Revenue	Total Cost	Profit (or Loss)
400	$_____	$_____	$_____
600	_____	_____	_____
800	_____	_____	_____
1,000	_____	_____	_____
1,200	_____	_____	_____
1,400	_____	_____	_____
1,600	_____	_____	_____

Problem 3. Exhibit S23.4 shows three alternative short-run supply curves and three alternative short-run demand curves for a typical perfectly competitive industry. In answering the following questions, assume that input prices do not change as industry output changes, unless you are told to assume otherwise.

Exhibit S23.4

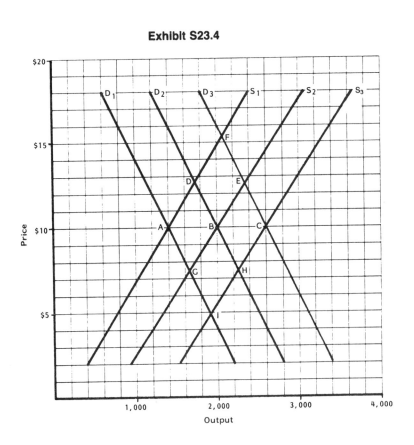

(a) Suppose that initially, supply curve S_2 and demand curve D_2 apply and that the industry is in long-run equilibrium at Point B. Then, the price of a good that is a substitute for the product of this industry increases. Of the curves and points shown, which would best represent the path to a new short-run equilibrium for this industry? Which would best represent the path to long-run equilibrium? As the industry moves first to a new short-run and then to a new long-run equilibrium, how would a typical individual firm in the industry react? Would any entry or exit of firms occur?

(b) Repeat the analysis required by the previous question for the case in which, beginning from Point B, an increase takes place in the price of a good that is a complement to the product of this industry.

(c) On the basis of your answers to parts a and b of this problem, sketch the industry's long-run supply curve. Label it LS$_1$.

(d) Assume now that for this industry, input prices tend to increase as industry output increases. Sketch an alternative long-run industry supply curve, passing through Point B, to illustrate this case. Label it LS$_2$.

(e) Suppose finally, that the supplier of an important input to this industry experiences strong economies of scale, so that input prices for this industry tend to drop as industry output increases. Sketch a long-run supply curve LS$_3$ to illustrate this case.

APPLICATION

1. List four characteristics of a perfectly competitive industry. Ignore dairy marketing boards - why would or wouldn't the dairy industry fit these characteristics?

2. Who sponsored this advertisement which appeared in a national magazine? Would you expect one individual dairy farmer in New Brunswick, for example, to advertise his/her products in a national magazine? Why or why not?

3. Illustrate the desired effect of a successful advertising campaign on the dairy industry as a whole. Ignore dairy marketing boards - how could a successful dairy advertising campaign affect individual dairy farmers? Illustrate both parts of your answer with graphs.

4. Ignoring dairy marketing boards, would you expect an individual dairy farmer to be making more than a normal rate of return in the long run? Explain your answer, and graphically illustrate a probable long-run equilibrium position for a perfect competitor.

CHAPTER 24
THE THEORY OF MONOPOLY

WHERE
YOU'RE GOING

When you have mastered this chapter, you will be able to:

- Define pure monopoly and distinguish between natural monopolies and franchised monopolies.

- Demonstrate the relationship between output and revenue for a pure monopolist.

- Compare the short-run profit maximization decision of a pure monopolist with that of a perfectly competitive firm.

- Explain the sense in which pure monopoly is an imperfect market structure and discuss the limitations on the policy conclusions that can be drawn from this imperfection.

- Discuss the significance of indirect competition in monopolistic markets and define monopolistic competition.

- Define and illustrate price discrimination and discuss the pros and cons of price discrimination.

- Define a cartel and compare profit maximization for a cartel with profit maximization for a pure monopolist in a perfectly competitive industry.

- Discuss the stability problem encountered by all cartels.

WALKING TOUR

You have read the chapter at least once and have reviewed the summary in the text. Now you are going to walk through the material step by step, filling in the blanks and answering the questions as you go along. After you have answered each question, check yourself by uncovering the answer given in the margin. If you do not understand why the answer given is the right one, refer back to the proper section of the text.

Profit Maximization for the Pure Monopolist

The first step in understanding the pure monopolist's profit maximization problem is understanding the relationship between output and revenue for such a firm.

The first two columns of the following table give part of the demand curve for a hypothetical pure monopolist. Use these data to complete the total revenue and marginal revenue columns of the table.

Quantity	Price	Total Revenue	Marginal Revenue		
17	$46	_____	_____	$782	$10
18	44	_____	_____	$792	$6
19	42	_____	_____	$798	$2
20	40	_____	_____	$800	-$2
21	38	_____	_____	$798	-$6
22	36	_____	_____	$792	

Next, use the information in the table to sketch the demand and marginal revenue curves for the firm in Exhibit S24.1. Extend the demand curve all the way to the vertical and horizontal axes. The vertical intercept is _____ and the horizontal $80

intercept is _____ units. Extend the   40
marginal revenue curve to 25 units of output.

Exhibit S24.1

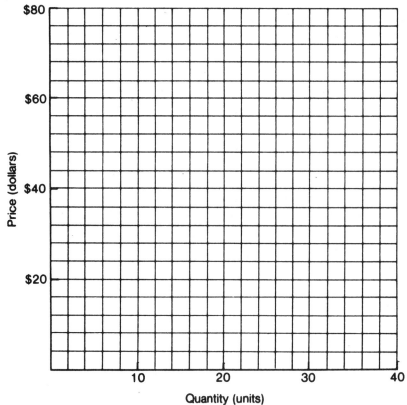

Note that the marginal revenue curve lies halfway between the demand curve and the vertical axis at all points.

Now, turn your attention to Exhibit S24.2, which shows a set of cost curves and two demand curves for a hypothetical pure monopolist.

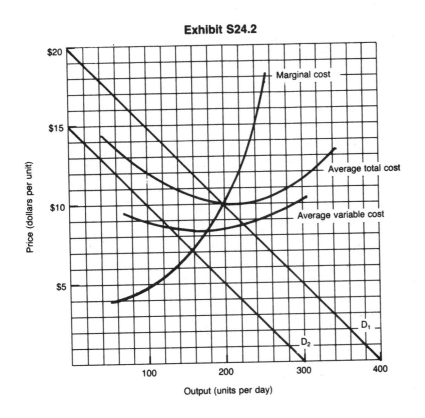

Exhibit S24.2

Begin by sketching in the marginal revenue curve corresponding to demand curve D_1. (Pay no attention to D_2 for the moment.) Label this curve MR_1; it should intersect the vertical axis at _____ and the

horizontal axis at _____ units of output. If demand conditions are represented by D_1, then the firm will maximize profits by producing at the point where the marginal cost curve intersects the _____ curve;

this happens at _____ units of output per day. The price at which this output will be sold is determined by the height of the _____ curve _____ at

this quantity; this price is _____

$20

200

marginal revenue

140

demand; D_1

$13

24-3

per unit. Average total cost at 140 units of output
is _____ per unit, so the firm makes a $11

total [profit/loss] of _____ under the   profit; $280
demand conditions indicated by D_1.
    Suppose now that because of a recession in the
economy at large or because of indirect competition
from other firms, this monopolist's demand curve
shifts to the position D_2. Sketch in the marginal
revenue curve corresponding to D_2, labeling it MR_2.
MR_2 should intersect the vertical axis at
_____ and the horizontal axis at $15

_____ units of output per day. Profit is   150

maximized at _____ units of output, given   100
the new demand conditions. This 100 units of output
will be sold at a price of _____ per unit. $10
This is [above/below] the average total cost of   below
_____ per unit, so the firm has a [profit/ $12

loss] of _____ under the demand conditions   loss; $200
given by D_2. However, note that at 100 units of
output, average total cost exceeds average variable
cost by _____ per unit, indicating a $3

total fixed cost of _____. This means $300
that if the firm were to shut down in the short run,
it would suffer a _____ loss per day, $300
which is more than it suffers at 100 units of output.
The firm thus should not shut down unless demand
conditions deteriorate still further.
    Go back now for a moment to the situation in
Exhibit S24.2, in which the demand curve D_1 called
for producing 140 units of output and selling them
at a price of $13 per unit. Starting from that point,
consumers would be willing to pay a [minimum/maximum]   maximum
of about _____ for the 141st unit of the $12.95

product. (This is indicated by the height of the
_____ curve at 141 units.) At the same   demand

time, the _____ curve indicates that   marginal cost
suppliers of labor, capital, and natural resources
would be willing to supply the input needed to
produce the 141st unit for a [minimum/maximum] of   minimum
about _____. It can be seen, then, that $6.05
a potentially mutually beneficial transaction between
consumers and resource owners is being passed up;
any price between $6.05 and $12.95 could satisfy both.
    However, if we continue to assume that the
monopolist must charge the same price for all units
sold, the 141st unit of output would not be produced.
Total revenue from selling 140 units at $13 per unit
is _____; total revenue from selling 141 $1,820

units at $12.95 would be _____, so the $1,825.95

141st unit would bring in _____ in new $5.95
revenue. As the marginal cost curve indicates,
however, the 141st unit would add _____ $6.05

to total cost. The monopolist's profit would thus
[rise/fall] by _____ if the 141st unit fall; $.10
were produced and sold.
     Note, though, that if the monopolist could
maintain the price of $13 for the first 140 units
while selling the 141st unit for any price between
_____ and _____, all three $12.95; $6.05
parties - consumers, resource owners, and the
monopolist - could be made better off. In principle,
_____ of this kind could result in price discrimination
production of as many as _____ units of 200
output per day, with the last unit sold at a price of
_____. $10.25

Cartels

A group of firms can enjoy monopoly power by forming
a _____, which involves an agreement among cartel
a number of independent suppliers of a product to
coordinate their [supply/demand] decisions so all of supply
them will earn _____ profits. When cartels monopoly
work well, their members tend to make large gains
(as in the case of OPEC), but most cartels are unstable
and [short/long]-lived. The two main problems faced short
by cartels are: (1) control over _____, entry
since, when new firms enter an industry,
_____ must be shared among a greater profits
number of members; (2) enforcement of _____ output
quotas, since if member firms produce [more/less] than more
their output quotas, the price of the product may be
forced [up/down] and the cartel broken. down

SELF TEST

These sample text items will help you check how much you have learned.
Answers and explanations can be found at the end of this book. Scoring
yourself: one or two wrong - on target. Three or four wrong - passing,
but you haven't mastered the chapter yet. Five or more wrong - not
good enough; start over and restudy the chapter.

Multiple Choice

1. Which of the following is true of a perfect competitor but not of a
   pure monopolist?
   a. The firm is a price taker.
   b. The firm maximizes profit by setting marginal cost equal to

marginal revenue.
   c. The firm may have to shut down in the short run if price does not
      cover average variable cost.
   d. The firm can earn a pure economic profit in the short run if
      demand conditions are favorable.

2. If a pure monopolist can sell 100 units of output at $50 per unit
   and 101 units of output at $49.90 per unit, marginal revenue in that
   range of output is approximately
   a. -$.10 per unit.
   b. -$10 per unit.
   c. $39.90 per unit.
   d. $49.90 per unit.

3. At the point where the marginal revenue curve intersects the horizontal
   axis, a monopolist's demand curve must be
   a. elastic.
   b. inelastic.
   c. unit elastic.
   d. perfectly elastic.

4. If a monopolist is operating at a point where its marginal revenue
   curve intersects its marginal cost curve, and if marginal cost is
   below average variable cost at that point, then to maximize profit,
   the firm should do which of the following?
   a. Increase output.
   b. Shut down.
   c. Charge a price determined by the demand curve at that level of
      output.
   d. Insufficient information given for an answer to be reached.

5. At an output of 100 units, a monopolist's marginal cost is $33, its
   marginal revenue is $33, its average variable cost is $30, and its
   average total cost is $38. To maximize profit or minimize loss in
   the short run, what should the firm do? (Assume that the price for
   which the firm sells its output is greater than average variable
   cost.)
   a. Produce more than 100 units of output.
   b. Produce exactly 100 units of output.
   c. Shut down.
   d. Insufficient information given for an answer to be reached.

6. Monopolistic competition resembles perfect competition
   a. in that the product of all firms is homogeneous.
   b. in that firms are likely to earn zero pure economic profit in the
      long run.
   c. in that all firms are price takers.
   d. in none of the above respects.

7. Other things being equal, we would expect a price discriminating monopolist to produce which of the following?
   a. More output than a nondiscriminating monopolist.
   b. Less output than a nondiscriminating monopolist.
   c. The same output as a nondiscriminating monopolist.
   d. No reason to expect one rather than another of the above.

8. Other things being equal, we would expect a price discriminating monopolist to charge the highest prices to the group with
   a. the least elastic demand.
   b. the most elastic demand.
   c. perfectly elastic demand.
   d. the least per capita income.

9. A cartel maximizes total profits for its membership by setting output at the point where the industry's marginal cost curve intersects
   a. the horizontal axis.
   b. the industry's demand curve.
   c. the industry's marginal revenue curve.
   d. none of the above.

10. If an individual member of a cartel could be certain of escaping detection, it would be tempted to cheat by
    a. increasing price.
    b. increasing output.
    c. doing both of the above.
    d. doing neither of the above.

HANDS ON

Now that you have reviewed the concepts introduced in this chapter, it is time for some hands-on practice with the analytical tools that have been introduced. Work through each problem in this section carefully, and then check your results against those given at the end of the book.

Problem 1. This problem is based on Exhibit S24.3. Part (a) of this figure shows total cost and total revenue curves for a typical pure monopolist.

(a) Using the figure in Exhibit S24.3(a) as your guide, fill in the total revenue, total cost, and total profit columns of the table given in Exhibit S24.3(b). What is the profit-maximizing level of output? What price does the monopolist charge to achieve maximum profit?

(b) Using the total revenue column as your guide, fill in the marginal revenue column of the table. Notice that the total revenue column moves in steps of 20 units of output. You can obtain a quick approximation of marginal cost in the range between each step by dividing the change in total revenue by 20. (Example: From 20 to 40 units of output, total revenue increases by $35, from $45 to $80. $35/20 = $1.75.) Fill in the marginal cost column in the same manner. Now, compare the marginal cost and marginal revenue columns to obtain an approximation of the profit-maximizing level of output. Does this agree with your previous answer?

Exhibit S24.3

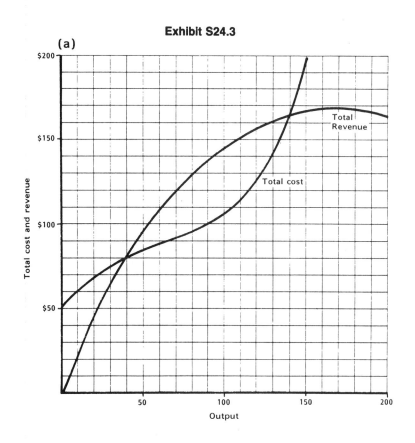

(a)

(b)

Price	Quantity of Output	Total Revenue	Marginal Revenue (approx.)	Marginal Cost (approx.)	Total Cost	Profit (or Loss)
0	0	$____	$____	$____	$____	$____
$2.25	20	____	____	____	____	____
$2.00	40	____	____	____	____	____
$1.80	60	____	____	____	____	____
$1.62	80	____	____	____	____	____
$1.45	100	____	____	____	____	____
$1.30	120	____	____	____	____	____
$1.17	140	____	____	____	____	____
$1.05	160	____	____	____	220	____

Problem 2. This problem is based on Exhibit S24.4, which shows a demand and a marginal cost curve for a typical pure monopolist.

Exhibit S24.4

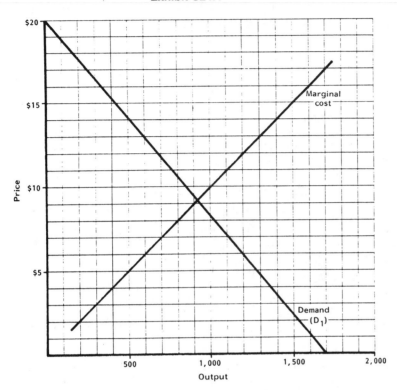

(a) Draw the firm's marginal revenue curve. What is its profit-maximizing price and level of output? If your answer to this part of the problem is 600 units of output and a price of $6, stop here and read this chapter's "Don't Make This Common Mistake!" section before you continue.

(b) Suppose now that demand conditions faced by the monopolist change, but that nothing disturbs the marginal cost curve. Specifically, let the demand curve shift to a new position that will keep the monopolist's profit-maximizing quantity at 600 units, as before, but will cause the profit-maximizing price to drop to $10. Draw the new demand curve and its associated marginal revenue curve. Make sure your new marginal revenue curve is consistent with your new demand curve. Label the new curves D2 and MR2.

(c) Now, suppose demand conditions change again, still with the marginal cost curve in its original position. This time, draw demand and marginal revenue curves that will give a profit-maximizing output of 1,000 units and a profit-maximizing price of $13. Label these curves D3 and MR3.

(d) A perfectly competitive firm has a supply curve that gives a 1:1 relationship between quantity and output for the firm. As changing demand conditions cause the price to rise and fall in a competitive market, each firm, and the industry as a whole, follows its supply curve like a train along a track. Each change in price produces a corresponding change in quantity. Does the monopolist shown in this figure also have a supply curve that gives a 1:1 relationship between price and quantity under changing demand conditions? Explain.

Problem 3.

Exhibit S24.5a

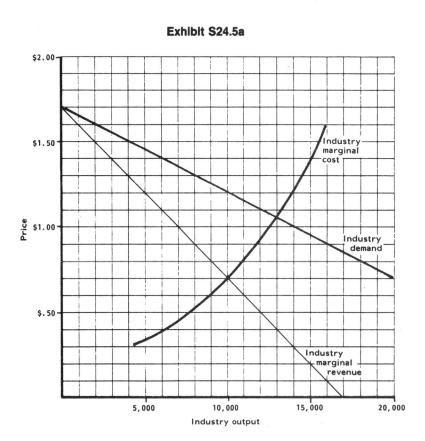

(a) Exhibit S24.5(a) shows demand, marginal revenue, and marginal cost curves for an industry composed of 100 identical small firms. Assume that the industry is organized as a cartel. What is the profit-maximizing quantity of output for the industry? The profit-maximizing price? If the 100 members of the cartel agree to share the profit-maximizing quantity of output equally, what is the output quota allowed to each firm?

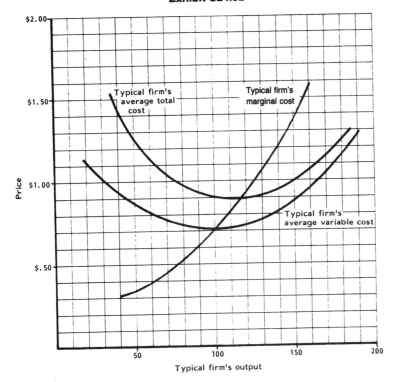

Exhibit S24.5b

(b) Exhibit S24.5(b) shows cost curves for one of the 100 identical firms making up the cartel. If the firm holds production to its 100 unit quota, how much profit will it earn? What will the relationship between marginal cost and marginal revenue be for this firm at 100 units of output?

(c) Suppose that this firm were to treat the cartel's profit-maximizing price of $1.20 per unit as a given. If it acted like a price taker with a fixed $1.20 per unit price, what would its profit-maximizing level of output be? How much profit would it make?

(d) Does this example tell you anything about the temptation of an individual member of a cartel to cheat on the cartel's agreed output quotas? Explain.

DON'T MAKE THIS COMMON MISTAKE!

Exhibit S24.6 is representative of one of the most common exam questions for this chapter. The figure shows a simple demand curve, a marginal revenue curve (sometimes you are asked to draw this yourself), and a marginal cost curve. <u>Question</u>: What is the profit-maximizing quantity and price for the firm?

Exhibit S24.6

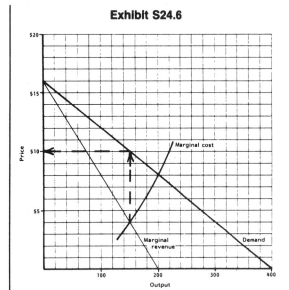

There's not much chance you'll miss the part about the quantity.
"I'm not dumb," you'll say to yourself. "I know the difference between
monopoly and perfect competition. This prof. can't fool me into thinking
the profit-maximizing quantity is 200 units. I know it is 150 units,
because that's where the marginal cost curve intersects the marginal
revenue curve."

So far so good. But, at this point, WATCH OUT for one of the most
common mistakes - one committed by thousands of economics students all
over the country every term! Just because the intersection of the marginal
cost and marginal revenue curves gave you the profit-maximizing quantity,
don't think it gives you the profit-maximizing price. The profit-
maximizing price for this firm is NOT $4 per unit. To find the correct
profit-maximizing price, FOLLOW THE ARROW UP from the MC=MR intersection
to the DEMAND CURVE. The correct profit-maximizing price, as shown in
the figure, is $10 per unit.

What would happen if the managers of this monopolistic firm put
their product on the market at $4 per unit? They would be SWAMPED by
customers! Quantity demanded at $4 is some 300 units. At 300 units of
output and a price of $4, the firm would not even come close to covering
its marginal costs, let alone its fixed costs. It would make a disastrous
loss, not the handsome profit available at a price of $10. So remember
to follow the arrow!

CHAPTER 25
OLIGOPOLY: COMPETITION AMONG THE FEW

WHERE
YOU'RE GOING
_____

When you have mastered this chapter, you will be able to:

- Explain what is meant by <u>oligopoly</u> and compare business rivalry
  under oligopoly with competition of the kind that takes place
  in perfectly competitive markets.

- Discuss the relative importance of various determinants of market
  concentration.

- Explain what is meant by <u>oligopolistic interdependence</u> and why such
  interdependence makes it difficult to develop formal theories of
  oligopoly.

- Discuss in an informal way various factors on which the performance
  of oligopolistic markets may depend.

- Discuss the conclusions reached by various attempts at empirical
  measurement of market performance under oligopoly.

- Explain the meaning and significance of the following additional
  terms and concepts:

      concentration ratio
      market performance
      market power
      price leadership

WALKING TOUR
_____

You have read the chapter at least once and have reviewed the summary
in the text. Now you are going to walk through the material step by
step, filling in the blanks and answering the questions as you go along.
After you have answered each question, check yourself by uncovering
the answer given in the margin. If you do not understand why the answer
given is the right one, refer back to the proper section of the text.

Market Concentration and Its Determinants

Concentration ratios are the most commonly used
measure of market concentration. Consider, for
example, the following hypothetical sales data

APPLICATION

Note: This letter was written when the United States government set gasoline prices to avoid price inflation as a result of gasoline shortages.

Dentist emergency fee called price-gouging

Dear Ann Landers: Recently the TV showed a service station owner being hauled off to jail because he charged more for gasoline than was permitted under law. It was called "price-gouging."

What would you call this? I overheard my dentist's receptionist tell a patient on the telephone, "The dentist will be able to fit you in at 11 o'clock today. There will be a $25 emergency fee." After a pause, she said, "Well—call us back if you continue to have trouble." Within minutes the phone rang again. That patient was told, "Yes, 11 o'clock is fine. The doctor can see you."

What kind of system lets professionals enrich themselves because people are in trouble? Don't they realize not everyone has health insurance? I am aware of how much it costs to become a doctor or a dentist. But are they justified in demanding, "Your money or your life?"— **Outraged**

Dear Out: My dentist, Dr. Jordan Block, said he never charges extra for emergencies—but many dentists do.

To my surprise, he added, "It's not a bad idea." When I said I felt this was unethical, he explained, "Some people will have a toothache for several days and ignore it until it becomes severe. They then call a dentist they have never gone to before. If he takes the patient, he must work time in between his regulars. This causes him to run late all day... When the emergency fee is mentioned, it is easy to discover how genuine the emergency is."

We then checked the Chicago Dental Society and found agreement with what Block had said. So maybe the emergency fee isn't such a bad idea after all.

From **Winnipeg Free Press**, *September 10, 1980. Reprinted by permission.*

1. What is the economic term for the "price-gouging" referred to in the article?

2. Your text states two conditions that must be met before price discrimination can occur. What are these two conditions and have they been met in the case of the dentist? Explain.

3. How are the dentist's emergency fee and the "price-gouging" by the service station owner different?

for the Canadian auto industry in a certain year:

Firm	Units Sold
GM	9.0 million
Ford	2.5 million
Chrysler	1.0 million
Volvo Canada	1.0 million
American Motors	0.5 million

On the basis of this data, you would calculate the four-firm concentration ratio for the Canadian auto industry to be _____ percent and the five-firm concentration ratio to be _____ percent. Because these figures do not take foreign sales in Canada into account, however, they represent an [understatement/ overstatement] of the actual degree of competition in the Canadian auto market.

96.4

100

understatement

In looking for explanations of the degree of concentration in this industry, you would think first of the cost advantages of making large numbers of cars - that is, of _____. In the auto industry, these would include [plant level/multiplant/both plant level and multiplant] economies. You would also want to know if there were any factors that prevented potential new auto firms from duplicating the performance of firms already in the industry - that is, if there were any _____. _____ influences might explain much of the remaining extent of concentration.

economies of scale

both plant level and multiplant

entry barriers; Random

Coordination and Interdependence Under Oligopoly

Imagine now that the auto industry consists of just two firms, Ford and GM, and that these firms are of equal size. At the beginning of 1984, each is faced with the decision of whether to spend large sums making the traditional annual model change or whether to continue producing 1983 models for another year. Each calculates that if both change models, they will split the market and earn $1 billion profit apiece. If neither changes, they will again split the market, but cost savings will be so great that each will earn $2 billion. But if one changes and the other doesn't, the firm with the new model will steal so many of the other's sales that it will earn $2.5 billion, while the firm with the old models will earn just $.5 billion.

Under these conditions, if the firms explicitly

coordinated their activities to maximize joint
industry profits, _____ would change   neither
models and total industry earnings would be
_____ billion. Without a formal $4
agreement, a tacit assumption by each that the
other will do what is best for everyone would
bring the same result. However, suppose Ford
decides that, whatever GM does, it will take the
course that gives highest Ford profits, given
the GM decision. That means [making/not making]   making
the model change if GM makes it and [making/
not making] the change if GM does not. If GM   making
follows the same strategy, [both/neither] will   both
make the model change, and total industry profits
will be _____ billion. $2
     It is hard to say which of the above outcomes
would result in any given industry, but certain
rules of thumb have been suggested. Other things
being equal, tacit coordination is thought to be
more likely, the [more/less] concentrated the   more
industry and the [more/less] rapid the pace of   less
growth and innovation.
     The kinked demand curve theory of oligopoly
makes assumptions about the behavior of rival firms.
Since rivals are assumed not to follow a price
[rise/fall], an oligopolist will lose customers to   rise
other firms if it [raises/lowers] its price from   raises
the prevailing market price. If an oligopolist
[raises/lowers] its price, rivals are assumed to   lowers
follow by lowering their prices, allowing each firm
to [keep/expand/contract] its share of the market,   keep
and resulting in an [expansion/contraction/no change]   expansion
in industry output.
     The prevailing price in the market as shown in
Exhibit S25.1 is $_____. At prices above   2.00
this market price, the oligopolist will be on the very
[elastic/inelastic] portion of its demand curve [AB/BC].   elastic; AB
At prices below the prevailing market price, the firm
will be on the very [elastic/inelastic] portion of the   inelastic
demand curve [AB/BC].   BC
     The kink in the firm's demand curve at the
prevailing market price causes a _____   step
in the marginal revenue curve. When the oligopolist
operates on the elastic portion of its demand curve,
it is on part [AF/GH] of its marginal revenue curve,   AF
and when it is on the inelastic portion of its demand
curve, it operates on [AF/GH] of the marginal revenue   GH
curve.
     Since the marginal cost curve cuts the marginal
revenue step in Exhibit S25.1, a price [above/below/
equal to] the prevailing industry price is the firm's   equal to

equilibrium price. The marginal cost curve can move
within the step and the firm will charge a price
[above/below/equal to] the prevailing price. Only   equal to
if the marginal cost changes enough to move the
intersection of marginal revenue and marginal cost
out of the step will the firm [charge/break with]   break with
the prevailing price.

The major flaw of the kinked demand curve
theory is that it fails to explain how the
prevailing price was determined in an oligopolistic
industry.

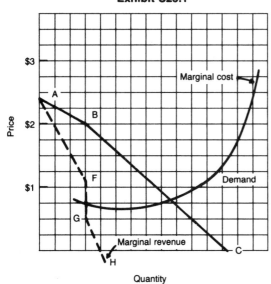

Exhibit S25.1

Assuming formal cartel agreements between firms
are illegal, an oligopolistic industry can operate
with so much _____ competition that pure   cutthroat
economic profit is eliminated. At the other extreme,
oligopolists can enjoy a _____ monopoly   shared
situation where firms tacitly coordinate their
activities in such a way as to earn maximum monopoly
profits for the industry as a whole. In reality,
most oligopolistic industries operate [somewhere
between/at one of] the two extremes.   somewhere between

These sample test items will help you check how much you have learned. Answers and explanations can be found at the end of this book. Scoring yourself: one or two wrong - on target. Three or four wrong - passing, but you haven't mastered the chapter yet. Five or more wrong - not good enough; start over and restudy the chapter.

Multiple Choice

1. Which of the following could be considered a barrier to entry into the interprovincial trucking industry?
   a. The necessity of raising capital to buy trucks.
   b. The necessity of advertising the newly offered service.
   c. The right of existing firms to protest, and often quash, applications from new firms for government trucking permits.
   d. The tendency of shippers to prefer doing business with familiar carriers.

2. An industry has two identical firms, A and B. If both firms do X, each will earn $1. If A does X and B does Y, A will earn $2 and B will earn $.10. If both do Y, each will earn $1.50. It can be concluded that
   a. both firms will do X.
   b. both firms will do Y.
   c. A will do X and B will do Y, or vice versa.
   d. not enough information is given for an answer to be reached.

3. If firms in an oligopoly follow the "golden rule" of doing unto others as they would have others do unto them, all firms are likely to earn
   a. higher than normal returns.
   b. normal returns.
   c. lower than normal returns.
   d. zero returns.

4. Which of the following is likely to make tacit coordination easier in an oligopolistic market?
   a. A small number of firms.
   b. An agreement among firms to exchange information on sales and prices.
   c. The presence of one clearly dominant firm.
   d. All of the above.

5. Which of the following is likely to make tacit coordination more difficult in an oligopolistic market?
   a. A small number of firms.
   b. The presence of a single dominant firm.
   c. Rapid growth and innovation.
   d. All of the above.

6. Which of the following statements best characterizes the relationship between information and market performance?
   a. Secrecy makes tacit coordination difficult, so the less information, the better market performance.
   b. Certain types of information exchange can facilitate tacit coordination and thereby be detrimental to good market performance.
   c. Improved communication can always be counted upon to improve market performance.
   d. Information is irrelevant to market performance.

7. Economists who have made empirical studies of the relationship between concentration and market performance have generally looked at data comparing
   a. quantities of output actually produced by firms in concentrated markets with quantities produced in less concentrated markets.
   b. prices charged by firms in concentrated markets with prices charged in less concentrated markets.
   c. rates of return in concentrated markets with rates of return in less concentrated markets.
   d. the gap between price and marginal cost in concentrated markets with the gap in less concentrated markets.

8. Which of the following might cause firms in more concentrated industries to earn higher rates of return, on average, than firms in less concentrated industries?
   a. Oligopolies operate much like formal cartels.
   b. Concentrated industries happen, on average, to grow faster than less concentrated industries.
   c. Data on rates of return are distorted by failure to account properly for advertising expenditures.
   d. Any of the above might cause such a relationship.

9. It is universally agreed among economists that
   a. rivalry among a few firms is just as good as perfect competition.
   b. oligopolies perform less well than perfectly competitive markets.
   c. oligopolies closely resemble formal cartels in terms of price and output decisions.
   d. all of the above conclusions are still being actively debated.

10. Which of the following aspects of decision making under oligopoly is a matter of pure economizing?
    a. Determining an optimal advertising strategy.
    b. Determining how to react to a rival's price changes.
    c. Determining how and when to enter a new market.
    d. None of the above.

Gulf Canada joining gasoline coupon spree

By Paul Taylor

Gulf Canada Ltd. of Toronto, anxious not to lose any more sales in the hotly competitive Ontario market, has become the latest oil company to offer special discount coupons on purchases of gasoline.

Gulf started placing full-page advertisements in various newspapers in Ontario yesterday. The ads contain three clip-out coupons, each worth 50 cents off on a minimum purchase of 25 litres of gasoline.

"We hope the coupons will help us hold on to our existing customers and possibly help us attract new ones," said Robert Scott, director of motorist markets for Gulf Canada Products Co., the marketing arm of Gulf Canada.

Three other oil companies are already accepting various discount coupons at their Ontario service stations. And the fact that more companies are accepting coupons is a sign of the intense competition in the industry.

Gasoline sales have fallen off sharply in recent months because of the recession, energy conservation and the switch to smaller cars. As a result, price wars have broken out in various regions as service stations try to cling to a piece of the shrinking market.

Oil executives dread price wars, which threaten to trim profit margins, so they have been looking for new ways to remain competitive without having to slash prices.

Imperial Oil Ltd. of Toronto, in conjunction with Loblaws Co. Ltd. of Toronto, was first in implementing the concept of discount coupons. Under its sales pitch, a customer can get a voucher worth $1 off on the purchase of gasoline by buying certain merchandise at Loblaws.

However, the coupon sales pitch is quickly taking on all the characteristics of a classic price war.

Soon after Imperial started accepting discount vouchers, Shell Canada Ltd. of Toronto unveiled a similar offer. It joined forces with Dominion Stores Ltd. of Toronto, which offers $1 gasoline discount vouchers with a $25 grocery purchase.

And in a move last week, Texaco Canada Inc. of Toronto said it will redeem both the Dominion and Loblaws discount coupons at its Ontario service stations.

Mr. Scott said Gulf has not noticed a "significant" drop in its sales since the other oil companies began accepting discount coupons. But he said Gulf decided to offer its own coupons because "we wanted to ensure that we didn't lose any business."

Gulf plans to accept the discount coupons until October, although a final cut-off date has not been set. "A lot depends on the competitive activity," Mr. Scott said.

Meanwhile, other oil companies are keeping an eye on the market, wondering whether they should also accept coupons. Sandy Hunter, a spokesman for Petro-Canada, said the federal oil company has no plans at present to introduce discount coupons.

*From **The Globe and Mail**, August 27, 1982.*

1. Are companies such as Gulf Canada Ltd., Imperial Oil Ltd., and Shell Canada Ltd., perfect or imperfect competitors? If they are imperfect competitors, into which category do they fall? What facts about these firms led you to your conclusions?

2. Imperial Oil started to offer gasoline discount coupons and other oil companies soon followed its lead in Ontario. What term or terms from your text describe this type of behavior? Cite a passage from the article to support your answer.

3. Why would the major oil firms be so sensitive to price changes by a rival? Cite a passage(s) from the article to support your answer.

4. Are price wars the typical way large oil companies compete with each other? If your answer is no, why would firms like to discourage price wars, and how would they prefer to compete? If your answer is yes, why are price wars a preferred form of competition?

5. Is it likely that the gasoline coupon price wars will spread to other areas of Canada? Why or why not?

CHAPTER 26
ADVERTISING AND MONOPOLISTIC COMPETITION

WHERE
YOU'RE GOING

When you have mastered this chapter, you will be able to:

- Distinguish the entrepreneurial element in consumer decision making from the element of pure economizing.

- Discuss a variety of mechanisms through which advertising affects consumer behavior.

- Summarize the normative economic cases for and against advertising.

- Discuss the evidence for and against the proposition that advertising is a barrier to entry into concentrated markets.

- Demonstrate the conditions for short-run and long-run equilibrium under monopolistic competition and outline the controversy over market performance under monopolistic competition.

- Distinguish between static and dynamic efficiency and discuss the debate over the Schumpeter hypothesis in terms of these two types of efficiency.

WALKING TOUR

You have read the chapter at least once and have reviewed the summary in the text. Now you are going to walk through the material step by step, filling in the blanks and answering the questions as you go along. After you have answered each question, check yourself by uncovering the answer given in the margin. If you do not understand why the answer given is the right one, refer back to the proper section of the text.

Advertising and the Consumer

To the extent that consumers seek to maximize utility
by choosing among known alternatives with given
constraints, they are acting as _____.   pure economizers
Advertising plays relatively little role in this
aspect of consumer choice but advertising is important
because consumers also engage in _____   entrepreneurial
decision making, seeking out new ways to satisfy old
needs and new needs to satisfy. Advertising affects
entrepreneurial consumer decisions by giving consumers

_____ about new alternatives and sources of supply, by changing _____ and _____, and by building or destroying _____.

information
tastes
perceptions
brand loyalties

Harvard professor John Kenneth Galbraith has attacked advertising on the grounds that it violates _____. This idea that advertising deflects consumers from "true" needs to "false" needs is also sometimes referred to by the term consumer _____. Many economists are skeptical about the concept of "true" needs, however, suggesting that it may simply reflect the preferences of a self-appointed elite.

consumer
   sovereignty

alienation

Advertising has also been attacked on the grounds that it is a barrier to entry. In a 1967 study, Comanor and Wilson found evidence that industries with high advertising outlays earn, on average, [higher/lower] rates of return than those doing less advertising. However, University of Chicago economist Yale Brozen has challenged the statistical methodology of the Comanor and Wilson study and has also argued that advertising is most important to firms [entering/already in] a market.

higher

entering

Advertising also plays an important role in monopolistically competitive markets; that is, in markets where there are [few/many] firms, [high/low] barriers to entry, and [homogeneous/differentiated] products. Exhibit S26.1 will help you to understand how equilibrium is achieved under monopolistic competition.

many; low
differentiated

The exhibit contains demand, marginal cost, and average total cost curves for a typical monopolistically competitive firm. Begin by adding the marginal revenue curve for the firm. It lies _____ between the demand curve and the [vertical/horizontal] axis; it thus intersects the vertical axis at _____

halfway
vertical
$14

and the horizontal axis at _____ units of output. Next, determine the quantity of output that will maximize profit for the firm in the short run. This quantity is found where the marginal cost curve intersects the _____ curve, which happens

875

marginal revenue

at _____ units of output, as the diagram is drawn. At that output, the product can be sold for _____ per unit, and average total cost per

500

$10

unit is _____. The firm's total profit is

$8

thus _____ per day.

$1,000

Under monopolistic competition, this state of

affairs [can/cannot] persist in the long run. Because this firm and others like it are earning higher than normal rates of return, [entry into/exit from] the market will be expected. As new firms enter with competing products, the demand curve shown in Exhibit S26.1 will [rise/fall]. If the firm tries to defend its market share by advertising or product innovations, its average total cost curve will [rise/fall]. Eventually, the firm (and others like it) will end up in a position where the average total cost curve is _____ the demand curve at the quantity of output for which marginal cost is equal to _____. When this position is reached (sketch it in the diagram), pure economic profit for the firm will be _____ and entry will cease. The industry will then be in long-run equilibrium.

cannot

entry into

fall

rise

tangent to

marginal revenue

zero

Exhibit S26.1

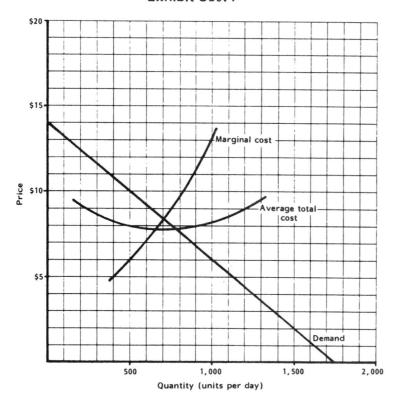

Quantity (units per day)

Market Dynamics and Competition Among
Entrepreneurs

A distinction can be made between a type of economic
efficiency that consists of getting the most out of
available resources, called _____   static
efficiency, and a type that consists of successfully
expanding output through growth and innovation,
called _____ efficiency. In earlier   dynamic
chapters, it was noted that many economists think
perfect competition to be superior to monopoly,
oligopoly, and monopolistic competition in terms
of _____ efficiency. However, according   static
to the Schumpeter hypothesis, perfect competition
may be inferior in terms of _____   dynamic
efficiency. Attempts have been made to test this
hypothesis empirically; these tests have for the
most part been [conclusive/inconclusive], largely   inconclusive
because of the difficulty of measuring the rate of
_____ in an industry.   innovation

SELF TEST
_____

These sample test items will help you check how much you have learned.
Answers and explanations can be found at the end of this book. Scoring
yourself: one or two wrong - on target. Three or four wrong - passing,
but you haven't mastered the chapter yet. Five or more wrong - not
good enough; start over and restudy the chapter.

Multiple Choice

1. Which of the following consumer decision making situations would
    involve an element of entrepreneurship?
    a. Getting competing bids from several contractors on a plumbing job.
    b. Trying a new brand of low-calorie beer.
    c. Looking at fall fashion ads in a popular magazine.
    d. All of the above.

2. On the basis of studies presented in this book, advertising is least
    likely to be able to do which of the following?
    a. Cause consumers to perceive an advertised brand of food as tasting
        better than a physically identical unadvertised brand.
    b. Cause consumers to try an unknown, newly advertised brand.
    c. Induce repeat purchases of a product that consumers perceive as
        inferior to an unadvertised brand.
    d. Strengthen existing brand loyalties.

3. According to John Kenneth Galbraith, advertising
    a. is a method by which firms that fill wants, at the same time create
        wants.

b. is an essential source of information for consumers to use in entrepreneurial decisions.

c. is a major protection against consumer alienation.

d. should be treated as an investment, not a current business expense.

4. To say that advertising is a barrier to entry implies, among other things,

a. that advertising is not available to newly entering firms on the same terms as it is available to existing firms.

b. that advertising represents a large share of total cost.

c. that advertising conveys little useful information to consumers.

d. all of the above.

5. Concern over advertising as a potential barrier to entry is highest for which of the following market structures?

a. Natural monopoly.

b. Oligopoly.

c. Monopolistic competition.

d. Perfect competition.

6. Which of the following is true in long-run equilibrium for both perfect competition and monopolistic competition?

a. Long-run average cost equals price.

b. Marginal cost equals price.

c. Long-run average cost is at its minimum.

d. All of the above.

7. Which of the following best characterizes the effect of introducing advertising into the legal profession?

a. Lower prices and an increased variety of services.

b. Lower prices and a decreased variety of services.

c. Higher prices and an increased variety of services.

d. Higher prices and a decreased variety of services.

8. A study showing that, other things being equal, legal services cost less in provinces where advertising was permitted than in provinces where it was prohibited would be evidence that

a. advertising is an important barrier to entry.

b. legal firms are not monopolistically competitive.

c. advertising is not detrimental to market performance.

d. the market for legal services is perfectly competitive where no restrictions on advertising exist.

9. According to the Schumpeter hypothesis, which of the following market structures would be most likely to exhibit good dynamic efficiency?

a. Perfect competition.

b. Monopolistic competition.

c. Oligopoly.

d. Natural monopoly.

10. Policies designed to break up large firms into small ones would tend to be supported by which of the following?
   a. A finding that the existing degree of concentration in most markets is the result of artificial barriers to entry.
   b. Confirmation of the Schumpeter hypothesis.
   c. A finding that larger firms spend a higher portion of their revenues on research and development than smaller firms.
   d. A finding that monopolistic competition is just as efficient as perfect competition.

APPLICATION

"Coke is it!" campaign unveiled

By Michael Weiss
Staff Writer of The News

Chances are that if you haven't already seen the new Coca-Cola theme, you will.

"Coke is it!" replaced the 2-year-old "Have a Coke and a Smile" campaign and, company officials claim, its introduction will be part of the most expensive ad blitz ever by the company.

Since presenting the new theme to officials representing Coke's 550 bottlers late last week, the company has purchased a pair of 3-network blocks of air-time aimed at reaching 90 million consumers, company officials said.

Coca Cola, whose stock closed Friday at 32¹/₈, has been performing well despite a strong challenge from Pepsico Inc., its principal competitor, according to a recent report by Sanford C. Bernstein & Co. Inc.

"Coke's long-term prospects on all fronts are quite positive. . . . Domestically, Coke has markedly improved its performance in food stores (the source of some disappointment in years past), gaining share even in the face of Pepsi's substantial gains," the report said.

Coca-Cola officials, in printed material, say the campaign "focuses directly on the superior qualities of the product, emphasizing as well the lifestyle of its consumers."

The "Coke is it!" campaign was test marketed against four alternates and a theme song was reviewed against

six others, officials said. The new standard's lyrics (chosen, in the words of one executive, "because of its power to present our product") revolves around a familiar theme of good times:

"It's the smile you can't hide
'Cause it comes from inside
Like the time that you spend
With your family and friends
It's the way that you feel
When you know it's real,
Coke is it!

The company said the "Coke is it!" campaign is the latest of a series beginning in the 1960s that have "accurately reflected attitudes of the times, often anticipating changing lifestyles and the national temperament."

In the 1970s, the company attempted to depict Coke as a wholesome alternative with the theme "It's the real thing." That was followed by "Look up America," and "Coke adds life."

Not prone to understatement, Coke officials, who sent no fewer than five press releases announcing the new campaign including one with the little-known fact that Coke is consumed 95 million times daily in the United States, say the "Coke is it!" campaign " . . . promises the consumer that the most popular drink in the world is also the best."

*From **Dallas Morning News**, February 8, 1982, p. 1. Permission granted by The Dallas Morning News.*

1. How would you characterize the structure of the soft-drink industry on the basis of this article? Explain.

2. Focus for a moment on those aspects of the soft-drink industry that resemble monopolistic competition. Using the graphical analysis developed in this chapter for monopolistic competition, discuss the effects of an intensive advertising rivalry between Coke and Pepsi.

What would the rivalry do to the firms' cost curves? Demand curves? Profits?

3. The huge cost of the "Coke is it!" campaign, if successful, will ultimately be passed along to consumers as part of the price of Coke. Why do you think consumers are willing to pay a higher price for heavily advertised Coke than for much less expensive generic-brand colas available in every supermarket? Do you think consumers get their money's worth?

4. Do you drink Coke? Do you have a brand loyalty in soft drinks, or do you just grab any can that comes within reach? If you do drink Coke, do you think you personally have been influenced by present or past advertising campaigns? How do you justify paying more for Coke than for a generic-brand cola? Have you ever done a scientific blind taste test of Coke (or whatever your favorite brand is) against cheaper generic brands?

CHAPTER 27
MARKET FAILURE AND GOVERNMENT REGULATION

WHERE
YOU'RE GOING
_____

When you have mastered this chapter, you will be able to:

- Distinguish between and give examples of <u>direct regulation</u> and
  <u>indirect or social regulation</u> by governments.

- Explain the main provisions of Canada's <u>anticombines legislation</u>,
  including policies in the areas of price fixing, price discrimination,
  tied selling, and mergers.

- Describe the regulatory approach to the problem of <u>natural monopoly</u>.

- Define <u>destructive competition</u> and explain how it applies to the
  agricultural industry.

- Describe federal and provincial government policies that have
  helped farmers, and explain how farmers are permitted to realize
  some of the benefits of membership in a cartel.

- Compare the effects of <u>price supports</u>, <u>acreage controls</u>, and <u>subsidy
  prices</u> as alternative methods of securing higher and more stable
  farm prices than would result from perfect competition.

- Define the concept of <u>externality</u> and explain how externalities
  can be positive or negative.

- Describe possible adjustments for externalities that might be
  arranged in the private sector or through government intervention.

- Explain the meaning and significance of the following additional
  concept:

      very short run

WALKING TOUR
_____

You have read the chapter at least once and have reviewed the summary
in the text. Now you are going to walk through the material step by
step, filling in the blanks and answering the questions as you go along.
After you have answered each question, check yourself by uncovering
the answer given in the margin. If you do not understand why the answer

given is the right one, refer back to the proper section of the text.

Scope of Government Regulations

Government regulation of economic activity can be divided into two categories. The first, _____ regulation, involves government   direct
control over price and [supply/demand] in a specific   supply
industry. The second, _____ or   indirect
_____ regulation, involves control of   social
the attributes of a product or service and can
involve the provision of better information and
_____ conditions. This second type of   working
regulation usually involves [one/many] industry(ies).   many
A recent survey shows that approximately
_____ percent of gross domestic product   29
(GDP) is subject to some form of direct regulation.

The Case Against Big Business and Anticombines Laws

The first anticombines legislation was passed in
Canada in 1889. The Anticombines Act made it illegal
to _____, _____, agree, or   conspire; combine
arrange to "restrain trade" or "lessen
_____." The act was later put under the   competition
Criminal Code and provisions were made to provide
administrative and investigative support for those
in charge of the legislation.
        Canadian legislation has been milder than
similar _____ legislation, and it has   American
made no attempt to break up monopolies. Canadian
law has primarily concerned itself with the
prevention of price _____ and price   fixing
_____.   discrimination
        Until recently, large sectors of the economy,
such as _____ and real estate, have   banking
been exempt from prosecution, and few funds have
been allocated by the government to anticombines
legislation.
        Since 1967, the Department of _____   Consumer and
Affairs has been responsible for combines, mergers,   Corporate
monopolies, and other forms of _____ of   restraint
trade. Before 1967, the Department of Justice
administered the law.
        Over the years, anticombines legislation has
successfully prosecuted offenses including
_____, where firms agree to sell their   price fixing
similar products at a set price; _____,   price discrimination
where customers are charged different prices for
no justifiable economic reason; and
_____ dealing and _____   exclusive; tied
selling, where products are supplied on the condition

that the purchaser buy other products as well.

_____ price maintenance, where a retailer
is forced to sell at a certain price, is illegal in
Canada.

Resale

Under given conditions of cost, competitive
markets perform more _____, but critics
of anticombines laws point out that cost conditions
are not always given. It is possible that
_____ may result in economies of scale
and cost cutting.

efficiently

mergers

Direct Government Regulation of Natural Monopoly

Under natural monopoly, costs are minimized by having
just one firm serve the entire market. This implies
that a firm must produce at least 50 percent of
industry output, and perhaps more, to achieve a minimum
efficient scale. In order to realize all potentially
mutually beneficial transactions in such a market, as
in any market, output should be expanded to the point
where _____ is equal to _____.

marginal cost; price

However, an unregulated, profit-maximizing monopolist
would produce at the point where marginal cost is equal
to _____, at which point output is [lower/
higher] and price [lower/higher] than the optimum.

marginal revenue
lower; higher

If a regulator could determine the optimal price
and output for the firm, a price [ceiling/floor]
could be set at that level, causing the regulated
firm to act as a _____ and to produce
the desired output. In order to keep the firm in
business without subsidy in the long run, the
price charged would have to be at least equal to
_____ cost, so that the firm could earn
a _____ rate of return.

ceiling

price taker

average total

normal

If the regulators were not able to directly
determine the quantity of output making marginal
cost and price equal, they could work backward
along the line of reasoning described above. First,
they would determine the firm's rate of return;
then, if it were higher than normal, they would
[raise/lower] the price, and if it were lower than
normal, [raise/lower] the price. This would work if
there were just one level of cost and output for
which a normal rate of return were possible. However,
when the regulators set a price, the firm may respond
by adjusting its costs upward to bring its rate of
return down to the normal level rather than by
adjusting its output. Even worse, if in error the
regulators set a target rate of return that is higher
than the true _____ cost of capital to the
firm, the firm may be tempted to invest without limit

lower
raise

opportunity

in questionable facilities. This would force the
regulators to raise the price continually, in order
to keep the rate of return at the target level.

The Structural Origins of the Farm Problem

The farm problem in Canada has traditionally been seen
as one of unstable prices and low farm incomes. The
short-run problem of unstable prices is in part caused
by the relatively [low/high] [price/income] elasticity   low; price
of demand for farm output. The inelastic demand means
that in a year of good crops, farm incomes tend to be
[higher/lower] than in a year of poor crops.   lower
  The long-term problem of low farm incomes and
rural poverty is caused in part by low [price/income]   income
elasticity of demand for farm products and in part
by increasing farm _____. In combination,   productivity
these factors have reduced the number of farmers
needed to produce the national farm output. In a
competitive market, the normal way to encourage
exit from an industry is through a prolonged period
of [high/low] _____.   low; earnings

Farm Policy

A number of policies have been devised for shielding
farmers to some extent from the effects of competition
in agricultural markets.
  There are essentially three ways that government
agencies can help farmers to control prices and
therefore their incomes: price supports, acreage
controls, and subsidy prices. Exhibit S27.1 provides
an exercise in comparing the effects of these three
policies.
  The diagram shows hypothetical supply and demand
curves for soybeans. Under competitive conditions,
the price of soybeans would be _____ per $350
tonne, and _____ million tonnes per year   1,600
would be produced. If farmers were not satisfied
with the $350 price and instead wanted to receive
$500 per tonne, one of the three policies mentioned
above, or a combination of them, could be employed.
  First, consider price supports. On the diagram,
draw in a dotted line to indicate a $500 support price.
At that price, the quantity supplied would be
_____ million tonnes per year, and the   2,000
quantity demanded would be just _____   1,000
million tonnes per year. This would result in a
[surplus/shortage] of _____ million   surplus; 1,000
tonnes per year, which the government would have
to buy and store or somehow dispose of without

27-4

depressing the market price. Under this price control
scheme, consumers would spend _____ billion $500
for _____ million tonnes, the total revenue   1,000
of soybean growers would be _____ billion, $1,000
and the total cost to the government (exclusive of
administrative costs) would be _____ $500
billion.

Alternatively, the price of $500 per tonne could
be achieved through acreage controls. Show how this
policy would work by sketching in a new supply curve,
S₂, parallel to S₁ and intersecting the demand curve
at a price of $500. Under this program, there would
be [a shortage/a surplus/neither a shortage nor a   neither a shortage
surplus]. Total farm revenue would be   nor a surplus
_____ billion and consumer expenditures $500

Exhibit S27.1

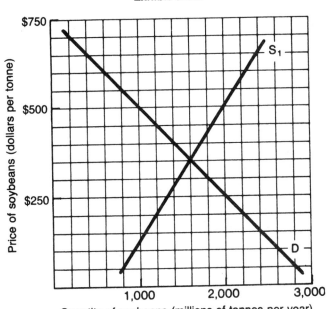

would be _____ billion. Note that the $500
marginal cost of producing the 1,000 millionth tonne
of soybeans (indicated by the height of the supply
curve at that quantity) would be _____ $500
per tonne under acreage controls, compared to about
_____ without them. $125
Finally, the government could establish a
subsidy price of $500 and agree to make up the
difference between that and the market price
through deficiency payments. Total production at the
$500 target price would be _____ million   2,000
tonnes per year, and total revenue would be

_____ billion. The market price would $1,000
fall to _____ per tonne; consumers would $250
pay a total of _____ billion and get $500

_____ million tonnes for their money. 2,000
The government would have to make a deficiency
payment of _____ per tonne on all $250
soybeans sold, for a total budgetary cost of
_____ billion. $500

Market Failure in the Form of Externalities

Even efficiently operating markets may not provide
for the best allocation of some goods and services.
Such a market failure involves _____, where externalities

an incidental benefit or _____ accompanies cost
an economic activity and affects people whom the
market does not compensate for the _____ cost
or charge for the _____. Pollution is benefit
an example of a [positive/negative] externality. negative

    Total social costs of air pollution, for instance,
are the sum of the total _____ costs private
incurred by the polluting producer to produce a
certain amount of output, and the total
_____ costs incurred by farmers, whose social
crops die from the pollution and by others, whose
lives or livelihoods are damaged by the air pollution.
The _____ social cost of pollution is marginal
the sum of the marginal private cost and the
marginal external cost. Left to itself, the perfectly
competitive air-polluting producer will produce a
quantity of output, where marginal [private/social] private
cost is equal to marginal _____. This is revenue
the point at which the firm's demand curve is cut by
the marginal [private/social] cost curve. private

    Label the three lines on Exhibit S27.2 to
illustrate the answers you gave above. The
horizontal line is the perfectly competitive
firm's _____ and _____ demand; marginal
curve, while the curve nearest the vertical   revenue
axis is the marginal _____ cost social
curve. The remaining curve is the marginal
_____ cost curve for the polluting private
producer, showing that output would be reduced
if marginal _____ cost was used to social
determine optimal output levels.

    In the case of such positive externalities
as those that arise from parks or public green
areas in a city, [costs/benefits] exist for those benefits
people living near by. Marginal _____ private
cost indicates the extra cost a private firm would

Exhibit S27.2

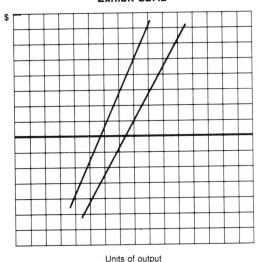

$

Units of output

incur for each acre of park it provided. The quantity
of park facilities provided by the owner would be
determined by the intersection of the marginal
[private/social] cost curve and the marginal   private
                        curve for park services.   revenue
_____
    If the government decides that parks provide
a benefit to society as a whole, or that the
marginal social cost of providing park services is
[less/more] than the marginal _____ cost,   less; private
it may tax city residents in order to provide parks.

    In the case of positive externalities, the
marginal private cost curve is usually graphed to the
[left/right] and [above/below] the marginal social   left; above
cost curve. Thus, the private market will
allocate too [few/many] units of the good if left to   few
itself.

SELF TEST
_____

These sample test items will help you check how much you have learned.
Answers and explanations can be found at the end of this book. Scoring
yourself: one or two wrong - on target. Three or four wrong - passing,
but you haven't mastered the chapter yet. Five or more wrong - not
good enough; start over and restudy the chapter.

Multiple Choice

1. Direct regulation
   a. can involve government regulation of price and output in a specific industry.
   b. affects approximately 29 percent of Canadian Gross Domestic Product.
   c. is very rare in the Canadian economy because most provinces oppose it.
   d. a and b, but not c.

2. The Anticombines Act of 1889 prohibited any action that would
   a. lessen competition.
   b. restrain trade.
   c. prevent competition.
   d. all of the above.

3. In comparing Canadian anticombines legislation to similar American laws, it is clear that
   a. the Canadian legislation concentrates on dissolving monopolies more than does American law.
   b. the Canadian law is generally less aggresive than the American law.
   c. American officials only prosecute very small firms.
   d. all of the above.

4. The following are common examples of natural monopolies regulated by government.
   a. Telephone companies.
   b. Hydro companies.
   c. Water and gas companies.
   d. All of the above.

5. Natural monopolies are regulated by government because
   a. competition by two or more firms is usually wasteful.
   b. the firms would take a loss without regulatory commission management.
   c. their long-run average cost curves rise quickly.
   d. a and b, but not c.

6. The structure of the market for wheat, in the absence of restrictive policies, would best be described as
   a. perfect competition.
   b. pure monopoly.
   c. monopolistic competition.
   d. a cartel.

7. Sharp year-to-year fluctuations in farm prices are a likely result of
   a. high-income elasticity of demand.
   b. low-income elasticity of demand.
   c. high-price elasticity of demand.
   d. low-price elasticity of demand.

8. Which of the following policies is likely to be most detrimental to productive efficiency in the farm economy?
   a. Price supports.
   b. Acreage controls.
   c. Subsidy prices.
   d. All of the above are about equal with regard to efficiency.

9. Which of the following farm policies would result in the lowest prices paid by consumers?
   a. Price supports.
   b. Acreage controls.
   c. Subsidy prices.
   d. All of the above would be about equal from the consumers' point of view.

10. When the spillover effects of production are negative,
    a. the market will allocate too few resources to the production of that good.
    b. the market will allocate too many resources to the production of that good.
    c. production of that good will be discontinued.
    d. production of that good will be greatly increased.

HANDS ON

Now that you have reviewed the concepts introduced in this chapter, it is time for some hands-on practice with the analytical tools that have been introduced. Work through the problem in this section carefully, and then check your results against those given at the end of the book.

Problem 1.

(a) Mark the competitive price for this grain, as Exhibit S27.3 is drawn. What is this price per tonne?

(b) If the government wants to supplement farmers' incomes through a direct price support of $175 per tonne, it will pay farmers the subsidy price for each tonne of grain produced that is not sold on the market. Indicate on Exhibit S27.3 any surplus or shortage this direct price support program creates. Using the values in Exhibit S27.3, state how much this program will cost the government.

(c) How, if at all, does the direct price support program affect the price the consumer pays for this grain?

(d) If, instead of a direct price support, a subsidy price program is used by the government to supplement farm incomes, by how much will farmers increase their grain output? (Assume a subsidy price of $175 per tonne.) What is the market price as a result of this increase in production? Indicate the market price on Exhibit S27.3.

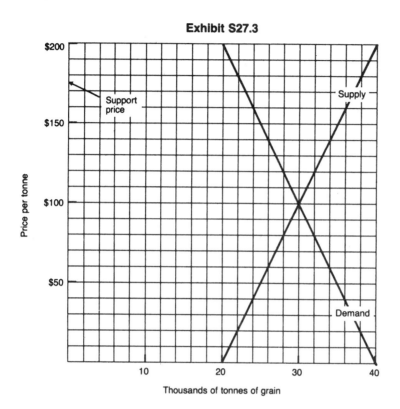

Exhibit S27.3

(e) What is the value of the deficiency payment per tonne made by the government to farmers? Mark the deficiency payment on Exhibit S27.3. What is the cost to the government of this subsidy price program?

(f) How, if at all, does the subsidy price program affect the price the consumer pays for this grain?

(g) Given the values in Exhibit S27.3, and assuming administrative costs for both plans are similar, state which program, the direct price support or the subsidy price program, is more expensive for the government. Would this conclusion necessarily hold if the demand for grain became very price elastic? Explain.

Alberta beekeepers swarming to increase honey production

By George Yackulic

Spurred by high prices for honey, Alberta's beekeepers are setting the stage for strengthening the province's reputation as Canada's biggest producer of the product.

Provincial agriculture officials estimate Alberta will have a record number of more than 2,000 beekeepers operating this year and that they will have more than 180,000 colonies of honeybees working for them.

"Depending on the weather and the nature of blossoms this summer, Alberta could produce around 25 million pounds of commercial honey worth more than $15-million this year," a provincial government official said.

"That's not really such an enormous amount of money spread about Alberta; but because beekeepers have virtually free workers in the bees bringing in the honey, many operators do obtain a good living from this business." Many people, however, practice beekeeping as a hobby and because it supplies them with top-quality honey.

On the basis that a beekeeper is rated as a commercial operator when he has more than 200 colonies, Alberta has only 230 such operators. Most of them are within a 100-mile radius of Edmonton or farther north in the Peace River region.

"With all the wild flowers and vast acreages of such crops as rapeseed, clover and alfalfa, an operator can make a very good living by running 400 colonies of bees in Alberta," Mr. Topping said. "Many of the operators average more than 200 pounds of honey a year in the Peace River region," where the summer daylight hours are longer than in the south.

As a result of such yields, some commercial operators have developed large-scale ventures; some in the Edmonton and Peace River regions have 4,500 colonies each.

Most of Alberta's honey is produced in two main surges. The first is in late June and early July when rapeseed crops are in bloom. Then there is a longer, heavy flow when the clover and alfalfa crops are blooming. The flow ends when the first frosts kill the wild flowers in the fall.

*From **The Globe and Mail**, April 27, 1981, p. B5 (excerpts from the original article). Reprinted by permission.*

1. Define the concept of externalities. Do farmers provide any externalities to beekeepers? If so, explain what these externalities are.

2. Do beekeepers provide any externalities in the Alberta economy? If yes, explain what externalities are provided.

3. If Alberta farmers provide benefits to beekeepers, could they charge beekeepers who put hives on or near their land? Would they? Evaluate, in terms of costs and benefits.

4. If beekeepers provide benefits to farmers through pollination of crops, could beekeepers charge farmers for this service? What problems might be involved?

CHAPTER 28
THE ECONOMICS OF ENERGY

WHERE
YOU'RE GOING
_____

When you have mastered this chapter, you will be able to:

- Use the theory of the mine to explain the basic principles of the
  allocation of nonrenewable resources over time.

- Compare the allocation of nonrenewable resources over time under
  competitive markets with their allocation under a cartel.

- Discuss in normative terms whether the rate of use of nonrenewable
  resources in competitive markets is optimal.

- Briefly discuss the roles of private companies, provincial governments,
  and the federal government in the determination of oil and natural
  gas prices and output.

- Explain the basic features of the 1980 National Energy Program (NEP).

- Use the concepts of consumer surplus and producer surplus to analyze
  government oil and natural gas pricing and output policies.

- Discuss the relative advantages and disadvantages of coal, solar
  power, electricity, and nuclear power as alternatives to oil and
  natural gas.

WALKING TOUR
_____

You have read the chapter at least once and have reviewed the summary
in the text. Now you are going to walk through the material step by
step, filling in the blanks and answering the questions as you go along.
After you have answered each question, check yourself by uncovering
the answer given in the margin. If you do not understand why the answer
given is the right one, refer back to the proper section of the text.

The Economics of Oil and Natural Gas

The theory of the mine, like most other branches of
microeconomic theory, assumes that resource owners
want to maximize their total income or wealth. The decision
facing the mine owner is simply one of how to distribute
sales of the nonrenewable contents of the mine over time.
   Suppose, for example, that you own an oil well and

that you want to decide whether to pump out one more barrel this year or to leave that marginal barrel in the ground until next year. Suppose you expect the price both this year and next to be $20 per barrel, and you know you can earn a 10 percent return on any funds that you invest this year outside the oil business. If you sell the barrel of oil this year and invest the proceeds, you will have $_____ by next year. If you wait until next year to sell the oil, you will have $_____ next year. So you will decide to sell the oil [this/next] year.

22

20

this

As you and your fellow oil producers decide to produce another and then another and another barrel this year, however, this year's market price will [rise/fall]; and because reserves left for next year will have been diminished, the expected future price will [rise/fall]. Suppose that this year's output is increased enough to push this year's price down to $19.10 per barrel and that in view of this greater rate of reserve depletion, next year's price is expected to rise to $21 per barrel. Now, if you extract the marginal barrel and sell it this year, investing the proceeds at 10 percent interest, you will have $_____ by next year, whereas if you hold the same quantity of oil for sale until next year, you will have $_____. You will decide to produce the marginal barrel [this/next] year. However, if this year's price falls by even one cent more, it will pay to produce the marginal barrel [this/next] year. A limit is thus placed on the rate of depletion: you and your fellow producers will stop producing this year and start conserving for next year as soon as the percentage increase of next year's price over this year's price equals the rate of interest.

fall

rise

21.01

21
this

next

Price Controls and Subsidies: Government Policies in the Oil and Gas Field

Oil and natural gas prices and output levels are determined by the interaction of three key "players" involved in the industry. These players are large private oil companies, _____, and the federal government. The province of _____, which produces 85 percent of Canada's oil and between 80 and 85 percent of its natural gas, has been particularly involved in natural resources policymaking.

provincial governments
Alberta

Rising world oil and natural gas prices and [increased/decreased] federal government involvement in energy resources through companies like Petro-Canada, have led to conflicts between Ottawa and the

increased

provinces. The federal government has looked for ways
to lessen regional _____ caused by higher   disparities
oil and gas prices and the concentration of these
resources in western provinces. Federal taxes and
policies have met with considerable resistance,
especially in provinces like _____. The   Alberta
_____ instituted in the fall of 1980   National Energy
was designed to slow the increase in the price of   Program
_____ and _____, to increase   oil; gas
[federal/provincial] government revenues, and further   federal
Canadianize the oil and gas industry. NEP continues
to be the topic of much debate and disagreement today.

An Economic Assessment of Oil and Natural Gas Policies

The energy policy pursued by the federal government in
keeping the domestic oil price at levels [higher than/
lower than/equal to] world prices has resulted in   lower than
economic inefficiency. The world oil price provides
a measurement of the [private cost/social benefit] to   social benefit
Canada of its oil resources, since the world price
represents the value world buyers place on Canada's
oil. Any loss in consumer _____ (the   surplus
difference between what consumers actually spend
on a product and what they would be willing to
spend) that would occur by raising Canadian oil prices
to world levels would be more than compensated for
by the [losses/gains] experienced by producers and   gains
taxpayers.

The Economics of Alternative Energy Sources

_____, _____ energy,   Coal, nuclear

_____, and solar energy are all   electricity
alternative sources of energy for Canada. Presently,
however, all of these energy sources require
[greater/lesser/the same] capital expenditure per unit   greater
of energy output than oil and natural gas to meet
health, _____, and environmental safeguards.   safety

SELF TEST
_____

These sample test items will help you check how much you have learned.
Answers and explanations can be found at the end of this book. Scoring
yourself: one or two wrong - on target. Three or four wrong - passing,
but you haven't mastered the chapter yet. Five or more wrong - not
good enough; start over and restudy the chapter.

Multiple Choice

1. If this year's price of oil is $30 per barrel and the rate of interest is 10 percent, how high must next year's expected price be in order to encourage a competitive producer to conserve a marginal barrel of oil for production next year?
    a. More than $27.
    b. More than $30.
    c. More than $33.
    d. None of the above; a competitive firm will never conserve.

2. Over time in a competitive resource market, other things being equal,
    a. price will rise and the rate of use will fall.
    b. price will fall and the rate of use will rise.
    c. both price and the rate of use will rise.
    d. both price and the rate of use will fall.

3. Suppose you studied past behavior of oil prices and found that over the past ten years they had risen more rapidly than the rate of interest. Which of the following would be the most reasonable explanation?
    a. A previously competitive market had become a cartel.
    b. Oil companies do not really try to maximize profits.
    c. The demand for oil increased, as oil companies had expected it would.
    d. None of these special explanations is necessary; what happened is just what the theory of the mine predicts.

4. Other things being equal, a cartel
    a. sells more but charges less than a competitive industry.
    b. sells less but charges more than a competitive industry.
    c. sells less and charges less than a competitive industry.
    d. sells more and charges more than a competitive industry.

5. According to the theory of the mine, other things being equal, future generations will best be served if
    a. today's resource markets are organized as cartels.
    b. today's resource markets are competitive.
    c. today's resource markets are subject to price controls.
    d. today's capital markets are subject to interest rate controls.

6. Price controls that depress both the price paid by consumers and the price received by domestic producers below the world price level are likely to
    a. cut domestic production.
    b. increase domestic consumption.
    c. increase imports.
    d. do all of the above.

7. The National Energy Program (NEP) was instituted to
    a. speed the rise of Canadian domestic oil and natural gas prices to the world price level.

b.　provide the provinces with a greater share of revenues while
　　　　greatly reducing the federal government's revenues.
　　c.　slow the increase in the price of oil and natural gas, and to
　　　　further Canadianize these two industries.
　　d.　allow foreign oil companies greater control over their Canadian-
　　　　based operations.

8.　When oil prices are artificially held below the world price by
　　government action,
　　a.　economic inefficiency results.
　　b.　consumers buy more of the product than they would at the world
　　　　price.
　　c.　resources are shifted out of the oil industry and into other
　　　　industries by producers.
　　d.　all of the above.

9.　Which of the following technologies for electric power generation
　　has the lowest capital cost per megawatt?
　　a.　Coal.
　　b.　Nuclear.
　　c.　Direct solar.
　　d.　All three have the same cost.

10.　Which of the following opportunity costs of nuclear power generation
　　is not borne entirely by nuclear power consumers?
　　a.　Health and safety costs.
　　b.　The cost of disaster insurance.
　　c.　The cost of dismantling existing plants when they become obsolete.
　　d.　None of the above costs are fully borne by consumers.

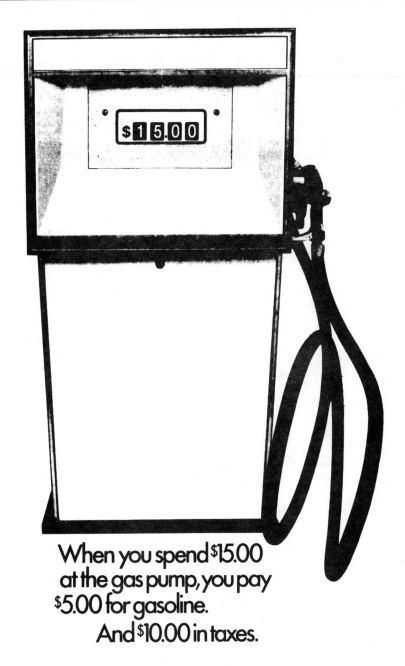

When you spend $15.00 at the gas pump, you pay $5.00 for gasoline. And $10.00 in taxes.

Of every dollar you spend for gasoline in Ontario, the petroleum industry receives 33¢. The remainder, 67¢ out of every dollar, goes to governments in the form of taxes and royalty payments.

Just thought you'd like to know.

If you'd like to know more about what the industry does with its share, write the P.R.C.F. If you'd like to know more about the sixty-seven cents, contact your M.P. or M.P.P.

A message from the 115 members of the Petroleum Resources Communication Foundation.   105,309 - 2nd Avenue, S.W. Calgary, Alberta T2P 0C5.

1. Explain why the government taxes gasoline so heavily.

2. Define consumer surplus. Explain how government taxes on gasoline affect the amount of this surplus enjoyed by consumers.

3. How would producer surplus be affected by government taxes on gasoline? (Exhibit S28.6 may be helpful to you in answering this question.)

4. Who would you expect to be members of the Petroleum Resources Communication Foundation? Suggest a possible reason for the Foundation sponsoring an advertisement like this.

CHAPTER 29
FOREIGN OWNERSHIP AND CONTROL OF CANADIAN BUSINESS

WHERE
YOU'RE GOING

When you have mastered this chapter, you will be able to:

- Discuss the extent of foreign ownership in Canadian business.

- Explain the difference between <u>portfolio investment</u> and <u>direct investment</u> in Canadian business.

- Define the concept of <u>multinational firms</u> and explain their significance in Canadian industry.

- List various costs and benefits of foreign ownership in Canadian business.

- Explain policies used to control foreign ownership and investment in Canadian business.

- Explain the meaning and significance of the following additional terms and concepts:

    truncation
    extraterritoriality

WALKING TOUR

You have read the chapter at least once and have reviewed the summary in the text. Now you are going to walk through the material step by step, filling in the blanks and answering the questions as you go along. After you have answered each question, check yourself by uncovering the answer given in the margin. If you do not understand why the answer given is the right one, refer back to the proper section of the text.

The Extent of Foreign Ownership of Canadian Business

Historically, Canada has encouraged foreign investment, especially by Great Britain and the United States.
Today, about _____ percent of total foreign   75
assets in Canada are owned by Americans.
    The foreign ownership that is of the most concern
to Canadians allows investors to control the company
through securing voting rights. This type of investment
is called _____ investment and is popular   direct

with many American investors. _____   Portfolio
investment, on the other hand, does not give
investors control of corporate decisions. This
type of investment often involves the sale of
bonds, and is a type of loan to the company.

    Direct investment is usually carried on by
firms called _____, who carry on business   multinationals
in a number of countries. These firms usually
operate from central headquarters in one country
and in some cases, exert a great deal of control
over their _____ in other countries.   subsidiaries

Examples of _____ operating in Canada   multinationals

are Ford, Alcan, _____ and   General Motors

_____. There is particular concern over   Imperial Oil, Canada
foreign ownership or control of Canada's natural   Safeway, Chrysler,
resources.   Shell Canada, and
                                                          many others

The Benefits and Costs of Foreign Ownership of Canadian Business

Foreign ownership of Canadian business limits the
choices available to Canadians concerning their
own resources, thus limiting the sovereignty of
Canadians. There are also definite benefits and
costs of foreign ownership.

    Benefits from foreign ownership involve the
introduction of new _____ and management   technology

skills. If investors were limited to _____   portfolio
investment and had no vote in decisions, they might
be less willing to risk their best ideas and
production techniques in plants outside their own
countries. Studies have shown that Canada has
[benefited from/been hurt by] foreign investment.   benefited from

    The costs of foreign investment can involve
_____, that is, the parent company limiting   truncation
the growth and development of its subsidiary by
confining certain services and operations to the head
office.

    Some studies show that foreign-owned companies
may do less research and _____ work than   development
domestically-owned companies. Similarly, foreign-owned
firms may import more goods, which affects Canada's
current account deficit. Large capital inflows to
finance foreign investment also affect the
_____ and the Canadian dollar foreign   balance of payments
exchange rate.   capital account
    Finally, there is the problem of _____, extraterritoriality
since the United States insists that all subsidiaries
of U.S. firms are subject to American laws.

Policies to Curb the Foreign Ownership of
Canadian Business

As Canadians become more concerned about foreign
investment in Canada, laws have been passed to curb
foreign ownership of Canadian businesses. Legislation
limits [direct/portfolio] foreign investment in sectors   direct
of the economy "deemed crucial to Canadian cultural
and financial development." Laws have been passed in
the areas of publishing, broadcasting, and

_____.   banking

    The _____ (FIRA) was established in   Foreign Investment
1973 by the federal government to monitor prospective   Review Agency
foreign _____, to encourage more Canadian   takeovers

participation at the _____ level, and to   management
promote the use of more Canadian resources and skills
by foreign corporations operating in Canada. The
effectiveness of FIRA is [debated/agreed upon] by   debated
economists.
    In 1980, the National Energy Program (NEP) was
announced with measures to [decrease/increase]   increase
Canadian ownership in the petroleum industry. A
main concern was that [more/less] oil revenues should   more
accrue to Canadians and Canadian governments. The goal
of the NEP was to [decrease/increase] Canadian ownership   increase
of the petroleum industry from about 30 percent at that
time, to at least [50/75/95] percent by 1990.   50
    Guidelines have also been developed for
multinational firms with subsidiaries in Canada. The
guidelines try to limit interference with the operation
of the Canadian firm. Other policies encourage increased
[Canadian/foreign] ownership of business firms.   Canadian

SELF TEST
_____

These sample test items will help you check how much you have learned.
Answers and explanations can be found at the end of this book. Scoring
yourself: one or two wrong - on target. Three or four wrong - passing,
but you haven't mastered the chapter yet. Five or more wrong - not
good enough; start over and restudy the chapter.

Multiple Choice

1. Historically, Canada has actively encouraged foreign investment by
    a. selling bonds abroad to finance large public and private
        undertakings.
    b. selling shares abroad to finance large public and private
        undertakings.
    c. negotiation with the American government.
    d. all of the above.

2. Multinationals are
   a. companies that carry on business in many different countries.
   b. companies with head offices in Canada.
   c. companies with head offices in the United States.
   d. companies that own a controlling interest in several other firms.

3. For which of the following subsectors of Canadian industry is foreign control of assets the greatest?
   a. Petroleum and coal.
   b. Utilities.
   c. Construction.
   d. Retail trade.

4. Canadians benefit from foreign ownership of Canadian business when
   a. superior technology and management skills are brought in with the foreign capital.
   b. research and development is concentrated in foreign countries.
   c. truncation of foreign-owned Canadian firms occurs.
   d. dividends from Canadian companies are paid to foreigners.

5. Canadian businesses that are 100 percent foreign-owned include
   a. General Motors of Canada.
   b. Canada Safeway.
   c. IBM Canada Ltd.
   d. all of the above.

6. Costs of foreign ownership in Canadian business are
   a. a loss of Canadian sovereignty.
   b. decisions by multinational parent firms that may not be in the best interest of the Canadian subsidiary.
   c. a larger balance of payments current account deficit caused by heavy importing.
   d. all of the above.

7. Some businesses that are owned by Canadians but heavily influenced by foreign interests include
   a. many movie houses that show films produced outside of Canada.
   b. many fast-food franchises.
   c. Eaton's.
   d. a and b.

8. The Foreign Investment Review Agency (FIRA)
   a. has prohibited all new foreign investment in Canada since 1973.
   b. allows only portfolio investment in Canada.
   c. monitors prospective foreign takeovers of Canadian firms and encourages greater Canadian participation at the management level in foreign firms already operating in Canada.
   d. only allows direct investment from the United States.

9. Attempts have been made by the government to establish a strong Canadian publishing industry
   a. by offering interest-free loans to new firms.
   b. through favorable tax laws and government subsidies.
   c. by prohibiting foreign-owned firms from publishing in Canada.
   d. by prohibiting firms with any foreign ownership from publishing magazines.

10. The government has made a number of efforts to encourage Canadian ownership of businesses by
    a. giving large interest-free loans to new businesses.
    b. allowing corporations that are partly Canadian-owned to pay lower dividend taxes than those corporations that are wholly foreign-owned.
    c. allowing managers in Canadian-owned firms to pay lower personal income taxes.
    d. b and c.

HANDS ON

Now that you have reviewed the concepts introduced in this chapter, it is time for some hands-on practice with the analytical tools that have been introduced. Work through the problem in this section carefully, and then check your results against those given at the end of the book.

Problem 1.

Exhibit S29.1
Direct Investment
in Canada by Foreigners

Year	(Millions of Dollars)
1978	85
1979	675
1980	585
1981	-4,600
1982	-1,425

Source: Bank of Canada Review, April 1983, p. S134, "Canadian Balance of International Payments: Capital Account."

(a) Under what circumstances do you think foreigners would be willing to pay more for Canadian assets than Canadians? Give at least two possible explanations.

(b) How might the Canadian government influence any of the reasons mentioned in your answer to part (a)?

(c) Using the concepts in your answer to part (a), state what circumstances could have caused the large change in direct investment in Canada by foreigners, that is illustrated in Exhibit S29.1. (You may want to reread Case Study 29.3 and the discussion of the National Energy Program before answering this question.)

APPLICATION

Branch plant imports seen hurting economy

OTTAWA (CP) — Foreign-owned companies spend too much money outside the country, thus contributing to economic hardship in Canada, says Stuart Smith, chairman of the Science Council of Canada.

No matter how much the dollar falls relative to other currencies, branch plants here continue to import from foreign parent companies, Smith told the final day of the annual meeting of the Canadian Advanced Technology Association yesterday.

These branch plants import up to three times as much as Canadian firms and make no effort to substitute domestically-made materials, he said.

This pattern is a major reason for the deficit in the balance of payments, in Smith's opinion. While Canada had a surplus of $6.5 billion in merchandise trade in 1981, that bulge was more than wiped out by a $15-billion deficit in service transactions.

Merchandise trade refers to the exchange of actual goods, while service transactions include such items as the $1 billion spent on foreign travel last year, the $7 billion in dividend and interest payments to foreigners, and a variety of other financial transactions.

The problem will exist "as long as we have our major industries in foreign hands and as long as major industries are not behaving in a way that assists Canada," said the psychiatrist and former leader of the Ontario Liberal party.

He noted that although a lower dollar makes Canadian exports more competitive, it also brings inflation because it increases the price of imports.

The long-term answer to strengthening the economy is building up the capacity of Canadian companies in fields that have a future — particularly the high-technology industries, although some medium- and low-technology industries are also worth supporting.

Although Canada is ahead in some aspects of high technology, the electronics trade deficit is still $2.5 billion.

For a start, government should cut the number of myriad and confusing programs aimed at helping industry and make them simpler, said Smith.

"Right now, they intimidate small- and medium-sized firms."

*From **Winnipeg Free Press**, May 20, 1982, p. 39. Reprinted by permission of Canadian Press.*

1. How is the activity by foreign-owned firms that is described in the article "contributing to economic hardship in Canada?"

2. If Canadian branch plants continue to import the same amount from their parent firms "no matter how much the (Canadian) dollar falls relative to other currencies," what does their demand curve for imports look like?

3. What account in the Canadian balance of payments is likely to run a larger deficit as a result of activities by foreign-owned companies? What must be done to balance this deficit?

4. How might a sustained inflow of foreign investment into Canada affect the exchange rate and therefore, the price of exports and imports?

CHAPTER 30
FACTOR MARKETS AND MARGINAL PRODUCTIVITY THEORY

WHERE
YOU'RE GOING

When you have mastered this chapter, you will be able to:

- Explain the role played by factor markets in the functional and personal distribution of income.

- Derive a firm's marginal revenue product curve from data on marginal physical product and marginal revenue.

- Explain why the marginal revenue product curve is the factor demand curve for a firm that is a price taker in the market where it purchases the factor.

- Derive marginal factor cost curves from factor supply curves for both competitive and monopsonistic firms.

- Explain the origin and shape of an individual's factor supply curve in terms of the income and substitution effects.

- Compare factor market equilibrium under competition and monopsony.

- Discuss the marginal productivity theory of distribution in both positive and normative terms.

- Define and give examples of pure economic rent.

- Explain how a perpetual rent can be capitalized to give the market value of the asset on which the rent is earned.

- Explain why borrowers are willing to pay interest on consumption loans and production loans.

- Discuss the relationship between profit, on the one hand, and risk, arbitrage, and innovation on the other.

- Explain the relationship of monopoly profits, windfall profits, and loot to pure economic profit and entrepreneurship.

WALKING TOUR

You have read the chapter at least once and have reviewed the summary in the text. Now you are going to walk through the material step by step, filling in the blanks and answering the questions as you go along. After you have answered each question, check yourself by uncovering the answer given in the margin. If you do not understand why the answer given is the right one, refer back to the proper section of the text.

The Demand for Factors of Production

The factor demand curve for a firm that is a price taker in the market where it buys its inputs is that firm's marginal ________________ curve for the factor. — revenue product

Marginal revenue product is equal to marginal ________________ times marginal ________________. — physical product; revenue

Complete the following table, which shows the derivation of the marginal revenue product curve:

Quantity of Factor	Total Physical Product	Marginal Physical Product	Marginal Revenue	Marginal Revenue Product	
120	2,000				
		________	$100	$________	10; 1,000
121	2,010				
		________	98	________	9; 882
122	2,019				
		________	96	________	8; 768
123	2,027				
		________	94	________	7; 658
124	2,034				
		________	92	________	6; 552
125	2,040				

A firm maximizes profit by hiring each factor up to the point where marginal revenue product is equal to marginal ________________. — factor cost

If the firm is a price taker in the market where it buys the factors, marginal factor cost is equal to factor ________________. — price

Supply and Demand in the Labor Market

(Note: The following exercise is based on material covered in the appendix to Chapter 20. If you did not work through that appendix, do so now, or skip ahead to the next exercise in this section.)

Because households are the sellers in the labor market, a theory of the labor supply curve is an outgrowth of the theory of consumer choice. Exhibit S30.1 shows how the indifference curve version of this theory can be used to derive a labor supply curve for an individual worker. Suppose that the

indifference map drawn in Part (a) of that exhibit
represents your preferences regarding money income
(represented on the vertical axis) versus leisure
time (represented on the horizontal axis). Suppose
initially that you can obtain a job paying $5 per
hour and that you can work any number of hours
from zero to twenty-four per day. at this job.
Draw a budget line in the exhibit that shows the

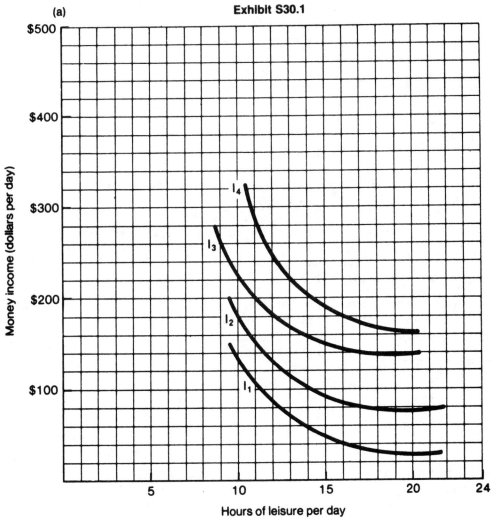

(a)   **Exhibit S30.1**

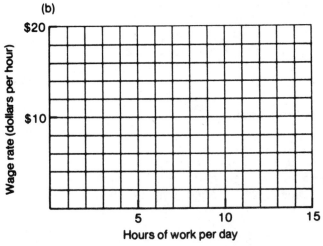

various combinations of money income and leisure time available to you under these circumstances, and label it "W = $5." This budget line should intersect the horizontal axis at _____ hours, indicating all leisure and no income. It should intersect the vertical axis at _____, indicating your hypothetical maximum income if you work around the clock.

twenty-four

$120

According to the indifference map shown in the exhibit, you will choose to work about _____ hours per day at $5 per hour, earning a total income of _____. This preferred position corresponds to the point where the indifference curve _____ is _____ to the budget line you just drew. Label this Point A. Note that you choose _____ hours of leisure at Point A, leaving eight hours for work in a twenty-four-hour day.

eight

$40

I_1; tangent

sixteen

Suppose now that the wage available to you rises to $10 an hour. Draw a new budget line, labeling it "W = $10." This budget line intersects the horizontal axis at _____ hours as before. It intersects the vertical axis at _____. With this new budget line, you will work about _____ hours per day and earn a total income of _____. This corresponds to the tangency of the $10 per hour budget line with the indifference curve _____. Label the tangency Point B.

twenty-four

$240

ten

$100

I_2

Repeat the steps for wages of $15 per hour and $20 per hour. The $15 per hour wage gives a Point C, with _____ hours of work per day and a total income of _____. The $20 per hour wage gives a Point D with _____ hours of work per day and _____ total income.

twelve

$180

eleven

$220

Now, use Points A, B, C, and D from Exhibit S30.1(a) to plot your labor supply curve in Exhibit S30.1(b). Notice that the axes in Part (b) are different - the horizontal axis now has hours of work rather than hours of leisure, and the vertical axis has the wage in dollars per hour rather than total income in dollars per day. At Point A in Exhibit S30.1(a), you worked _____ hours per day at _____ per hour, so plot this point in Exhibit S30.1(b), labeling it Point A. At B, you worked _____ hours at _____ per hour, so this becomes Point B in S30.1(b), and so forth. Your completed diagram should look like the one shown in the solutions section at the end of this book. Note the backward-bending individual labor supply curve.

eight; $5

ten; $10

Turn your attention now to Exhibit S30.2, which you can use to compare labor market equilibrium under conditions of competition and monopsony in the labor market. As drawn, the exhibit shows a downward-sloping labor demand (marginal revenue product) curve and an

Exhibit S30.2

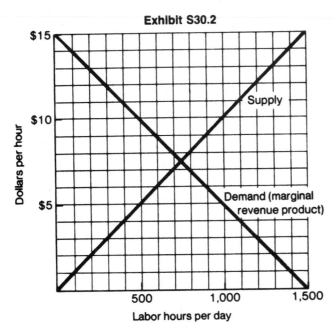

upward-sloping labor supply curve. If employers behave as price takers in hiring labour, the equilibrium wage rate will be _____ per hour and the quantity of labor hired will be _____ labor hours per day. Label this equilibrium E$_c$ in the exhibit.

$7.50

750

Suppose now that the marginal revenue product curve shown is that of a single monopsonistic employer. To determine equilibrium under monopsony, first construct the marginal factor cost curve corresponding to the supply curve shown. Do this by plotting two sample points and drawing a straight line through them. For example, consider first the range from 400 to 401 labor hours. As the supply curve is drawn, you can see that to attract one extra labor hour at any point, the wage rate must be raised by _____. Thus, to hire 400 labor hours per day, the firm must pay _____ per hour,

one cent
$4

and to hire 401 labor hours, it must pay _____ per hour. The total wage bill for 400 labor hours comes to _____, and the total wage bill for 401 labor hours comes to _____. Marginal labor cost in the range 400 to 401 labor hours is thus _____ per

$4.01

$1,600

$1,608.01
$8.01

hour. Plot a point at 400.5 hours and $8.01; label
it Point A. Proceeding in the same manner, calculate
marginal labor cost in the range 500 to 501 labor
hours per day. To get 500 labor hours, the wage must
be _____ per hour, and the total wage bill $5

will thus be _____. To get 501 labor $2,500

hours, the wage must be _____ per hour $5.01

for a total wage bill of _____. Marginal $2,510.01
labor cost in the range 500 to 501 labor hours is
thus _____ per hour. Plot Point B at $10.01
500.5 labor hours and a wage of $10.01. Draw a
straight line through Points A and B, and label it
"marginal labor cost."
    Now that you have the monopsonist's marginal
labor cost curve, it is a simple matter to discover
the equilibrium wage rate and quantity of labor.
The monopsonist will hire workers up to the point
where marginal _____ is equal to marginal   labor cost

_____. In Exhibit S30.2, this happens at   revenue product

_____ labor hours. To hire this many   500
labor hours, the firm must, according to the supply
curve, pay a wage of _____ per hour. So $5
the point corresponding to 500 labor hours and $5 per
hour is the monopsony equilibrium; label it E_m.
    In comparing the competitive equilibrium E_c
with the monopsony equilibrium E_m, note the following
points: under monopsony, the number of labor hours
hired per day is [higher/lower] than under competition,   lower
and the wage rate is [higher/lower]. Under competition,   lower
the wage rate is [greater than/less than/equal to]   equal to
marginal revenue product; under monopsony, the wage
rate is [greater than/less than/equal to] marginal   less than
revenue product. These results will be of interest
when labor unions are discussed in the next chapter.

Rent, Interest, and Profits

Pure economic rent is the income earned by a factor
of production that is in perfectly _____   inelastic
supply. The supply curve of such a factor is a
_____ line. The rental value of the   vertical
factor is determined in a competitive market by the
intersection of the vertical supply curve with the
marginal _____ curve of the factor.   revenue product
    If a rent-earning factor of production, such as
a parcel of land, is sold outright, its rental value
becomes capitalized into the rental price. In the
simplest case, where a resource is expected to earn
a constant annual rent in perpetuity, the capitalized
value of the resource can be calculated by dividing the

_____ by the _____ . For example,   annual rent;
given a 5 percent rate of interest, a property   rate of interest
producing an annual rental income of $2,000 would have
a capitalized value of _____ . Interest $40,000
can be earned both on loans made for consumption
purposes and on those made for productive investment.

Interest and Capital

The term _____ is used to express the price   interest
borrowers pay to lenders for the use of funds, and to
express the market return earned by _____   capital

as a factor of _____ . Interest is paid on   production

_____ loans when households borrow to   consumption
consume [more/less] than their current income allows.   more
Funds are also borrowed, and interest paid on the
loan, to create or purchase capital for production.
Using capital is referred to as a _____   roundabout
method of production. Loans of funds used for
increasing productivity are called _____   investment
loans. These loans allow the producer to increase
output by using a more _____ intensive   capital
(or more roundabout) production method.

Profit and Entrepreneurship

According to one theory, profit is a reward that
entrepreneurs earn for bearing risk. This theory
assumes that most people [like/dislike] risk, other   dislike
things being equal, and hence are willing to pay to
avoid it. For example, an entrepreneur starting a
new business contracts to pay workers and suppliers
even if the firm fails and is thus able to buy their
labor and resources at a [higher/lower] price than   lower
would be the case if they were to share more of the
risk.
　　According to a second theory, profits are earned
by buying [high/low] and selling [high/low]. This   low; high
activity is known as _____ . Still another   arbitrage
theory sees profits as a reward for innovation. This
theory was popularized by the economist _____ .   Joseph Schumpeter
In practice, it seems reasonable to take an eclectic
view of profits, considering them a reward for a
mixture of risk bearing, arbitrage, and innovation.

SELF TEST
_____

These sample test items will help you check how much you have learned.
Answers and explanations can be found at the end of this book. Scoring
yourself: one or two wrong - on target. Three or four wrong - passing,

but you haven't mastered the chapter yet. Five or more wrong - not good enough; start over and restudy the chapter.

Multiple Choice

1. The increase in quantity of output resulting from a one-unit increase in a variable factor, with the quantities of fixed factors held constant, is known as
   a. the marginal physical product of that factor.
   b. the marginal revenue product of that factor.
   c. the marginal factor cost of that factor.
   d. the diminishing marginal product of that factor.

2. In equilibrium, the wage rate for each factor will be equal to the marginal physical product of the factor times product price, if the firm is
   a. a monopolist in its output market.
   b. a perfect competitor in its output market.
   c. both of the above.
   d. none of the above.

3. Which of the following would cause the demand curve for a factor of production to shift to the left?
   a. An increase in demand for the product.
   b. An increase in the price of a good that is a substitute for the product.
   c. An improvement in technology that increases the marginal physical product of the factor.
   d. A decrease in the price of a factor that is a substitute for the factor in question.

4. Which of the following is represented graphically by a movement along a given labor demand curve?
   a. The effects of a change in the wage rate.
   b. The effects of a change in raw materials prices.
   c. The effects of a change in output prices.
   d. None of the above.

5. In equilibrium in a perfectly competitive labor market, the wage rate is equal to
   a. marginal revenue product.
   b. marginal factor cost.
   c. the height of the supply curve.
   d. all of the above.

6. Which of the following might be said to earn a pure economic rent?
   a. A parcel of farmland.
   b. An operatic tenor with a voice of rare quality.
   c. A cab owner in a city where the supply of cab licenses is perfectly inelastic.
   d. All of the above.

7. Assuming a 5 percent rate of interest, what would be the capitalized value of an apartment building that produced a rental income of $100,000 per year and was expected to become worthless at the end of twenty years?
   a. $2 million.
   b. Less than $2 million.
   c. More than $2 million.
   d. Insufficient information is given for an answer to be reached.

8. The term "interest" can be used to mean
   a. the income earned from consumption loans.
   b. the income earned from production loans.
   c. the return to capital as a factor of production.
   d. any of the above.

9. The theory of profit as a reward for risk bearing implies that most people, given the choice between a $100 bill and a lottery ticket having one chance in a thousand of winning $100,000, would show which preference?
   a. They would prefer the lottery ticket.
   b. They would prefer the $100 bill.
   c. They would be indifferent between the two.
   d. None of the above is implied by the theory.

10. A person who, on a certain date, bought 100 ounces of gold in the London gold market at $402 per ounce and simultaneously sold 100 ounces of gold in the Zurich market at $403.50 per ounce would be said to earn an income primarily through
    a. risk bearing.
    b. arbitrage.
    c. innovation.
    d. looting.

HANDS ON

Now that you have reviewed the concepts introduced in this chapter, it is time for some hands-on practice with the analytical tools that have been introduced. Work through each problem in this section carefully, and then check your results against those given at the end of the book.

Problem 1. This problem is based on Exhibit S30.3, which shows marginal revenue product and supply curves for a monopsonistic employer.

(a) If these supply and marginal revenue product curves applied to a perfectly competitive labor market, what would be the equilibrium wage rate and the equilibrium quantity of labor employed?

(b) Instead, we assume that the employer is a monopsonist. On this assumption, fill in the blanks in Exhibit S30.3(b). Using the completed table as your guide, draw in the monopsonist's marginal labor cost curve. What is the equilibrium quantity of labor

Exhibit S30.3

(a)

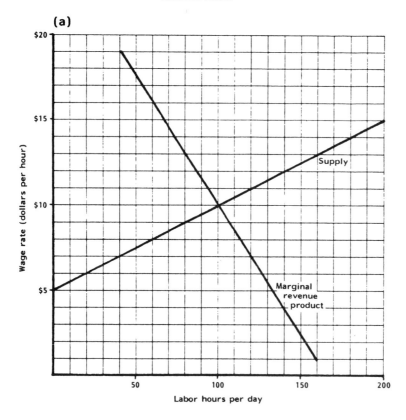

(b)

Labor Hours Per Day	Wage Rate	Total Labor Cost	Marginal Labor Cost
49	$_____	$_____	
50	_____	_____	$_____
51	_____	_____	_____
⋮			
99	_____	_____	
100	_____	_____	_____
101	_____	_____	_____

employed by the monopsonist? The equilibrium wage rate?

(c) Does the position of the marginal labor cost curve in Exhibit S30.3(a) suggest to you a shortcut method of drawing such a curve when the supply curve is a straight line? Can you prove that the shortcut method works?

Problem 2. This problem relies on indifference curve analysis, introduced in the option appendix to Chapter 20 of Basic Economics (Chapter 5 of the paperback Basic Microeconomics). If you did not cover that appendix, skip this problem.

Exhibit S30.4a

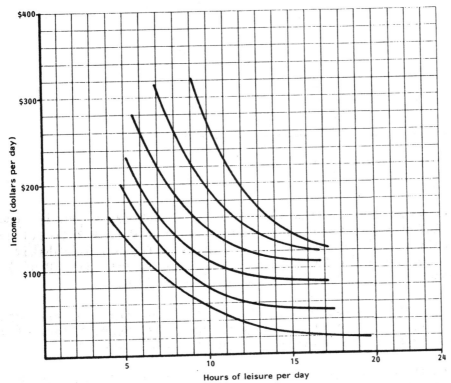

(a) The horizontal axis of this figure shows hours of leisure per day for one individual worker. The vertical axis shows dollars of income earned per day. At any given wage rate, the worker faces a budget line, indicating that earning more income requires giving up some leisure hours. Draw budget lines corresponding to wage rates of $2.50, $5, $7.50, $10, $12.50, and $15 per hour.

(b) Using the budget lines you have just drawn, locate the equilibrium points for each wage rate. Label these points A through F, beginning with the lowest wage rate.

Exhibit S30.4b

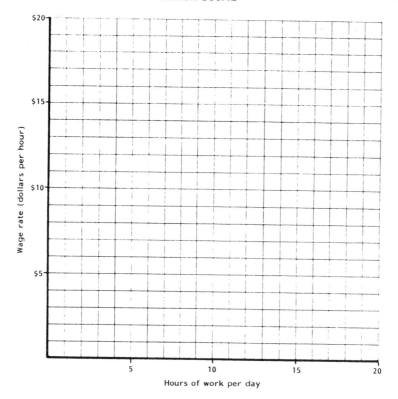

(c) The budget lines and equilibrium points you have drawn provide you with the information you need to construct this worker's individual labor supply curve. First, locate points a through f in Exhibit S30.4(b), corresponding to points A through F in Exhibit S30.4(a). Then, connect the points with a smooth freehand curve.

(d) Is leisure time a normal or an inferior good for this worker? How can you tell? At about what wage rate does the income effect of a wage increase begin to outweigh the substitution effect?

Problem 3. Calculate the market price or the capitalized value of the rent for a piece of land with an expected real rental value of $2,000 per year for perpetuity. Assume a real interest rate of 3 percent, and use the formula R/r, where R is the perpetual expected real annual rental value per year and r is the real rate of interest. How much does the capitalized value of the land decrease if the real interest rate is 2 percent?

Problem 4. Calculate the interest paid on a $2,000 loan if the borrower makes a payment of $50 per year plus the eventual repayment of the principal. What is the rate of interest if a payment of $150 is made per year? $250 per year?

Problem 5. If a firm buys a machine for $2,000 and earns $50 per year by employing the productive services of that machine, what rate of interest does the firm earn on its capital purchase? What rate is earned if the firm receives $150 per year? $250 per year?

Problem 6. What is the profit rate for a firm with a net income of $100,000, when $1,600,000 of investors' funds or assets have been committed to the operation? If the firm could purchase government bonds paying 8 percent interest per year and the firm could realize $1,600,000 from the sale of its assets, should it sell? Explain.

DON'T MAKE THIS COMMON MISTAKE!

When you used Exhibit S30.2 to determine the equilibrium quantity of labor employed under monopsony, you went straight to the intersection of the marginal revenue product curve and marginal factor cost curve. Your correct answer: 500 labor hours per day hired by the monopsonist. If you then put down $10 per hour as the equilibrium wage rate under monopsony, you made the most common mistake for the material covered in this chapter.

If you look at the supply curve for this labor market, you will see that at a wage rate of $10 per hour, not 500, but 1,000 labor hours per day would be supplied by workers. Twice as many workers as needed would apply for the available jobs. Instead, to maximize profit, the monopsonist will offer a wage rate just high enough to attract the quantity of labor needed. Given this supply curve, only $5 per hour need be offered to obtain 500 labor hours per day.

In short, after you find the equilibrium quantity at the intersection of the marginal revenue product and marginal factor cost curves, look straight down to the supply curve to obtain the equilibrium wage. Don't let a long line of disappointed workers pile up at your factory gate!

Knitters paid $27 for $400 sweaters

LONDON (AP) — American designer Ralph Lauren is paying British senior citizens $10 to $27 to knit sweaters he sells in the United States for $400, *The Sunday Times* reported.

The London weekly published a picture of grey-haired Mabel Foxwell of the London borough of Blackheath holding a sweater which she said takes her about two days to knit. Alongside it was a picture of a Lauren buyer, identified only as Torna, holding a sweater she said would sell at the firm's Bond Street boutique in London for $290.

"We have no problem selling as many as we can get," Torna was quoted as saying. "But I do feel bad about how much the knitters receive."

Foxwell was quoted as telling *The Sunday Times* she enjoys the work, despite the low pay, because, "Tricky knitting keeps my brain active."

With the cost of materials, the sweater costs about $44 to make.

The Sunday Times said Lauren justifies the disparity between cost and price by saying he also must pay his London agent's commission, shipping charges to the U.S., a U.S. import duty of 30 per cent and other handling charges on each garment.

The article said the sweater wholesales in the U.S. at about $185 and retails for about $400.

The Sunday Times quoted Foxwell as saying the small fee is not Lauren's fault.

"It's up to the worker to ask for more," she was quoted as saying.

From **Winnipeg Free Press**, October 25, 1982, p. 27. Reprinted by permission of Associated Press.

1. Define marginal revenue product (MRP) of labor. What is the MRP on the London market to Lauren's firm of hiring another knitter for approximately two days?

2. Define marginal factor cost (MFC). Roughly, what is the MFC to Lauren's firm of hiring another knitter for approximately two days?

3. How does a profit-maximizing firm decide how much of a factor input to hire? Would you suggest that Lauren's firm hire more or fewer knitters if it wants to maximize profits (even after allowing for middlemen expenses)? Explain your answer.

4. Could the profits made by Lauren's firm be considered monopoly profits? If yes, explain how Lauren has established a monopoly. If no, how can these profits be explained?

CHAPTER 31
LABOR UNIONS AND COLLECTIVE BARGAINING

When you have mastered this chapter, you will be able to:

- Distinguish between <u>craft unions</u> and <u>industrial unions</u> and explain the place of each in the history of the labor movement in Canada.

- Recount the origins of the AFL led by Samuel Gompers and explain its influence on Canadian unionism.

- List various goals that a labor union might pursue in its bargaining with employers and explain how it might be able to achieve those goals by means of a strike or strike threat.

- Compare the effects of unionization in a monopsonistic labor market with its effects in a competitive labor market.

- Explain the meaning of <u>bilateral monopoly</u>.

- Discuss the effects of unionization on the relative wages of union members and on the average wages of all workers.

- Describe the historical evolution of labor and management relations in Canada and list major pieces of legislation that have influenced this relationship.

- Explain the meaning and significance of the following additional term:

    featherbedding

WALKING TOUR

You have read the chapter at least once and have reviewed the summary in the text. Now you are going to walk through the material step by step, filling in the blanks and answering the questions as you go along. After you have answered each question, check yourself by uncovering the answer given in the margin. If you do not understand why the answer given is the right one, refer back to the proper section of the text.

The History of Canadian Unionism

The labor movement in Canada has been described as "decentralized, fragmented, weak," and heavily influenced by _____ unionism. The first [United States] small unions appeared in Canada in the 1820s and 1830s. These were mainly _____ unions that limited [craft] their membership to workers practicing the same trade. In the 1870s, an American union, the _____, [Knights of Labor] organized many Canadian workers into a/an _____-type union. Anyone who worked for a [an industrial] living was welcome to join. Membership in the Knights of Labor declined in the 1880s.

The _____ Council (TLC), founded in [Trades and Labour] 1886, was one of the first successful confederations of labor in Canada. It affiliated itself with the American _____ (AFL), led by Samuel Gompers. [Federation of Labor] Gompers had a great deal of influence on Canadian labor union philosophy. He based his philosophy on the following three principles: (1) the AFL was a _____ union whose members were skilled [craft] workers; (2) the AFL devoted its main energies toward improving rates of _____ and working [pay] conditions, and not toward attempting to overthrow the capitalist system; (3) the AFL's political role was limited to _____ and there was no [lobbying] attempt to form a separate labor political party.

A more radical form of unionism developed in Canada between 1914 and 1917. The _____ [One Big] Union was formed in the West in 1918, and in 1919 a _____ occurred in Winnipeg. [General Strike]

After this short radical period, unions made few advances until the 1940s and 1950s. In 1940, the _____ of Labour (CCL) was formed and [Canadian Congress] established a loose affiliation with the American _____ (CIO). In 1956, the TLC and the [Congress of Industrial Organizations] CCL merged into the _____ Congress (CLC), [Canadian Labour] which included craft and industrial unions.

Between the 1950s and the 1970s, union membership increased by [a great deal/little], as a [little] percentage of the nonagricultural labor force. Recent membership drives have concentrated on organizing [professional and clerical/blue collar] workers. [professional and clerical]

Collective Bargaining and Wage Rates

Exhibit S31.1 can be used to analyze the effects of union activities on wage rates and employment in a competitive industry. The supply and demand curves shown there indicate an equilibrium wage rate of _____ per hour and an equilibrium employment [$5] of _____ labor hours per day. [20,000] Suppose now that the workers in the industry in question form a union and threaten to strike if they are not paid at least $7.50 per hour. In terms

of the diagram, this action can be represented as a
change in position of the [supply/demand] curve.   supply
This curve will now be a [vertical/horizontal] line   horizontal
at _____ .   Sketch in this modified $7.50

Exhibit S31.1

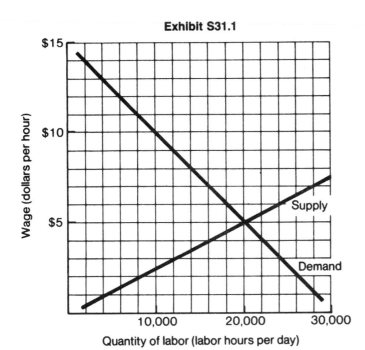

Quantity of labor (labor hours per day)

supply curve. With the modified supply curve in place,
the equilibrium wage rate will be _____ $7.50
per hour and the equilibrium quantity of labor will be
_____ labor hours per day.   15,000
        Note that the wage rate is [higher/lower] and the   higher
number of labor hours employed is [higher/lower] than   lower
without the union. At $7.50 per hour, workers will
want to supply _____ labor hours per day,   30,000
leaving an excess labor supply of _____   15,000
hours per day. The available work will somehow have
to be _____ among the workers. Note also   rationed
that total labor income, with the union, is
_____ per day. This is [up/down] from its $112,500; up

level of _____ without the union. However, $100,000
raising the wage higher than $7.50 would begin to
reduce total labor income. At $8 per hour, for
example, total labor income would be down to
_____ per day. Total labor income would $112,000
fall below its level in competitive equilibrium if the
wage rate were forced above _____ per hour. $10
In general, raising the wage rate will raise total
labor income only so long as the demand for labor
is [elastic/inelastic].   inelastic
        Turn your attention now to Exhibit S31.2, which
can be used to show the effects of unionization in a

monopsony labor market. The supply curve of labor
shown there is the same as in Exhibit S31.1, and the
marginal revenue product curve for this monopsonist
is the same as the demand curve shown in the previous

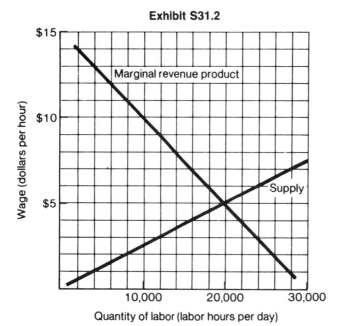

Exhibit S31.2

exhibit. Begin by sketching in the marginal labor cost
curve for the monopsonist, as you learned to do in
Chapter 30; it is a straight line starting at the
origin and intersecting the marginal revenue product
curve at a height of _____. The quantity $7.50
of labor hired in equilibrium by the monopsonist
can thus be seen to be _____ labor hours   15,000
per day and the equilibrium wage rate to be
_____ per hour. (Note that the wage rate $3.75
is given by the height of the supply curve, not the
height of the marginal revenue product curve!) In comparison with the competitive equilibrium, the wage rate
under monopsony is [higher/lower] and the quantity of   lower
labor hired is [higher/lower].   lower
    If the labor force is unionized and refuses to
work for any wage below a certain level, the marginal
labor cost curve facing the monopsonist effectively
becomes a [horizontal/vertical] line, corresponding   horizontal
to the wage demanded up to the point where it
intersects the labor supply curve; beyond that point,
the marginal labor cost jumps to its previous level.
Sketching in such a marginal labor cost curve
corresponding to a union demand of $4 per hour, for
example, shows that the monopsonist would hire
_____ labor hours per day at that wage.   16,000
If $5 per hour were demanded, _____ labor   20,000

hours per day would be used. A demand of $6 would cause _____ labor hours to be hired;   18,000

and $7.50 per hour, _____ labor hours.   15,000
Thus it can be seen that, beginning from a monopsony equilibrium, the union can force the wage rate as high as $7.50 per hour without a loss of work. Maximum employment for union members is obtained at a wage of _____ per hour. $5

SELF TEST

These sample test items will help you check how much you have learned. Answers and explanations can be found at the end of this book. Scoring yourself: one or two wrong - on target. Three or four wrong - passing, but you haven't mastered the chapter yet. Five or more wrong - not good enough; start over and restudy the chapter.

Multiple Choice

1. Approximately what percentage of the nonagricultural labor force belonged to unions in Canada in 1980?
   a. 19 percent.
   b. 23 percent.
   c. 33 percent.
   d. 50 percent.

2. Which of the following did not characterize the American Federation of Labor in its early years?
   a. Craft unionism.
   b. Business unionism.
   c. Lobbying in support of labor.
   d. Support of a national labor party.

3. Which of the following unions was the most radical in its political activities?
   a. American Federation of Labor.
   b. All-Canadian Congress of Labour.
   c. One Big Union.
   d. Trades and Labour Council of Canada.

4. A union formed in a previously competitive labor market, in which the competitive equilibrium lies on an elastic portion of the labor demand curve, can reasonably hope to be able to increase which of the following in the market where it operates?
   a. The wage rate.
   b. Total labor income.
   c. Total employment.
   d. All of the above.

5. A union facing a straight-line labor demand curve maximizes the total income of its members by setting the wage at
    a. the highest possible level.
    b. the point of unit demand elasticity.
    c. the competitive equilibrium wage.
    d. b or c, whichever is the higher wage.

6. A union formed in a monopsonistic labor market can, at least within limits, reasonably hope to raise which of the following for its members?
    a. Wages.
    b. Total employment.
    c. Both of the above.
    d. None of the above.

7. A union formed in a previously monopsonistic labor market has already raised the wage of its members up to the equivalent of the competitive equilibrium wage. Which of the following will happen if it raises the wage further?
    a. Employment will increase and total labor income will decrease.
    b. Employment will decrease and total labor income will increase.
    c. Employment and total labor income will both decrease.
    d. Insufficient information is given for an answer to be reached.

8. In a situation of bilateral monopoly in a labor market, the equilibrium wage rate will be
    a. equal to the competitive equilibrium wage.
    b. above the competitive equilibrium wage.
    c. below the competitive equilibrium wage.
    d. impossible to determine from the information given.

9. Empirical studies indicate that unions have often been successful in raising
    a. the share of wages in GNP.
    b. the relative wages of their members.
    c. both of the above.
    d. none of the above.

10. The Rand Formula requires
    a. only union members to pay union dues.
    b. both union and non-union members to pay union dues.
    c. all firms with more than 250 employees to be unionized.
    d. none of the above.

HANDS ON

Now that you have reviewed the concepts introduced in this chapter, it is time for some hands-on practice with the analytical tools that have been introduced. Work through the problem in this section carefully, and then check your results against those given at the end of the book.

Problem. The following questions are based on Exhibit S31.3, which shows demand and supply curves for a typical labor market in which employers are perfectly competitive.

Exhibit S31.3

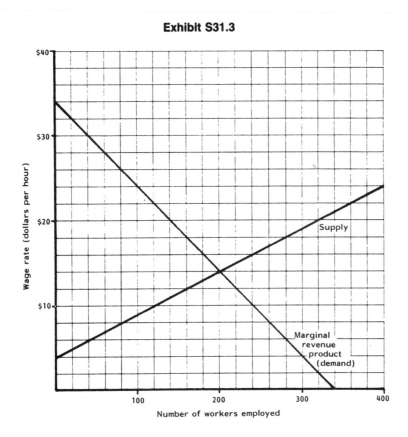

(a) If workers behave competitively and are non-unionized, what will be the equilibrium wage rate and number of workers employed?

(b) What wage rate would a union bargain for if its objective were to maximize the total sum of wages paid to all workers in this labor market?

(c) What is the opportunity of taking a job in this labor market to the 100th worker to take a job there? To the 120th? To the 140th? At what wage rate does the increase in total wage income of all workers become less than the opportunity cost to the added worker of taking a job in this labor market? Why might a union seek this "rent" maximizing wage?

(d) If this union were controlled by an elite group of 100 workers who were interested only in getting jobs for themselves at the highest possible wage, what wage would the union bargain for?

Won't accept pay cuts, Steelworkers' union says

By Mike Lowe
Special to The Globe and Mail

SUDBURY — Like the Canadian wing of the United Auto Workers, Canada's largest industrial union has no intention of negotiating concessionary contracts, even if it means putting companies out of business, two top officials of the United Steelworkers of America said yesterday.

David Patterson, director of the Steelworkers' Ontario district, acknowledged that his union's hard line on concessions has cost some jobs and even hastened the demise of a few union locals because of plant closings.

"But not one of our locals is working under a take-away agreement and we have no intention of signing any in the future. If a company isn't making money, we say, 'Don't prolong the agony — close it down.' Any wage concessions we make aren't going to make any difference.

"It's one thing to bite the bullet; it's another thing to swallow it."

The Steelworkers' Ontario district has been hit hard by the recession. Membership has dropped to 84,000 from 100,000 in the past year, and the number of dues-paying members continues to dwindle weekly.

But Mr. Patterson said the UAW will have the full backing of his union when it resists granting wage concessions at the bargaining table this fall. "Once the bosses knock off one of the largest industrial unions in Canada, it's only a matter of time before we all go down."

Clement Godbout, the Steelworkers' director in Quebec and the Maritimes, agrees with Mr. Patterson, adding that Quebec Steelworkers also plan to throw their support behind the province's public-sector employees in their fight to resist wage concessions in forthcoming negotiations.

In the Quebec and Maritimes district, Steelworkers membership has dropped to 51,000 from 63,000 over the past 12 months, and Mr. Godbout said 30 per cent of his membership in Newfoundland and Nova Scotia is now out of work.

The largest employer in his district, the Iron Ore Co., has laid off 3,000 Steelworkers in Northern Quebec, even though it made $125-million in profits last year, Mr. Godbout added.

"They've closed the mine in Schefferville, while they've opened one in Brazil to take its place. In Sept-Iles right now, half the people are out of work. Why should we be granting concessions to people like this?"

Mr. Patterson said he has been made wary of management demands for wage concessions by their past performances. "Look at U.S. Steel in the States. For years they've been telling our members they couldn't afford to modernize their steel mills to keep them open, and then last fall they bought Marathon Oil for $6.8-billion."

*From **The Globe and Mail**, May 13, 1983, p. 11. Reprinted by permission.*

1. Given Mr. Patterson's statements, what exactly do you think the Ontario branch of the Steelworkers' union is attempting to maximize?

2. If the Steelworkers' members face an elastic demand curve, and if Mr. Patterson's statement that "Any wage concessions we make aren't going to make any difference (to a plant already in financial trouble)," is the Steelworkers' insistence regarding no wage concessions in the best interests of its members? Explain.

3. Do you agree with the statement that "Any wage concessions we make aren't going to make any difference?" Cite information from the article to support your answer.

4. What three factors mentioned in your text determine a union's ability to raise the relative wages of its members? Given these three factors, and the information in the article, do you think the Steelworkers' union is likely to raise its members' relative wages? Explain.

CHAPTER 32
THE PROBLEM OF POVERTY

When you have mastered this chapter, you will be able to:

- Discuss the relative distribution of income in Canada and changes in this distribution over time.

- Discuss alternative definitions of poverty, including the one established by Statistics Canada and the Economic Council of Canada.

- Describe the demographic and geographic characteristics of poverty in Canada.

- Describe the various programs or solutions to the problem of poverty, including the negative income tax and job market strategies.

WALKING TOUR

You have read the chapter at least once and have reviewed the summary in the text. Now you are going to walk through the material step by step, filling in the blanks and answering the questions as you go along. After you have answered each question, check yourself by uncovering the answer given in the margin. If you do not understand why the answer given is the right one, refer back to the proper section of the text.

A Profile of Poverty in Canada

According to 1980 figures for personal income distribution, about _____ percent of all   twenty
households received less than half of the median
Canadian income. When income figures are altered
to reflect government _____ and   taxation
_____ programs, one study shows that   expenditure
income is redistributed from the higher to the
lower income groups. Other studies doubt these
results, saying that the structure of Canadian
households has changed in recent years, and that
it is difficult to say that government welfare
programs have significantly changed the
_____ of income in Canada.   distribution
    Inequality of income distribution can also be
measured by dividing families into five equal-sized
groups called _____. If income were   quintiles

equally distributed, each group would receive _____ percent of the income. In Canada, however, the lowest income group has received approximately _____ percent of family income, and the highest income group has received thirty-eight to over thirty-nine percent of the income since 1965.

     A _____ curve is a graphical method of illustrating income inequality. The cumulative percentage of _____ units is plotted along one axis and the cumulative percentage of income received by those units is plotted along the other axis. If income were evenly distributed, the _____ curve would be a [curve/straight line at a 45° angle from the axes]. In reality, however, the Lorenz curve is a [curve/straight line] illustrating that income distribution is unequal in Canada.

     The degree of inequality is more accurately portrayed by the _____ coefficient, which calculates the ratio of inequality. This ratio is determined by measuring the area between the Lorenz curve and the 45° line (OE in Exhibit S32.1) and the area of the entire triangle OPE.

     In Exhibit S32.1, Lorenz curve [OABE/OCDE] shows the greatest inequality of income distribution and therefore has a [lower/higher] Gini coefficient than Lorenz curve [OABE/OCDE].

twenty

six

Lorenz

income

Lorenz
straight line at a
  45° angle from
  the axes
curve

Gini

OCDE

higher
OABE

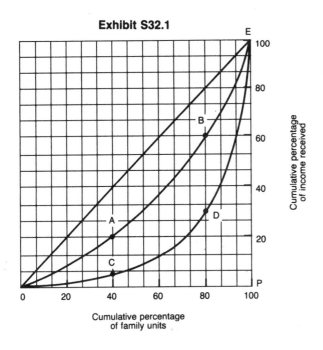

Exhibit S32.1

Cumulative percentage
of income received

Cumulative percentage
of family units

Poverty and Income Distribution

It is hard to find a universally acceptable definition
of poverty, but useful guidelines have been established
by Statistics Canada and the Economic Council. Today,
a household that spends _____ percent of   58.5
its income on essential food, shelter, and clothing
is considered to be poor.
       In 1980, about three million Canadians, or
_____ percent of the population, was living   15
below the poverty line. The [majority/minority] of the   majority
poor live in cities with populations of 100,000 or
more, but a [higher/lower] proportion of rural families   higher
were poorer than city families. The [Maritimes/Prairies]   Maritimes
had more families living below the poverty line; more
families headed by a [man/woman] were poor; and more   woman
families with very young and very old heads were poor.
Labor force participation was also important. [Very
few/Many] unemployed family heads lived with their   Many
families in poverty.
       A special Senate Committee classified the poor
into _____ categories: (1) the   three

_____ of the poor who are not able to work   one-quarter

because of a severe _____; (2) the   disability

_____ of the poor who are working, but who   one-half
do not make an adequate income; and (3) the remaining
one-quarter who are able to work but who are

_____.   unemployed

What Is to Be Done About Poverty?

A variety of programs to help the poor have been tried
or suggested, but many economists feel that all income
transfers to the poor should be combined into a single
negative _____. Exhibit S32.2 provides a   income tax
place for you to illustrate how a negative income tax
program might work. Construct a line showing after-tax
incomes at various levels of earned income, assuming
that the program will provide a minimum benefit of
$5,000 and will incorporate a 50 percent benefit
reduction rate. Assume that households not qualifying
for any payments under the negative income tax pay
a marginal tax rate of 20 percent. Your schedule
should be a straight line intersecting the vertical
axis at a height of _____ and intersecting $5,000

the 45° line at a height of _____. Beyond $10,000
$10,000 of income, the schedule should continue with
a slope of _____.   0.8
       Reading now from your negative income tax
schedule, you see that a family with no earned income

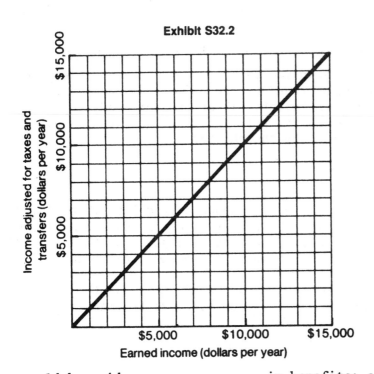

Exhibit S32.2

would be paid _____ in benefits; a family $5,000
with a $5,000 earned income would be paid
_____ in benefits; and a family with $2,500
$9,000 earned income would be paid _____ $500
in benefits. A family earning $12,000 would pay
taxes at a marginal rate of 20 percent on the extra
$2,000 and would have _____ of after-tax $11,600
income.

Helping the Poor: Job Market Strategies

Income transfer strategies for helping the poor are
based on the idea that the poor are poor because they
do not have enough _____. Another point of   money (or income)
view says that poverty results from a failure of the
_____ market to allocate human resources   factor
properly.
  Some economists argue that a _____   dual
labor market exists. One market with high-paying
jobs offers opportunities for advancement and some
security from economic fluctuations, and the other
offers _____-paying insecure jobs with   low
little chance for advancement. Antipoverty programs
that agree with this theory aim at breaking down the
barriers of discrimination and poor work habits that
keep some workers in the lower labor market.
  Other economists view education and training as
a very significant part of an antipoverty program.
They point out that education not only benefits the
individuals involved but _____ as a whole.   society

These sample test items will help you check how much you have learned. Answers and explanations can be found at the end of this book. Scoring yourself: one or two wrong - on target. Three or four wrong - passing, but you haven't mastered the chapter yet. Five or more wrong - not good enough; start over and restudy the chapter.

Multiple Choice

1. In 1980, approximately
   a. 25 percent of the households in Canada earned less than $16,000.
   b. 40 percent of the households in Canada earned less than $16,000.
   c. 50 percent of the households in Canada earned less than $16,000.
   d. 75 percent of the households in Canada earned less than $16,000.

2. According to the text, the province in Canada that has the largest percentage of its families living below the poverty line is:
   a. British Columbia.
   b. Quebec.
   c. Newfoundland.
   d. Nova Scotia.

3. A household is more likely to be living below the poverty line when
   a. it is headed by a woman.
   b. the head is very young or very old.
   c. the head is unemployed.
   d. all of the above.

4. According to the text, the province in Canada that has the lowest percentage of its families living below the poverty line is:
   a. Prince Edward Island.
   b. Ontario.
   c. Manitoba.
   d. British Columbia.

5. The Senate Committee on poverty found that
   a. over one-half of Canada's poor are able to work but unwilling to take a job.
   b. one-third of Canada's poor are able to work but unwilling to take a job.
   c. about one-half of the poor are working, but are not able to earn an adequate income.
   d. two-thirds of Canada's poor are unable to work because of severe disability.

6. Which of the following solutions to Canada's poverty problem have been tried?
   a. Social assistance involving transfer payments.
   b. Government pension plans and unemployment insurance.
   c. Manpower training programs.
   d. All of the above.

7. A negative income tax experiment
   a. has never been tried in Canada.
   b. does nothing to encourage people to work.
   c. pays benefits or collects taxes from families according to a
      schedule based on earnings.
   d. that was tried in New Jersey was a total failure.

8. A negative income tax experiment in Canada
   a. was conducted in Manitoba.
   b. guaranteed a minimum level of income to families.
   c. was concluded with uncertain results.
   d. all of the above.

9. The negative income tax scheme has not been adopted for all of Canada
   because
   a. political realities have kept it in the experimental stage.
   b. it would be hard to set an acceptable level of benefits for
      the very diverse regions of Canada.
   c. economists have decided that the scheme will not work.
   d. a and b but not c.

10. The dual labor market theory
   a. finds that some people tend to get locked into the secondary
      labor market.
   b. states that it is impossible to move from the secondary labor
      market to the high-wage labor market.
   c. places most unionized workers in the secondary labor market.
   d. finds that workers in the secondary labor market have numerous
      opportunities for advancement.

Big-city family poor on $18,243

OTTAWA (CP) — You are poor if you are single and living on an annual income of less than $8,970 in a large city such as Toronto, Montreal or Calgary, says the federal government's National Council of Welfare.

A family of four is poor if it is surviving in a big city on less than $18,243 annually. The same family in a rural area is poor with an income below $13,419.

Couples in a big city are poor if their income is less than $11,835, and if they are in a rural area, less than $8,669.

The figures are contained in a new poverty line chart issued yesterday by the council, a body that advises the government on social welfare policy.

The poverty lines are basically an up-to-date version of two-year-old Statistics Canada figures on low-income Canadians, roughly defined as those who spend nearly 60 per cent of their money on the essentials of life: food, clothing and shelter.

Based on the most recent government study, in 1978, families spend an average 38.5 per cent of their income on essentials. Those spending 20 percentage points above the average are thus considered poor.

While the council can bring the poverty line up to date by calculating how inflation has eaten income in the last two years, it does not have fresh figures on the number of poor in Canada.

The 1980 figures showed there were 3.475 million Canadians under the poverty lines and council director Ken Battle said if the figure has changed, it is no doubt higher.

That is probably safe to say, he said, because economic conditions have deteriorated and recipients of welfare, unemployment insurance and other social benefits have been on the increase.

The 3.475 million poor represented 15.1 per cent of the total population, including men, women and children. There were especially high rates of poverty among single mothers and the elderly.

The council said there is no single poverty line for the country as two factors which affect living costs are taken into account — size of a family and where they live. Taking that into account produces 35 different poverty lines.

Battle said most poor Canadians live on incomes that are hundreds, often thousands, of dollars below the poverty lines. Eighty per cent of poor families are 10 to 20 per cent below the poverty lines and 75 per cent of poor single persons are more than 20 per cent under the poverty lines.

To bring the figures up to date, the council made calculations that assume income was eroded by inflation of 12.5 per cent in 1981 and will be eroded by 11.5 per cent in 1982.

Here's the difference between 1980 and 1982 poverty lines for six of the 35 categories. The 1980 figures are in brackets.

In a large metropolitan city: Single person $8,970 ($7,152), couple $11,835 ($9,436), family of four $18,243 ($14,545).

In a medium city with a population under 500,000 but over 100,000: Single person $8,519 ($6,792), couple $11,231 ($8,955), family of four $17,337 ($13,823).

In a rural region: Single person $6,633 ($5,289), couple $8,669 ($6,912), family of four $13,419 ($10,699).

*From **Winnipeg Free Press**, August 27, 1982. Reprinted by permission of Canadian Press.*

1. Does the article define poverty in absolute terms, relative terms, or both? Cite information from the article to support your answer.

2. Why do the National Council of Welfare's poverty lines vary among metropolitan cities, medium cities, and rural regions?

3. Why are there "especially high rates of poverty among single mothers and the elderly?"

4. What is a negative income tax and how might it help alleviate the problem of poverty in Canada?

CHAPTER 33
THE ECONOMICS OF POPULATION AND DEVELOPMENT

WHERE
YOU'RE GOING
_____

When you have mastered this chapter, you will be able to:

- Compare various interpretations of the process of economic development.

- Explain the conditions under which a population can grow or can achieve equilibrium.

- Describe the demographic transition, and explain the circumstances under which a country may be caught in a population trap.

- Describe the role of food production in economic development.

- Explain the meaning and significance of the following additional terms and concepts:

      depauperization
      the dual economy
      crude birth rate
      crude death rate
      rate of natural increase
      net reproduction rate

WALKING TOUR
_____

You have read the chapter at least once and have reviewed the summary in the text. Now you are going to walk through the material step by step, filling in the blanks and answering the questions as you go along. After you have answered each question, check yourself by uncovering the answer given in the margin. If you do not understand why the answer given is the right one, refer back to the proper section of the text.

Three Faces of Economic Growth

The way that less-developed countries differ from developed countries is that less-developed ones have lower _____ incomes. Higher per capita incomes result from economic _____ and _____. Economic growth does not necessarily mean a better life for everybody, but it is hard to have a better life for everybody without _____.

_____ accumulation is usually seen

per capita

growth
development

economic growth

Capital

as a key to economic _____. Without   growth
_____ accumulation, it is difficult   capital

to increase _____, improve the   employment

level of _____, or to make use of   education

improved _____.   technology

    A proper emphasis on _____ is also   industrialization
seen as a means to economic growth. Industrialization
offers employment and helps to meet the demand for
_____ with domestic sources of supply.   manufactured goods
    Economic growth and industrialization [may not/
will always] mean a better life for the very poor.   may not
Some economists feel that special programs of
_____ should be developed. These programs   depauperization
would benefit the very poor, providing them not only
with the material necessities of life, but also with
access to education, status, security, self-expression,
and power.
    There are two basic development strategies. The
first of these is an _____-first approach.   industry
With this approach, developing nations may suffer
from a _____ economy that is sharply   dual
divided into a modern, westernized industrial sector
capable of rapid growth and a traditional, rural
sector that remains stagnant. The second strategy
places emphasis on _____ of income and   redistribution

mass _____ first and growth second.   education
Israel, Japan, and China are examples of the countries
that have followed this strategy.

Population and Development

Immigration and emigration aside, a population can
grow only if the crude _____ exceeds the   birth rate

crude _____. The difference between the   death rate

two is known as the rate of _____. These   natural increase
measures are usually expressed in terms of births or
deaths per _____ of population. For   1,000
example, a population with a birth rate of 50 and
a death rate of 36 would have a rate of natural
increase of _____ per 1,000 per year.   14
This could also be expressed as a population growth
rate of _____ percent per year.   1.4
    Still another way to express population growth
is in terms of the number of years required for the
population to double, were a particular rate of growth
to continue. Population doubling times can be
calculated by the "rule of 70": the doubling time equals
70 divided by the percentage rate of population growth.

A population growth of 1.4 percent per year would thus be equivalent to a fifty-year population doubling time.

A birth rate of 50 and a death rate of 35 would be typical of a country at a [very low/medium/high] level of development. As such a country began to develop economically, the [birth rate/death rate] would first begin to fall. The rate of natural increase would [rise/fall] as a result. However, as long as the rate of economic growth stayed above the rate of population growth, per capita income would [rise/fall]. The eventual result of increasing per capita income would be a drop in the [birth rate/death rate], once again reducing the rate of population growth. Eventually, the country would reach a population equilibrium, with a [high/low] birth rate and a [high/low] death rate. This complete sequence is known as the _____.

very low

death rate

rise

rise

birth rate

low
low
demographic
  transition

Suppose now that, beginning from a birth rate of 50 and a death rate of 36, modern public health measures were able to reduce the death rate of a country to 15 over a very short period. The rate of natural increase would thus rise to _____. If the best the country could manage was a 3 percent rate of economic growth, per capita income would [rise/fall] at a rate of _____ percent per year. As per capita income fell, the [birth rate/death rate] would rise until population growth fell to the rate of economic growth. Per capita income would stagnate, and the country would be said to be in a _____.

35

fall; 0.5

death rate

population trap

Looking at a country's crude birth rate and crude death rate gives a snapshot of population dynamics at a moment in time; to predict long-term population trends, one must look at other statistics. One of the most revealing population statistics, for example, is the number of daughters born, on the average, to each female child over her lifetime. This is known as the _____ rate. If the net reproduction rate is greater than 1, population will _____ in the long run;

net reproduction

grow

if it is less than 1, it will _____;

shrink

and if it is exactly 1, it will be _____. However, when the net reproduction rate of a country first falls to 1, population growth does not stop immediately. That is because a population that has been growing in the recent past will tend to have a relatively [large/small] portion of its members in the prime child-bearing years. Only after more than a generation with a net reproduction rate of 1 will the age structure of the population reach

stable

large

a long-run equilibrium, so that the rate of natural
increase drops to zero. Of course, if the net
reproduction rate drops below 1, as it has done in
West Germany, for example, actual population growth
will slow and even become negative.

SELF TEST

These sample test items will help you check how much you have learned.
Answers and explanations can be found at the end of this book. Scoring
yourself: one or two wrong - on target. Three or four wrong - passing,
but you haven't mastered the chapter yet. Five or more wrong - not
good enough; start over and restudy the chapter.

Multiple Choice

1. Emphasis on which of the following aspects of development is most
    likely to create a so-called dual economy?
    a. Industrialization.
    b. Rural development.
    c. Land reform.
    d. Depauperization.

2. Depauperization is thought to be aided by
    a. land reform.
    b. mass education for literacy.
    c. development of labor-intensive industry.
    d. all of the above.

3. The number of daughters born to each female child during her lifetime
    is known as the
    a. crude birth rate.
    b. rate of natural increase.
    c. rate of population growth.
    d. net reproduction rate.

4. If a country's population is currently growing, it must have a net
    reproduction rate of
    a. 1.
    b. less than 1.
    c. greater than 1.
    d. not necessarily any of the above.

5. A country with a crude birth rate of 35 and a crude death rate of 10
    would have a rate of natural increase, per 1,000 per year, of
    a. 13.
    b. 25.
    c. -25.
    d. 40.

6. A population can be in equilibrium when
   a. excess births among the rich are balanced by excess deaths among the poor.
   b. everyone in the population is living just at the subsistence level.
   c. the per capita income is so high that the net reproduction rate falls to 1.
   d. any of the above is the case.

7. During the demographic transition,
   a. first the birth rate falls, then the death rate.
   b. first the death rate falls, then the birth rate.
   c. first both the birth rate and death rate fall, then they both rise.
   d. first both the birth rate and death rate rise, then they both fall.

8. For a country to be caught in a population trap requires
   a. that the rate of population growth at some point exceed the rate of economic growth.
   b. that the rate of economic growth at some point exceed the rate of population growth.
   c. that the birth rate rise above its initial level at some point.
   d. that the death rate exceed the birth rate at some point.

9. Population control experience in Pakistan
   a. is a major success story for modern techniques.
   b. shows that the inundation technique works.
   c. shows that availability of birth control devices is not enough without the widespread desire to use them.
   d. demonstrates the political risks of compulsory population control.

10. Many development economists today emphasize the need for rural development, because
   a. food aid is not a long-term solution to the world food problem.
   b. it is nearly impossible to expand industrial jobs fast enough to keep up with urban growth in countries where the focus of development has been on the cities.
   c. rural development contributes to depauperization.
   d. all of the above are true.

China's food and people in precarious balance

By Timothy McNulty
Peking correspondent
Chicago Tribune Press Service

PEKING — The year that John Kennedy became President and Alan Shepard was launched into suborbital space, the peasants near Peking were stripping the bark off trees to grind into flour paste. They ate elm leaves like lettuce.

Few in the Western world knew the extent of the famine during the "Three Lean Years" except by the evidence of starving Chinese pushing against the metal fence on the border with Hong Kong and the presence of girls' photos hanging outside their Canton homes to signal that they would prostitute themselves for grain rations.

The cause of the 1960–62 famine, analysts now say, was a combination of the "lunacy of the Great Leap Forward" and weather disasters. It was also a result of extremely poor crop planning prompted by exaggerated and falsified production estimates.

It was a deadly combination. Even now the number who died of illnesses associated with malnutrition and those who starved to death can only be guessed. Sinologists using newly released grain and birth-rate statistics suspect that from 16 million to 28 million could be the death toll.

Earlier this year Sun Yefand, director of the Economic Research Institute at the Chinese Academy of Sciences, said past economic and agricultural policies had cost "an enormous price in blood."

ALL STATISTICS here, if and when they are available, are staggering. China is one of the world's largest producers of food. It is also the largest consumer.

China boasts that it is "self-sufficient" in food production, and that is mostly true. But Western analysts believe the malnutrition rate may be more than 13 per cent — that is, more than 130 million people don't get enough of the right kind of food.

China has more than doubled its food production and tripled its grain crops since the middle 1950s, but the population, too, has more than doubled.

"The quantitative evidence is clear: Virtually no improvement has taken place in average Chinese per capita food consumption over the past two decades," wrote Canadian Professor Vaclav Smil in May's issue of Food Policy magazine.

He added that only rationing and a fairer distribution system show any difference between now and the early 1930s.

The demand for wheat, much like the demand for beer, has skyrocketed, especially in the colder northern provinces. Rice remains the unequaled staple in the South. . . .

Food can never be taken for granted when cropland is in almost constant use. In the northeast provinces, when rows of workers finish harvesting wheat, another wave of workers follows turning the soil to plant corn. Southern Sichuan Province, China's most fertile, has three rice plantings and harvests a year.

China's land area is approximately the same as the U.S., but only 11 per cent is arable compared with nearly 19 per cent in America. Double and triple harvests are the only way to feed a population about four times as large as the U.S.

YET EACH success and every effort to keep its people fed may prompt a new contradiction, a forced change in policy, and sometimes disaster:

● When Chairman Mao instructed his countrymen to "plant grain everywhere," of course they took him literally, tearing up natural windbreaks, forested areas, and grasslands. Over the years this has created huge spreading dust bowls where fertile land once lay. . . .

● New agricultural policies have allowed the peasants more land for private planting (food that isn't included in the commune quota and therefore doesn't have to be sold to the state).

That plus an increase in state-controlled prices has enriched many peasants until it has caused resentment from inflation-hit city dwellers and rancor even within the People's Liberation Army (PLA). "The peasants say now they can make more than a PLA general," reports a Sichuan county official. Some also complain that farmers discourage their sons from entering the army, which until recently was an honored position and one that benefited the soldier's family.

There are also indications that the new prosperity is acting against China's major social goal of birth control. Suburban peasants, as they're called, are making more money by bringing vegetables and fruits to the city to sell in private markets. The new money, some have said, means that they can now afford more children. . . .

Back on their communes, emergency measures allowed peasants to farm a portion of the land for their own needs instead of selling all to the state. Ironically, those long-since-banned private plots are again being encouraged and described as "innovative" production techniques.

CHINA FACES modern population, distribution, and political decisions on food supply, but in many respects it has to deal with them with centuries-old methods, from village to town by oxcart, planting and harvesting by hand.

In many places it is unable to fight natural disasters with adequate irrigation or flood control systems. In Fujian Province, along the southern coast, a visitor happened to see a Ming Dynasty silk drawing of a lone peasant in a straw hat and loinwrap treading a waterwheel to irrigate a vast rice field. Later that day the visitor was driven in a new Japanese tour bus past a vast rice field, and the peasant was still there, still slowly treading the waterwheel.

From **Chicago Tribune**, February 5, 1982, Sec. 1, p. 20. Reprinted by permission.

1. On the basis of this article, what stage of the demographic transition does China appear to be in? What evidence do you see in the article? Do you see any evidence that China may be in a "population trap?"

2. Under new policies, according to the article, "peasants say now they can make more than a PLA general." Do you think the new incentive structure is a sensible one, given China's stage of economic development?

3. What kind of a development strategy does China appear to be pursuing? What is the relationship between depauperization, industrialization, and rural development? On what evidence from this article do you base your conclusions?

CHAPTER 34
CAPITALISM VERSUS SOCIALISM

WHERE
YOU'RE GOING

When you have mastered this chapter, you will be able to:

- Define capitalism and distinguish between classical liberal capitalism and anarcho-capitalism (radical libertarianism).

- Define socialism and distinguish among centralized socialism, Oskar Lange's system of market socialism, participatory socialism, and European social democracy.

- Briefly describe the ideological and historical origins of the Soviet economic system.

- Describe the formal structure of the Soviet economy.

- Recapitulate the main points of the debate over the relative static and dynamic efficiency of capitalism and socialism.

- Outline the performance of the Soviet economy in terms of economic growth, explaining both the reasons for previous rapid growth rates and for currently declining growth rates.

- Explain the meaning and significance of the following additional terms and concepts:

        extensive growth
        intensive growth

WALKING TOUR

You have read the chapter at least once and have reviewed the summary in the text. Now you are going to walk through the material step by step, filling in the blanks and answering the questions as you go along. After you have answered each question, check yourself by uncovering the answer given in the margin. If you do not understand why the answer given is the right one, refer back to the proper section of the text.

Capitalism

Economic systems can be distinguished from one another in terms of a number of characteristics, including ownership of resources, mechanisms for coordinating economic activity, and distribution of income.

In the broadest terms, economic systems described as capitalistic emphasize [private/collective] ownership of nonlabor resources. They rely primarily on the [market/managerial] principle for coordinating relationships among firms, although within firms the [market/managerial] principle is used. Distribution of income follows, in the first instance, the _____ principle.

Within the broad category of capitalism, there are a number of more or less distinct possible systems. At one extreme is a hypothetical economic system in which there is no government at all; this system is known as _____-capitalism. (An-archy means "without rulers.") A capitalist system in which the government performs the limited function of protecting the property rights and enforcing the rules of the game is known as _____ capitalism.

private
market

managerial

marginal productivity

anarcho

classical liberal

Socialism

Socialism too comes in a number of varieties. The best-known socialist economy is that of the Soviet Union, which can be described as _____ socialism because it relies (in principle) on [market/managerial] coordination between, as well as within, firms.

centralized
managerial

Origins

The origins of the _____ socialist economic system of the Soviet Union can be traced to the writings of _____ and the revolutionary. practice of _____. For both men, the postrevolutionary economy was supposed to replace the "anarchy of the market" with the "planning principle," that is, to replace _____ coordination with _____ coordination at the national level.

After the revolution, Lenin [did/did not] attempt to implement many features of a centralized system. Coming during a period of civil war, these radical measures led to chaos. They were followed by a period of increased reliance on the market known as the _____. Central planning was once again instituted at the end of the 1920s, together with a policy of _____ of agriculture. At that time, the structure of the Soviet economy took on most of the important features it retains to this day.

centralized

Karl Marx

V.I. Lenin

market

managerial

did

New Economic Policy

collectivization

Structure

Under current practice, the activities of each firm
are guided by a technical-industrial-financial plan
that determines [inputs/outputs/both inputs and outputs]   **both inputs and**
for the firm.   **outputs**
    A socialist system in which capital and natural
resources are centrally owned, but in which the market
mechanism is used to coordinate the activities of
individual firms, is referred to as _____   **market**
socialism. Still another variety of socialism vests
ownership of capital not in the state but in the
workers of individual enterprises; this is known as
_____ socialism. An example of this kind   **participatory**
of system is that of _____. Finally,   **Yugoslavia**
many European countries are governed by parties that
are nominally socialist but which, in practice, rely
on private enterprise to nearly the same degree as
does state capitalism. These parties are collectively
referred to as _____ parties.   **social democratic**

Socialism: Pro and Con

The relative efficiency of capitalism and
socialism has been debated for many years. In the
1930s, the case for the superior efficiency of
socialism was forcefully argued by _____.   **Oskar Lange**

He envisioned a type of _____ socialism   **market**
that would duplicate the performance of a perfectly
competitive capitalist market in terms of
_____ efficiency, while avoiding problems   **static**
such as _____ and _____.   **monopoly; pollution**
    Lange's system was criticized as impractical,
but more fundamentally, it was criticized for
paying too little attention to _____   **entrepreneurial**
decision making. Other kinds of socialism, too,
are criticized for being inferior to capitalism
in terms of _____ efficiency as well as   **dynamic**
static efficiency.

Performance

During the 1930s, immediately after the introduction
of comprehensive central planning, official Soviet
data showed growth rates of 15 percent per year or
more for national output. Western observers believe
that these high growth rates were somewhat exaggerated
by the use of a very [early/late] base year for   **early**
constructing growth indexes. Nonetheless, growth rates
were clearly high at that time. The type of growth
that took place is best described as [extensive/
intensive] growth, because it was based largely on   **extensive**

mobilization of new factor inputs.

Since World War II, the growth rate of the Soviet economy has gradually slowed. This apparently indicates difficulties in achieving [extensive/intensive] growth   intensive through the more efficient utilization of available factor supplies. The declining growth rate [has/has not yet] led to comprehensive reforms of the   has not yet centralized planning system. As it has throughout the past fifty years, the _____ sector   agricultural

continues to lag behind the _____ sector.   industrial

SELF TEST
_____

These sample test items will help you check how much you have learned. Answers and explanations can be found at the end of this book. Scoring yourself: one or two wrong - on target. Three or four wrong - passing, but you haven't mastered the chapter yet. Five or more wrong - not good enough; start over and restudy the chapter.

Multiple Choice

1. Which of the following is not a characteristic of capitalism?
   a. Private ownership of capital.
   b. Owners of capital performing entrepreneurial functions.
   c. Market coordination between firms.
   d. All of the above are characteristics of capitalism.

2. Which of the following economic systems preserves the smallest role for government?
   a. Classical liberal capitalism.
   b. Radical libertarianism.
   c. Centralized socialism.
   d. All of the above are about the same with regard to the role of government.

3. In which of the following systems can government be thought of as a referee, concerned primarily with enforcing the rules of the game?
   a. Centralized socialism.
   b. Classical liberal capitalism.
   c. Radical libertarianism.
   d. Anarcho-capitalism.

4. Which of the following is not characteristic of all major varieties of socialism?
   a. Nonlabor resources must be government owned.
   b. Income must be distributed more equally than under classical liberal capitalism.
   c. Private ownership of all capital is not acceptable.
   d. All of the above are true of all types of socialism.

5. During which of the following periods did the Soviet economy rely least on central planning?
   a. War communism.
   b. The New Economic Policy.
   c. Collectivization.
   d. The postwar period.

6. Which of the following measures was not instituted by Stalin in 1928?
   a. The Five-Year Plan for industry.
   b. Collectivization of agriculture.
   c. Abolition of the use of money.
   d. All of the above were instituted.

7. Which of the following marginal rules would not be observed under Lange's form of market socialism?
   a. Marginal cost equals price.
   b. Marginal physical product per dollar's worth of each factor of production equals marginal physical product per dollar's worth of each other factor.
   c. Marginal revenue equals marginal physical product for all goods.
   d. All of the above would be observed.

8. Which of the following is characteristic of participatory socialism?
   a. Managerial coordination between firms.
   b. Government ownership of all capital.
   c. Both of the above.
   d. None of the above.

9. Which of the following economic systems believes that managerial coordination has no role to play anywhere in the economy?
   a. Radical libertarianism.
   b. Participatory socialism.
   c. Classical liberal capitalism.
   d. None of the above.

10. Which of the following best characterizes the economic advances of the past fifty years in the Soviet economy?
   a. Transformation of an essentially underdeveloped country into a modern superpower with moderate living standards.
   b. Reduction of living standards once as high as those of Italy to a level lower than those of Brazil today.
   c. Achievement of true parity with the United States in terms of living standards.
   d. Transformation of a country once as poor as Nepal into one now comparable to Brazil in living standards.

APPLICATION

"The proletariat (the modern working class) will use its political supremacy to wrest, by degrees, all capital from the bourgeoisie (owners of the means of production), to centralize all instruments of production in the hands of the state, i.e., of the proletariat organized as the ruling class, and to increase the total productive forces as rapidly as possible.

"Of course, in the beginning this cannot be effected except by means of despotic inroads on the rights of property and on the conditions of bourgeois production; by means of measures, therefore, which appear economically insufficient and untenable, but which, in the course of the movement, outstrip themselves, necessitate further inroads upon the old social order, and are unavoidable as a means of entirely revolutionizing the mode of production. . . .

" . . . in the most advanced countries the following will be pretty generally applicable:

1. Abolition of property in land and application of all rents of land to public purposes.
2. A heavy progressive or graduated income tax.
3. Abolition of all rights of inheritance.
4. Confiscation of the property of all emigrants and rebels.
5. Centralization of credit in the hands of the state, by means of a national bank with state capital and an exclusive monopoly.
6. Centralization of the means of communication and transport in the hands of the state.
7. Extension of factories and instruments of production owned by the state; the bringing into cultivation of wastelands, and the improvement of the soil generally in accordance with a common plan.
8. Equal liability to labor. Establishment of industrial armies, especially for agriculture.
9. Combination of agriculture with manufacturing industries; gradual abolition of the distinction between town and country, by a more equable distribution of the population over the country.
10. Free education for all children in public schools. . . .

"In place of the old bourgeois society, with its classes and class antagonisms, we shall have an association in which the free development of each is the condition for the free development of all."

1. What type of economic system does Marx appear to be proposing, according to the classification given in your text? What passages indicate this?

2. Marx lists ten characteristics of communism. Which of these are now common in basically capitalist countries like Canada? Given your general knowledge, would you say any of the ten points are found nowhere in the world today?

ANSWERS

CHAPTER 1

Self Test

1-d; 2-d; 3-c; 4-d; 5-b; 6-b; 7-c; 8-b; 9-d; 10-a.

CHAPTER 2

Self Test

1-c; 2-a; 3-c; 4-a: in Canada the trade-off ratio is 1 to 2; in the United States the trade-off ratio is 25 to 40, making Good A comparatively cheaper in Canada and Good B comparatively cheaper in the United States; 5-d; 6-b; 7-d; 8-a; 9-d; 10-c.

Hands On

Problem 1.

(a) For the XYZ Corp. job offer in Calgary

Budget of Out-of-Pocket Costs

Transportation	$1,500
Food	$1,200
Personal Expenses	$2,500
Apartment Rent	$4,500
	$9,700

Budget of Opportunity Costs

Salary foregone by turning down the Halifax job	$17,000
	$17,000

(b) For the ABC firm offer in Halifax

Budget of Out-of-Pocket Costs

Transportation	$1,500
Food	$1,200
Personal Expenses	$2,500
Apartment Rent	$4,500
	$9,700

Budget of Opportunity Costs

Salary foregone by turning down the job in Calgary	
	$15,000
	$15,000

(c) You should accept the ABC firm's job offer in Halifax since the opportunity cost is lower than the opportunity cost of accepting the job with the XYZ Corp. in Calgary.

Problem 2.

(a) Mexico has the absolute advantage in the production of oranges since a kilogram can be produced with 1 hour of labor while it takes 8 hours of labor to produce the same amount in Canada. Canada has the absolute advantage in the production of steel (4 hours compared to 8 hours in Mexico.)

(b) The opportunity cost of Canada producing a kilogram of oranges is 2 tonnes of steel since it takes Canada 8 hours of labor to produce a kilogram of oranges and 4 hours of labor to produce a tonne of steel. In Mexico, producing a kilogram of oranges means giving up the opportunity to produce 1/8 tonne of steel. In terms of opportunity cost, Mexico has the comparative advantage in the production of oranges. In terms of producing steel, Canada has the lowest opportunity cost and therefore, the comparative advantage. In Canada ½ kilogram of oranges must be given up to produce a tonne of steel, and in Mexico 8 kilograms of oranges must be given up to produce a tonne of steel.

(c) The oranges to steel price ratio will be 1 to 8 in Mexico and 8 to 4 or 2 to 1 in Canada.

(d)

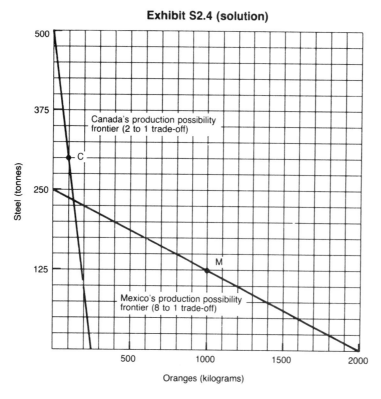

Exhibit S2.4 (solution)

Canada's production possibility frontier (2 to 1 trade-off)

Mexico's production possibility frontier (8 to 1 trade-off)

Steel (tonnes)

Oranges (kilograms)

(e) The graph above shows points C and M. The pretrade exhibit is below:

	Mexico	Canada	Total for both nations
oranges (kilograms)	1,000	100	1,100
steel (tonnes)	125	300	425

(f) The posttrade production and consumption for Mexico and Canada would be:

		Mexico	Canada	Total for both nations Posttrade	Pretrade
Oranges	Production	2,000	0	2,000	(1,100)
	Consumption	1,000	1,000	2,000	
Steel	Production	0	500	500	(425)
	Consumption	200	300	500	

CHAPTER 3

Self Test

1-d; 2-d; 3-c; 4-b; 5-d; 6-c; 7-d; 8-d; 9-d; 10-a.

Hands On

<u>Problem 1</u>. (a) Equilibrium price is 10¢ per kilogram and equilibrium quantity is 200 million kilograms per month. (b) Cane sugar is a substitute, so an increase in its price shifts the corn sweetener demand curve to the right. The supply curve does not shift. (c) An increase in production costs shifts the supply curve upward; the demand curve stays at D_2. (d) With supply curve S_1, corn sweetener production would drop to zero at about 6¢ per kilogram. Your completed diagram should look like this:

Exhibit S3.3 (solution)

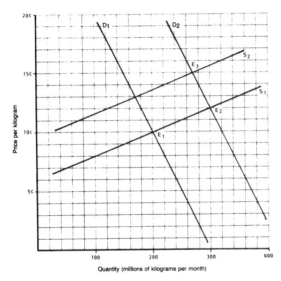

Problem 2. (a) Equilibrium quantity initially is 10,000 crates per day and equilibrium price is $10 per crate. (b) A $3 per crate decrease in production costs shifts the supply curve straight down by $3. The demand curve does not shift. The equilibrium price falls by $2 per crate to $8. (c) The fad for bean sprout salad (a lettuce substitute) shifts the demand curve to the left, as shown; the supply curve remains at S_2. The equilibrium price will fall to about $3.50 per crate and the equilibrium quantity to about 6,500 crates per day. (d) At the $8 support price, quantity demanded will be 5,500 crates per day, and quantity supplied will be 11,000 crates; the government will thus have to buy 5,500 crates per day at a cost of $44,000 per day. Quantity produced will be 4,500 crates per day above what it would be without the price support. Your completed diagram should look like this:

Exhibit S3.4 (solution)

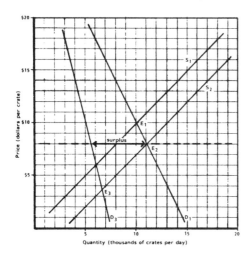

CHAPTER 4

Self Test

1-a; 2-b; 3-c; 4-c; 5-d; 6-c: the others are at least semi-mixed public goods; 7-a; 8-a; 9-d; 10-c.

CHAPTER 5

Self Test

1-d; 2-a: inventories of shoes fall by $1 million; 3-a; 4-d; 5-b; 6-d: the economy is in equilibrium only if imports equal exports; 7-a; 8-b; 9-d; 10-a.

Hands On

Problem 1. (Blanks in table): (1) $200,000; (2) $160,000; (3) $50,000;
(4) $210,000; (5) -$10,000; (6) $200,000; (7) $200,000; (8) $210,000;
(9) -$10,000. (a) Aggregate supply is $200,000 and aggregate demand
is $210,000. (b) The economy is not in equilibrium because aggregate
demand exceeds aggregate supply. Producers would react to the unplanned
inventory reduction by raising output, or prices, or both, causing the
circular flow to expand.

Problem 2. (a) Applying the first equation gives AD = 1,150. The
second equation tells us that I_u = AS - AD, so unplanned inventory
investment is 50. (b) For equilibrium, AD must equal AS. C + I_p
+ X - M = 675. 800 - 675 = 125 gives the required value of G, the
missing component of AD. (c) In the government sector, injections
exceed leakages by 100. In the foreign sector, injections exceed leakages
by 50. For total leakages to equal total injections, investment (the
remaining injection) must fall short of saving (the remaining leakage)
by 150. If planned investment falls short of saving by 150, then the
economy will be in equilibrium, with planned injections = total leakages.
(d) The statement is true. Injections exceed leakages in the government
sector. If the economy is in equilibrium, with no unplanned investment,
then injections also exceed leakages in the investment/saving sector.
To balance, leakages (imports) must exceed injections (exports) in the
foreign sector, i.e., negative net exports. If net exports are not
negative, the only way to make the equation balance is by reduced
injections, that is, unplanned inventory depletion, which would mean
disequilibrium.

CHAPTER 6

Self Test

1-b; 2-d; 3-d; 4-c; 5-d; 6-c; 7-b; 8-c; 9-a; 10-d.

Hands On

Problem 1. (a) The Kids' Consumer Price Index (KPI) for 1979 = 40.55;
1981 = 46.65; 1983 = 54.45. (b) To convert to a 1979 base year, set
the prices of the 1979 market baskets = 100, and for other years, divide
the current year number given by the 1979 index number given and multiply
by 100. For example, the KPI for 1981 = 46.64/40.55 x 100 = 115.0. The
complete figures are as follows:

      KPI 1979 = 100; 1981 = 115.0; 1983 = 134.3
      CPI 1979 = 100; 1981 = 123.2; 1983 = 144.7

The kids fared better between 1979 and 1981.
(c) The KPI for food was 2.15 in 1979; 2.50 in 1981; and 3.20 in 1983.
To calculate a kid food index based on the five-item weighted food market
basket alone, divide each year's food total by the 1979 total and multiply
by 100. The results:

The KPI food index rose faster than the KPI as a whole. Probably, kids do spend more than 5 percent of their incomes on food. If so, the KPI understates the true impact of inflation on kids.

(d) Real earnings of paper boys and girls rose from $.44 per customer per week in 1979 to $.53 per customer per week in 1983 ($.53 = .71/(134.3/100)). Real earnings of babysitters, deflated by the KPI, rose from $1.00 in 1979 to $1.19 in 1983 ($1.19 = $1.60/(134.3/100)). If the figures for babysitters' earnings were deflated by the kid food index, the heavy-eating babysitter would have found real earnings to have risen from $1.00 in 1979 to $1.08 in 1983 ($1.08 = 1.60/(148.8/100)).

CHAPTER 7

Self Test

1-a; 2-a; 3-a; 4-d; 5-c: the expected real rate of interest is equal to the nominal rate minus the expected rate of inflation; 6-b; 7-b; 8-a; 9-a: the rate of growth of nominal GNP is equal to the rate of growth of real GNP plus the rate of inflation; 10-b.

Hands On

Problem 1.   (a)*

Males	Population 15 Years and Over	Labor Force (Thousands) Total	Employment	Unemployment	% Participation Rate	% Unemployment Rate
15-24 years	2,251	(1,479)	1,068	411	(65.7)	(27.8)
25 years and over	6,933	(5,458)	4,844	614	(78.7)	(11.2)
All males 15 years and over	(9,184)	(6,937)	(5,912)	(1,025)	(75.5)	(14.8)
Females						
15-24 years	2,187	(1,327)	1,080	247	(60.7)	(18.6)
25 years and over	7,375	(3,630)	3,244	386	(49.2)	(10.6)
All females 15 years and over	(9,562)	(4,957)	(4,324)	(633)	(51.8)	(12.8)
Both sexes - 15 years and over	(18,746)	(11,894)	(10,236)	(1,658)	(63.4)	(13.9)

* Source: The Labour Force, Statistics Canada, March 1983, Table 3, p. 24.

(b) Workers in the 15 to 24 age bracket generally have less work experience, less education and training, less on-the-job training, and less seniority. For all of these reasons, the unemployment rate in this group is higher than for workers in the 25 and over age group.

CHAPTER 8

Self Test

1-a; 2-a; 3-c: the consumption schedule passes through the origin and
has a slope less than 1; 4-b; 5-d: this would produce a movement along
the schedule; 6-d; 7-d; 8-d; 9-d; 10-b.

Hands On

Problem 1. (a) The values for nominal savings are -50, -10, 30, 70,
110, 150, and 190; MPC = 0.8; MPS = 0.2. (b) Autonomous consumption is
50. The slope of the consumption schedule is 0.8 and the slope of the
saving schedule is 0.2. (c) Your graph should look like this:

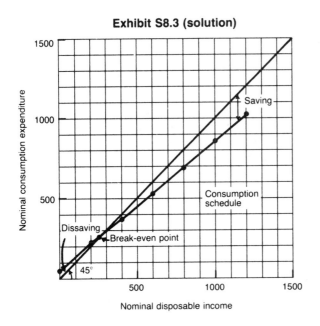

Problem 2. (a) The values for imports are 50, 70, 90, 110, 130, 150,
and 170. (b) The slope of the import schedule is 0.1, which is the
value of the marginal propensity to import. (c) The values for net
exports are 50, 30, 10, -10, -30, -50, and -70. Your graphs should
look like this:

Exhibit S8.4 (solution)

(a)

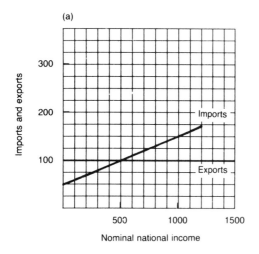

(b)

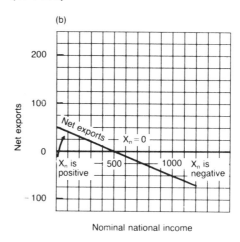

CHAPTER 9

Self Test

1-d: nothing can shift the aggregate nominal supply schedule; 2-b; 3-b;
4-c; 5-d; 6-d: the multiplier is 10 in this case; 7-c; 8-d; 9-a; 10-c:
a is a nonsense answer; b could be true but is not necessarily so.

Hands On

Problem 1. (a) Consumption is $150 when both disposable income and nominal
national income are zero, since Y=DI in this example because T is zero.
The consumption schedule intersects the vertical axis at $150 and has
a slope of 0.6, equal to the MPC. The AND schedule intersects the vertical
axis at $625 (add I=$200, G=$200, and (X-M)=$75 to the consumption
intercept.) The slope of the AND schedule is 0.5 (MPC-MPM).
(b) Equilibrium nominal national income is $1,250. At $1,500 there would
be unplanned inventory accumulation, and at $900 there would be unplanned
inventory depletion. (c) The new equilibrium level is $1,650 and the
multiplier is 2. You can find this by looking at the ratio of the
change in equilibrium national income to the change in AND ($400/$200=2)
or by applying the multiplier formula $1/(1 - MPC_D)$. In this problem
that is $1/(1 - .5)$, since the MPC is 0.6 and the MPM is 0.1, leaving
the MPC_D equal to 0.5. Your completed graph should look like Exhibit
S9.3 (solution).

Exhibit S9.3 (solution)

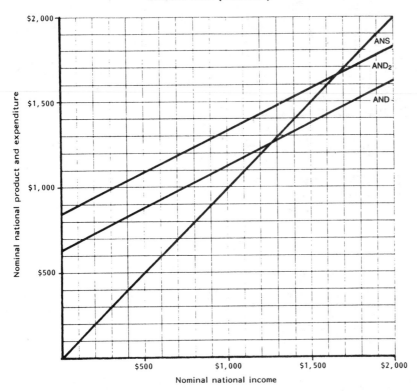

Problem 2. (a) When DI and Y are equal to zero, the value of savings is -$250, which is the negative of autonomous consumption. The total leakages when Y is zero are -$200, which is the sum of -$250 plus Ma of $50 and T of 0. The MPS is 0.4, which is 1 - MPC. The slope of the leakages schedule is the sum of the MPS and the MPM, which is 0.5 = (0.4 + 0.1). (b) Total planned injections are $300 when Y is zero. This is the sum of I = $125, G = $100, and X = $75. The slope of the injections line is 0/infinity. The injections schedule is a horizontal line. (c) The equilibrium level of Y is $1,000, where S + T + M = I + G + X. (d) A downward shift of $100 in the planned injections schedule lowers equilibrium nominal national income to $800. The multiplier is 2 from the formula $1/(1 - MPC_D)$, where the values are 1/(1 - 0.5). (e) If autonomous imports decline to $25, the leakages schedule shifts down by $25, increasing Y to $1,050. Your completed graph should look like Exhibit S9.4 (solution) below.

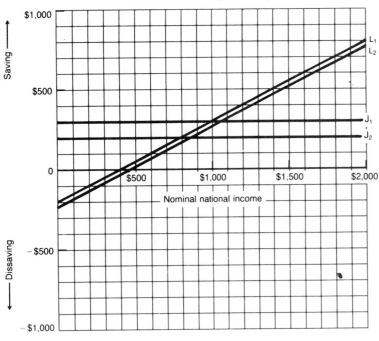

Exhibit S9.4 (solution)

CHAPTER 10

Self Test

1-b; 2-a; 3-b: the multiplier is 4; 4-b: the net tax multiplier is -4;
5-a; 6-d; 7-d; 8-c: the exact value of nominal national income is 1,116.67;
9-c; 10-b.

Hands On

Problem 1. (a) The slope of AND is the MPC - MPM, which is the same as
the $\overline{MPC_D}$, or 0.6 in this case. Using the multiplier formula $1/(1-MPC_D)$
gives us a multiplier of 2.5. (b) Unplanned inventory accumulation is
occurring at the target income since ANS is greater than AND. There is
a deflationary gap of $300. (c) Equilibrium nominal national income is
$750 and the target income is $1,500. With a multiplier of 2.5, a $300
increase in government purchases would be required to increase AND by
the necessary $750. The net tax multiplier is -1.5, when the formula
$-MPC_D/(1-MPC_D)$ is used. A decrease in taxes of $500 would be required
to reach the income target. (d) With a multiplier of 2.5 and a net
tax multiplier of -1.5, an increase in government purchases of $750
accompanied by an increase in taxes of $750 would allow the economy to
reach the target income while keeping the budget balanced. Effectively,
the multiplier is 1 in this case, which is the balanced budget multiplier
situation.

CHAPTER 11

Self Test

1-d; 2-b; 3-a; 4-d; 5-d; 6-c; 7-d; 8-b; 9-d; 10-a.

CHAPTER 12

Self Test

1-c; 2-d; 3-c; 4-c; 5-a; 6-b: the question asks about one bank, not the entire banking system; 7-c; 8-a; 9-b; 10-d.

Hands On

Problem 1. (a) The required reserve ratio is 10 percent, and the money multiplier is 10. (b) The bank would retain $5,000 of the funds as new required reserves and would extend $45,000 in new loans. (c) Sycombeville would lose $100,000 in deposits and reserves. That would give it -$75,000 in total reserves. It would have required reserves of $15,000, on the remaining $150,000 of deposits, so it would have a $90,000 reserve deficiency (negative excess reserves). It would have to call in, or allow to be repaid, $90,000 in loans before it could achieve balance sheet equilibrium. In the banking system as a whole, the $100,000 open market sale would cause a $1 million drop in the money supply.

Problem 2. (a) The required reserve ratio is 25 percent, and the money multiplier is 4. (b) The bank is not in equilibrium; it has a $5,000 reserve deficiency. Given the balance sheet as shown, its only recourse would be to call in, or allow to be repaid, $5,000 in loans. In the real world, it would have other ways to make up the deficiency. It could borrow from the Bank of Canada. It could also sell other assets it might own, such as securities. (c) The $10,000 deposit raises Random's required reserves by $2,500 and raises its excess reserves by $7,500. It would make $7,500 in new loans to achieve equilibrium. The money supply as a whole would grow by $40,000 once all banks reached a new equilibrium.

Problem 3. (a) Assets must equal liabilities, so assets are $500,000. Loans plus reserves must equal total assets, so total reserves are $130,000. Of these, $5,000 are excess, so required reserves are $125,000. The required reserve ratio is thus 25 percent, and the money multiplier for the system is 4. (b) It is not in equilibrium. In the simplified system, Tylertown would make $5,000 in new loans to businesses or consumers. In the real world, it might also buy securities. (c) Tylertown would now have the same $130,000 total reserves, but now only $100,000 would be required. It could make up to $30,000 in new loans, etc. The new money multiplier will be 5. With 10 banks, total system reserves are $1.3 million, so the money supply will rise from $5.2 million to $6.5 million as a result of the cut in required reserve ratios.

CHAPTER 13

Self Test

1-a: Py is equal to nominal national income in the formula MV = Py; 2-c; 3-a; 4-b: in both cases, there is a 10 percent return; 5-b; 6-a; 7-c; 8-b; 9-c; 10-c.

Hands On

Problem 1. (a) The equilibrium nominal interest rate is initially 6 percent. (b) The new money supply curve will be a vertical line drawn at a money supply of $100. (c) At the initial interest rate of 6 percent, people will want to hold more than $100 in the form of money, so there will be an excess demand for money. In a two-asset economy, this is equivalent to an excess supply of bonds. Individuals will sell bonds in order to obtain the additional money balances they want at the initial low rate of interest. (d) Sales of bonds by individuals do not increase the total supply of money in the economy, but such sales do depress the price of bonds. Falling bond prices mean a rising interest rate. As the interest rate rises, the quantity of money demanded falls--a movement up and to the left along the money demand curve. Eventually, when the interest rate reaches 12 percent, people are content with the $100 of money supplied by the Bank of Canada, and both the money market and bond market return to equilibrium.

Problem 2. (a) The initial nominal interest rate is 12 percent. (b) Given the new, lower nominal income but with the interest rate still at its initial 12 percent level, there will be an excess supply of money. Individuals will react to the excess supply of money by using the money to buy bonds, thereby creating an excess demand for bonds. (c) Individual purchases of bonds for money do not reduce the money supply in the economy as a whole - they just drive up the price of bonds. As bond prices rise, interest rates fall, moving the economy down and to the right along MD_2. A new equilibrium is eventually reached at a 6 percent interest rate, where people are content to hold $200 of money in their portfolios, even given the reduced nominal income.

CHAPTER 14

Self Test

1-d; 2-d; 3-c: an increase in exports would push up the AND curve, leading to a rise in interest rates; 4-a; 5-d; 6-b: the Bank of Canada adjusts the money supply to whatever level is needed to keep interest rates constant; 7-d; 8-d; 9-b; 10-b.

Hands On

Problem 1. (a) The interest rate is 9 percent as determined by the intersection of the money supply (MS) and the money demand (MD) curves. At 9 percent interest, planned investment is $200. The equilibrium level of nominal national income is $1,400, which is at the intersection of aggregate nominal supply (ANS) and aggregate nominal demand (AND). No, with an interest rate of 6 percent, planned investment would be greater than when the interest rate was 9 percent, causing AND to shift upward. The new equilibrium would be at a higher level of nominal national income than previously. (b) Your AND_1 curve should be below the original AND

curve by $200, as shown in the solution graph below. Yes, unplanned
inventory accumulation results, since ANS is now greater than AND at
the original equilibrium level of $1,400, which causes nominal national
income to start to fall. No crowding out effect would result from the
contractionary fiscal policy, since the crowding out effect is defined
as the drop in private planned investment as a result of expansionary
fiscal policy. (c) As nominal national income falls, the demand for
money will also fall, shifting the money demand curve downward to MD_1.
With a fixed money supply, the interest rate will fall and planned
investment will increase. See the solution graphs below. (d) Aggregate
nominal demand will increase as a result of the increased investment
and will settle at AND_2, a level greater than AND_1. (e) To strengthen
the effect of the government's contractionary fiscal policy, the Bank of
Canada could lower the money supply (to MS_1), keeping interest rates from
falling and thus stopping or reducing an increase in planned investment
that resulted in AND_2. Depending on the reduction in the MS, aggregate
nominal demand will stay at AND_1, or possibly fall to AND_3. See the
solution graphs below.

Exhibit S14.2 (solution)

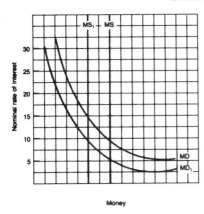

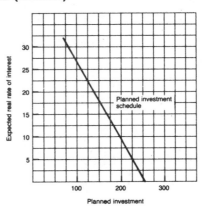

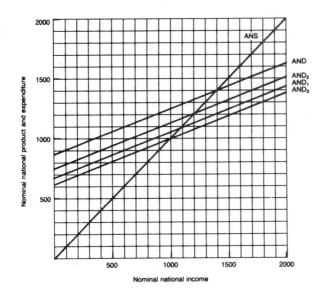

CHAPTER 15

Self Test

1-b; 2-a; 3-b; 4-d; 5-d; 6-b; 7-b; 8-b; 9-a; 10-c.

Hands On

Exhibit S15.1 (solution)

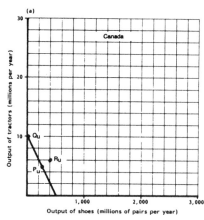

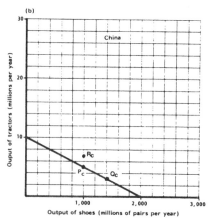

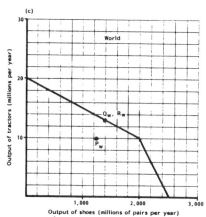

(a) In Canada, the opportunity cost of a tractor is 50 pairs of shoes.
In China, the opportunity cost of a tractor is 200 pairs of shoes. Canada
thus has a comparative advantage in tractors, and China in shoes. Canada
has an absolute advantage in both products. (b) See solution exhibit.
(c) Initially, Canada produces 5 million tractors and 250 million pairs

of shoes. China produces 5 million tractors and 1,000 million pairs of shoes. These points are marked "P" on the solution graphs. (d) Canada should export tractors and import shoes. Any trading ratio between 1 tractor for 200 pairs of shoes (the opportunity cost ratio in China) and 1 tractor for 50 pairs of shoes (the opportunity cost ratio in Canada) would be mutually advantageous. (e) Under these assumptions, Canada would produce 10 million tractors and no shoes. China would shift 1 billion labor hours from tractors to shoes, lowering tractor production to 3 million and raising shoe production to 1,400 million. These points are marked "Q" in the solution exhibit. Consumption points are 6 million tractors and 400 million pairs of shoes in Canada; 7 million tractors and 1,000 million pairs of shoes in China. These points are marked "R" in the solution exhibits. (f) Both countries are better off; Canada now consumes more of both products; China consumes more tractors and no fewer shoes. World production has gone up from 10 million to 13 million tractors, and from 1,250 million to 1,400 million pairs of shoes. Each individual country has moved outside its domestic production possibility frontier. The world as a whole has moved from an inefficient point inside its frontier to an efficient point on the frontier.

CHAPTER 16

Self Test

1-d; 2-b; 3-a; 4-b; 5-d; 6-a; 7-b; 8-b; 9-a; 10-b.

Hands On

Problem 1. (a) The equilibrium exchange rate at E is $1 Cdn. = $1 U.S., or the two dollars are at par. Increased American tourism in Canada would shift the demand curve for Canadian dollars upward to the right (a change in demand) along the supply curve (a change in the quantity supplied). The Canadian dollar has appreciated relative to the U.S. dollar since the Canadian dollar is now worth more in terms of United States currency than it previously was. (b) No, this should not be represented by a shift of either the demand or supply curves. The greater imports caused by the higher exchange rate reflect simply a movement along the supply curve from E to E_1. There has been a change in the quantity of Canadian dollars supplied.

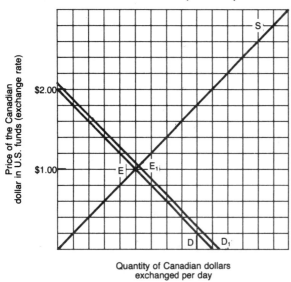

Exhibit S16.2 (solution)

Price of the Canadian dollar in U.S. funds (exchange rate)

Quantity of Canadian dollars exchanged per day

CHAPTER 17

Self Test

1-a; 2-a; 3-b; 4-a; 5-d; 6-d; 7-a; 8-c; 9-b; 10-d.

Hands On

<u>Problem 1</u>. Each column of the table becomes a separate aggregate real demand curve. The entries in the table are shown as dots on the graph (a few don't fit). Smooth curves have been sketched in to connect them.

Exhibit S17.2a (solution)

		Aggregate nominal demand		
		1,200	2,100	3,600
Price level	4.0	300	525	900
	3.0	400	700	1,200
	2.0	600	1,050	1,800
	1.5	800	1,400	2,400
	1.0	1,200	2,100	3,600
	0.5	2,400	4,200	7,200
		equals ARD_1	equals ARD_2	equals ARD_3

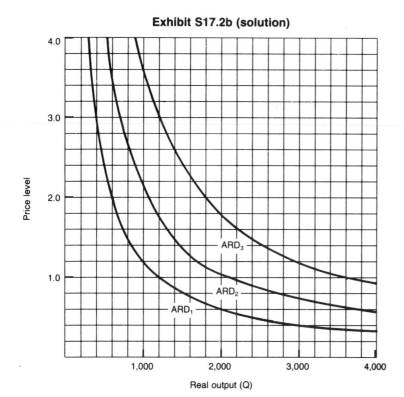

Exhibit S17.2b (solution)

Price level / Real output (Q)

ARD₁, ARD₂, ARD₃

Problem 2. (a) As drawn, the equilibrium level of real output is $2,000, the price level is 1.6, and the level of aggregate nominal demand is $3,200. (If you don't understand how to obtain these answers, check the "Don't Make This Common Mistake!" section for this chapter.) The equilibrium is shown as E_1 on the S17.3 solution exhibit. (b) See ARD_2 in the solution exhibit. (c) As the economy moves toward E_2, the economy experiences demand-pull inflation. The price level and real output at the new equilibrium level are higher. The new equilibrium level is $2,400.

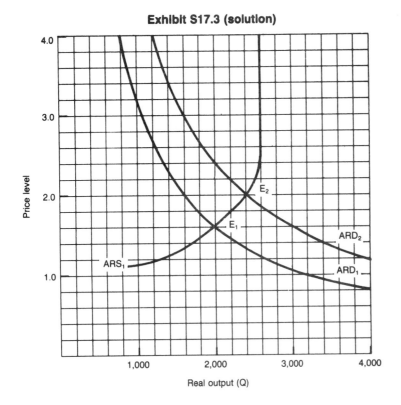

Exhibit S17.3 (solution)

Price level

Real output (Q)

CHAPTER 18

Self Test

1-d; 2-a; 3-b; 4-a; 5-b; 6-a; 7-b; 8-b; 9-a; 10-d.

Hands On

<u>Problem 1</u>. (a) The wage offer curve will rise as employers raise wages to attract workers. For a while, the reservation wage curve will remain constant because people have incomplete knowledge of current and future economic trends. The duration of unemployment will fall, as will the unemployment rate, because jobs will be easier to find with aggregate nominal demand increasing. (b) At point B, inflation will be 1 percent and unemployment will be 5 percent. 1 percent inflation plus 6 percent growth of real output equals a 7 percent increase in nominal GNP. (c) The Phillips curve will shift upward, showing that a 1 percent inflation rate is expected at each level of unemployment. For instance, the economy moves from point B on Ph1 to point C on Ph2 in Exhibit S18.3 (solution). (d) The economy will move to the left along Ph1 past point B to a point like B'. (e) If nominal GNP increases by 4 percent and real output rises by 1 percent, inflation must be 3 percent since 4 must equal 1 + the inflation rate. No, this is not a quick cure, since people take time to reduce their inflationary expectations and adjust their reservation wages downward. Firms also take time to reduce their prices. These events are called an inflationary recession.

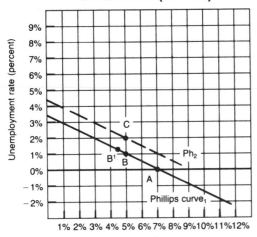

Exhibit S18.3 (solution)

CHAPTER 19

Self Test

1-d; 2-d; 3-b; 4-a; 5-b; 6-c; 7-d; 8-d; 9-d; 10-c.

CHAPTER 20

Self Test

1-c; 2-a; 3-d; 4-d; 5-d: any of the above might be true, but none need be true; 6-d: not enough information is given to determine elasticity; 7-b: elasticity is 0.5; 8-a: doubling the tax less than doubles the total price; 9-c; 10-a.

Hands On

Problem 1. (a) To construct the total revenue curve, first multiply price times quantity for a representative selection of points along the demand curve, such as Points A through E shown in the solution graph for Exhibit S20.2a. Plot these (and more if you want) in the next diagram (see Points a through e in the solution graph for Exhibit S20.2b). Connect the points with a smooth curve. (b) As shown in the solution graph, the elastic range of demand corresponds to the upward-sloping portion of the total revenue curve, and the inelastic range to the downward-sloping portion. The point exactly at maximum revenue is the point of unit elasticity.

Exhibit S20.2 (solution)

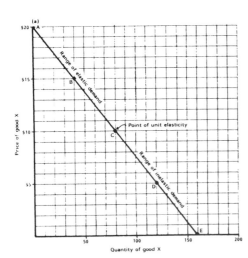

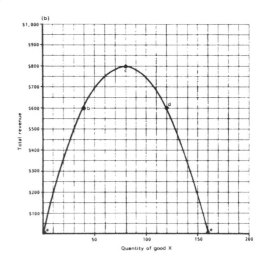

Problem 2. (a) The initial equilibrium is at a quantity of 10 tonnes per year and a price of $400 per tonne, shown as E₁ in the solution graph. (b) The cost reduction shifts the supply curve straight down by $300 to the position shown as S₂ in the solution graph for Exhibit S20.3. The new equilibrium is at E₂ - 12 tonnes at $300 per tonne. (c) Apply the elasticity formula as the price falls from $400 to $300 and the quantity increases from 10 tonnes to 12 tonnes. You should get an elasticity of 0.636. (d) The demand curve shifts to the right by 6 tonnes to the position D₂. The new equilibrium will be D₃, 14 tonnes at $500 per tonne. (e) Applying the elasticity formula should give you an elasticity of supply of 0.308.

Exhibit S20.3 (solution)

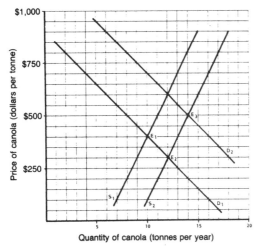

CHAPTER 21

Self Test

1-b; 2-b; 3-c; 4-c; 5-c: the marginal utility ratio must equal the price ratio in equilibrium; 6-c; 7-c: the theft eliminates the income effect, but the price effect acting alone is enough to cause her to consume more milk; 8-d: the first three are only remotely possible explanations; 9-d: d is clearly inferior both to a and to c; thus, it cannot be a member of an indifference set containing either a or c; 10-c: if substitutes, to the left and up; if complements, to the left and down.

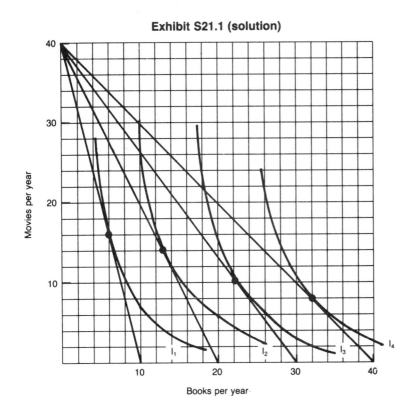

Exhibit S21.1 (solution)

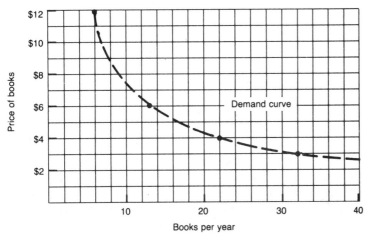

Hands On

Problem 1. (a) A standard downward-sloping convex indifference curve can be drawn through A, D, and H, but not through A, D, and I. At least part of the section from D to I would have a zero or positive slope. This would contradict the "more is better" assumption on which indifference curves are normally drawn. (b) An indifference curve through C, F, and I would be bent the wrong way - the marginal rate of substitution of flowers for cookies would increase rather than diminish. An indifference curve through B, E, and H would be a straight line with a constant marginal rate of substitution - also not normally possible. A curve through A, D, and G would be fine, with the normal convex shape and a diminishing marginal rate of substitution. (c) Taken individually, there is nothing the matter with indifference curves through Points A, E, and I or C, D, and G; but the two curves would cross, so they can't be part of the same indifference map. If they were, the principle of transitivity would be violated.

Exhibit S21.2 (solution)

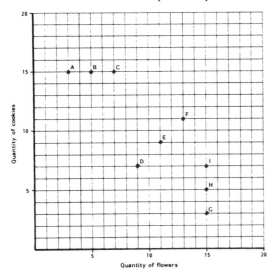

Problem 2. (a) The budget lines and equilibrium points are given in the solution graph to Exhibit S21.3. (b) In this context, meat is a normal good, because, with prices unchanged, the quantity consumed increases as income increases. Bread is an inferior good, because the quantity consumed decreases as income increases.

Problem 3. (a) See the solution graph for Exhibit S21.4. (b) This result strongly suggests a downward-sloping convex indifference curve. Other shapes (e.g., concave or straight) would, in most cases, correspond to a "corner solution," that is, a diet of all one good or all of the other. (c) The slope of the curve is changed to $-\frac{1}{4}$ by the change in relative prices. At the new prices, the rat would need 440 pushes for the 11 milliliters of root beer plus 40 pushes for the 4 milliliters of Collins mix, or a total of 480 pushes, to reach the same point as before.

A-23

This gives the budget line B_2 in the solution graph. (d) See the solution graph.

Exhibit S21.3 (solution)

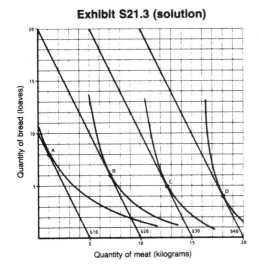

(e) You do know that I_1 is tangent to B_1 at E_1, and I_2 is tangent to B_2 at E_2. Also, you can assume that the curves are downward-sloping, convex, and noncrossing. The curves shown are reasonable choices. (f) The income effect is defined as the part of the consumption change caused by the change in real income when prices change. However, in this case, the budget, in terms of pushes, has been adjusted to keep real income the same, that is, to give sufficient purchasing power to buy the original selection. Any change, the reasoning continues, must thus be caused by the substitution effect alone. (Food for thought: Even though the rat's real income has not increased according to the reasoning just given, the rat is better off, that is, on a higher indifference curve after the price change. Compare the rat's situation to that of a worker whose wages are indexed to the consumer price index. Can you argue that the worker is made better off the more inflation there is, assuming inflation does not affect all goods equally?)

Exhibit S21.4 (solution)

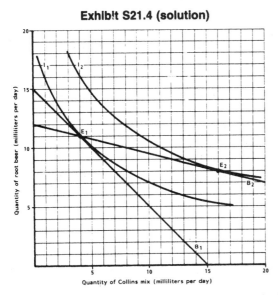

CHAPTER 22

Self Test

1-d; 2-b; 3-d: 15 ÷ 500 x 100 = 3% + 12% = 15%; 4-c; 5-d; 6-c: this is
a variant on the average marginal rule; 7-c; 8-c; 9-c; 10-a.

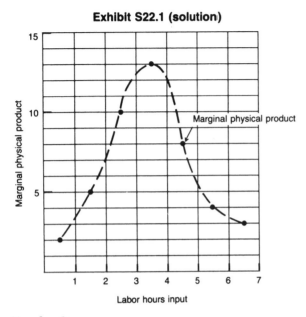

Exhibit S22.1 (solution)

Hands On

Problem 1. (a) Total fixed cost for this firm is $600. You can
determine this by noting where the average total cost curve intersects
the vertical axis. When output is zero, the only costs are fixed costs.
(b) To find average total cost, divide total cost (the vertical distance)
by quantity (the horizontal distance). Thus, average total cost is $20
at 50 units of output and about $11.50 at 100 units of output. Because
average total cost is the ratio of the vertical distance to the
horizontal distance, it can also be thought of as the slope of a line
from the origin to the total cost curve. Place one end of a ruler on
the origin and swing the edge up until it just touches the total cost
curve (at about 130 units of output). This is the point of minimum
average total cost. (c) Marginal cost is equal to the slope of the
total cost curve. Draw a tangent to the curve at 40 units of output -
the slope is about ½, so the marginal cost is about $5=(50/10). (Be
careful to notice that the units on the vertical axis are ten times as
large as those on the horizontal axis.) Marginal cost is at a minimum
at the point where the total cost curve has the least slope, that is,
where it just stops bending down and starts bending up. Find this point
(about 80 units of output) by sliding a ruler along the total cost curve,
keeping the ruler tangent. Marginal and average total cost are equal
at 130 units of output - the point where a line drawn from the origin
is just tangent to the total cost curve.

Problem 2. (a) At 40 units of output, average fixed cost is $8. At
80 units of output, average fixed cost is $4. Figure this out by measuring

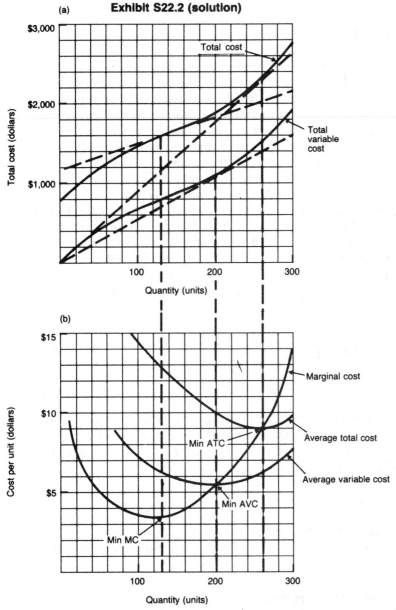

Exhibit S22.2 (solution)

(a) Total cost (dollars): $3,000, $2,000, $1,000

Total cost

Total variable cost

Quantity (units): 100, 200, 300

(b) Cost per unit (dollars): $15, $10, $5

Marginal cost

Min ATC

Average total cost

Min AVC

Average variable cost

Min MC

Quantity (units): 100, 200, 300

the gap between the average total cost and average variable cost curves. At either point, multiply average fixed cost by quantity to obtain total fixed cost, which is $320. (b) Marginal cost and average variable cost are equal where average variable cost is at a minimum, which is 70 units of output. Marginal cost at 70 units of output is thus $7. If you follow the same reasoning, you will find marginal cost is about $10.80 at 100 units of output. (c) As you discovered in answering the previous question, the marginal cost curve must pass through the average cost curves at their respective minimum points. Draw a smooth upward-sloping curve that does this. (d) Marginal cost is the difference between the total cost of producing a certain quantity of output and the total cost of producing one more unit of output. To calculate total cost, multiply average total cost by the quantity of output. At 50 units of output, marginal cost is approximately $7.5; at 110, it is approximately $14.5;

and at 130 units, it is approximately $17.85.

Problem 3.   (a) The output level that will minimize the short-run average
cost, given plant size A, is about 750 units - the minimum point on A.
The level of output for which plant size A produces minimum long-run cost
is found where short-run curve A is tangent to the long-run curve, or at
about 500 units. At larger levels of output, some larger plant size
with a short-run curve not shown, but tangent to the long-run curve,
would be better. (b) Short-run curve B is drawn wrong. It should not
intersect the long-run curve, but instead, be tangent to it from the inside.
As drawn, there is a range of output (1,600 units and up) for which
short-run total cost is lower than long-run total cost - an impossibility.
(Comment: Although the question asks which of the short-run curves is
drawn wrong, one could say instead that if B is a valid short-run curve,
the long-run curve is drawn wrong. It should be tangent to B at about
1,800 units of output. Redraw the long-run curve in this way.) (c)
Economies of scale continue to about 1,100 units of output, after which
diseconomies of scale begin.

CHAPTER 23

Self Test

1-c; 2-a; 3-d: although average cost is above price at 500 units, it may
(or may not) drop below price at some higher rate of output; 4-c; 5-d:
accounting profit is a matter of implicit versus explicit costs, about
which nothing has been said; 6-a; 7-a; 8-b; 9-d; 10-b.

Hands On

Problem 1.   (a) The slope of the total revenue curve tells you the price.
Along TR_1, for example, total revenue rises by $10 for each one unit of

Exhibit S23.2b (solution)

Output	Total Revenue $2.50	Total Revenue $5.00	Total Revenue $7.50	Total Revenue $10.00	Total Cost same for all prices	Profit (or Loss) $2.50	Profit (or Loss) $5.00	Profit (or Loss) $7.50	Profit (or Loss) $10.00
0	$ 0	$ 0	$ 0	$ 0	$ 400	$ (400)	$(400)	$(400)	$(400)
70	175	350	525	700	775	(600)	(425)	(250)	(75)
80	200	400	600	800	810	(610)	(410)	(210)	(10)
90	225	450	675	900	855	(630)	(405)	(180)	45
100	250	500	750	1,000	900	(650)	(400)	(150)	100
110	275	550	825	1,100	960	(685)	(410)	(135)	140
120	300	600	900	1,200	1,025	(725)	(425)	(125)	175
130	325	650	975	1,300	1,120	(795)	(470)	(145)	180
140	350	700	1,050	1,400	1,240	(890)	(540)	(190)	160
150	375	750	1,125	1,500	1,400	(1,025)	(650)	(275)	100

output, indicating a price of $10 per unit. (Note that the units on the vertical axis are in multiples of 100, whereas those on the horizontal axis are in multiples of 10.) The price of TR2 is $7.50 per unit; for TR3, $5 per unit; and for TR4, $2.50 per unit. (b) See solution for Exhibit S23.2b for details of the table. As you would expect, the quantity supplied increases as the price increases. (c) Marginal revenue is equal to the slope of the total revenue curve; marginal cost is equal to the slope of the total cost curve. Thus, the point of profit maximization for each output occurs where the appropriate total revenue schedule is parallel to the total cost curve.

Problem 2. To fill in the tables, remember total cost = average total cost x quantity, and total revenue = price x quantity. See solutions for Exhibit S23.3b and S23.3c for details. Answers given are approximate. To show the supply curve, shade the upward-sloping portion of the marginal cost curve that lies above its intersection with average variable cost. (a) Total fixed costs for this firm are $320. At 800 units of output, average fixed costs are $0.40, or the difference between the average total cost of $1.10 and the average variable cost of $0.70. Thus, total fixed costs are the average fixed cost times 800 units of output, or $320. Remember that total fixed costs do not vary with the level of output.

Exhibit S23.3b (solution)

Price	Profit-Maximizing Output	Total Revenue	Total Cost	Profit (or Loss)
$ .60	$ 0	$ 0	$ 320	$(320)
.70	800	560	880	(320)
.80	900	720	963	(243)
.90	960	864	1,018	(154)
1.00	1,040	1,040	1,092	(52)
1.10	1,100	1,210	1,166	44
1.20	1,140	1,368	1,208	160
1.30	1,200	1,560	1,284	276

Exhibit S23.3c (solution)

Output	Total Revenue	Total Cost	Profit (or Loss)
400	$ 520	$ 620	$(100)
600	780	744	36
800	1,040	880	160
1,000	1,300	1,060	240
1,200	1,560	1,284	276
1,400	1,820	1,610	210
1,600	2,080	2,080	0

Problem 3.   (a)   In the short run, the demand curve would shift to a position like D3, and the market would move up along S2 from B to E. As it did so, individual firms would be moving up along their marginal cost curves in response to the increase in market price.   In the long run, new firms would enter, shifting the supply curve to the right to a position like S3.   As the supply curve shifted, the market price would fall, and individual firms that had been in the industry all along would move back down along their short-run marginal cost curves.   The entire path to long-run equilibrium would thus be B to E to C.   (b) This time, the demand curve would shift to the left, toward D1.   The market would move toward a short-run equilibrium at G.   As it did so, individual firms would move down along their short-run marginal cost curves and would sustain losses.   Some firms would be driven out of the market by the losses, thereby shifting the supply curve toward S1 in the long run. As this happened, price would recover and the market would move toward equilibrium at A.   (c)   With constant input prices, the long-run supply curve would lie along the line ABC.   (d)   With rising input prices, the long-run curve would be steeper than ABC, but not as steep as GBE. (e)   With falling input prices, the long-run supply curve would have a negative slope, but not so steeply negative as DBH.

CHAPTER 24

Self Test

1-a; 2-c: total revenue for 100 units is $5,000 and $5,039.90 for 101 units; 3-c; 4-c; 5-b: exact location of demand curve is not known, but it must be above the marginal revenue curve. The short-run shut down price must be less than $30; 6-b; 7-a; 8-a; 9-c; 10-b.

Hands On

Problem 1.   (a)   The profit-maximizing level of output is 100 units.   See solution table for Exhibit S24.3(b) for details.   The profit-maximizing

Exhibit S24.3(b) (solution)

Price	Quantity of Output	Total Revenue	Marginal Revenue (approx.)	Marginal Cost (approx.)	Total Cost	Profit (or Loss)
0	0	$ 0			$ 50	$(50)
$2.25	20	45	$2.25	$ .90	68	(23)
$2.00	40	80	1.75	.60	80	0
$1.80	60	108	1.40	.40	88	20
$1.62	80	130	1.10	.35	95	35
$1.45	100	145	.75	.60	107	38
$1.31	120	157	.60	.95	126	31
$1.17	140	164	.35	1.90	164	0
$1.05	160	168	.20	2.80	220	(52)

price is $1.45 per unit, as you can see by dividing total revenue by output at the profit-maximizing quantity. (b) In the range from 80 to 100 units, marginal revenue is still higher, on the average, than marginal cost. By the time the firm reaches the 100 to 120 unit output range, marginal cost, on the average, is above marginal revenue. The two must be equal somewhere between 80 and 120 units, so this approach agrees with the 100 unit estimate from Part (a) of this problem.

Problem 2. (a) As drawn, the profit-maximizing price is $13 and the profit-maximizing quantity is 600. Note, as explained in the text, that the marginal revenue curve for a straight-line demand curve is a straight line falling halfway between the demand curve and the vertical axis. (See MR_1 in solution graph to Exhibit S24.4.) (b) This looks tricky, but it really is easy if you work step by step. To draw a straight line, you need just two points. Here is how to obtain two points each on the demand and marginal revenue curves: First, enter the point corresponding to the given profit-maximizing price and quantity - $10 and 600 units of output, in this case. This point is labeled Q in the solution graph. You know that this point must lie on the demand curve. Now, you can find your first point on the marginal revenue curve, which you know must pass halfway between Q and the vertical axis. Label the point halfway between Q and the vertical axis R. You also know that the marginal revenue curve must intersect the marginal cost curve at the 600 unit profit-maximizing level of output. Label this Point S. You now have your two points on the marginal revenue curve. Draw MR_2 passing through Points S and R. Label the point where MR_2 hits the vertical axis T. This Point T must also be on the demand curve, since the marginal revenue and demand curves both begin at the same point on the vertical axis. Now you have two points on the demand curve. Draw the new demand curve D_2 through Points T and Q, as in the solution figure. (c) Proceed as for Part (b), finding Points Q', R', S', and T'. See solution exhibit for details. (d) A monopolist has no supply curve in the sense that a perfectly competitive firm has one. As you see from this example, there is no 1:1 relationship between price and quantity produced. It is possible for demand to change in such a way that the price changes but not the quantity, or the quantity changes but not the price - or, in fact, for the profit-maximizing quantity and price to move anywhere within a wide range of possibilities.

Problem 3. (a) The profit-maximizing quantity is 10,000 units and the profit-maximizing price $1.20. If each firm produces an equal share of the total, the quota will be 100 units of output per firm. (b) At 100 units of output, this firm's average total cost is $.90 per unit. It would thus make $30 profit if it sold 100 units for $1.20 per unit, according to the cartel's plan. Under these circumstances, marginal revenue will exceed marginal cost at 100 units of output. (c) If the firm acted as a price taker with a price of $1.20, it would increase output to the point where marginal cost rose to $1.20. That would occur at 140 units of output. Average total cost at 140 units is about $.95, so the firm would earn a $35 profit. (d) In this, and every other cartel situation, each individual firm would be able to increase its

Exhibit S24.4 (solution)

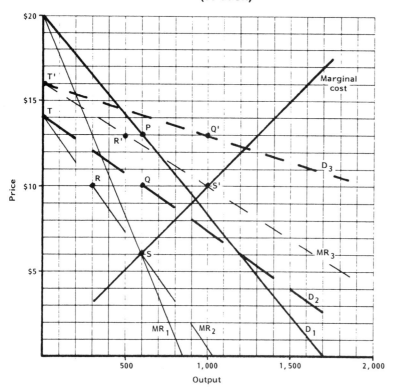

profit by producing more than its quota, provided all other firms stuck to their quotas, thus keeping the market price high. Of course, if all firms cheated, the price would fall to the competitive level, and no one would earn monopoly profits.

CHAPTER 25

Self Test

1-c; 2-d: one must also know how each firm expects its rival to act; 3-a; 4-d; 5-c; 6-b; 7-c; 8-d; 9-d; 10-d.

CHAPTER 26

Self Test

1-d; 2-c; 3-a; 4-a; 5-b; 6-a; 7-a; 8-c; 9-c; 10-a.

CHAPTER 27

Self Test

1-d; 2-d; 3-b; 4-d; 5-a; 6-a; 7-d; 8-b; 9-c; 10-b.

Hands On

Problem 1. (a) The competitive price is $100 per tonne. (b) A surplus of 15,000 tonnes of grain (37,500 t - 22,500 t) is created by the direct price support program. The cost of this plan to the government is $2.625 million, which is the 15,000 tonnes of surplus grain multiplied by the support price of $175 per tonne. (c) The price of grain for the consumer rises, since the price increases from $100 per tonne to $175 per tonne. (d) Farmers would increase their output by 7,500 tonnes, to a total of 37,500 tonnes, as a result of the subsidy price program. The market price would be $25 per tonne as a result of the increased output. (e) The deficiency price payment made to farmers is $150 per tonne ($175 - $25). The price to the government of this subsidy price program is the deficiency price of $150 per tonne multiplied by 37,500 tonnes, or $5.625 million. (f) The price to the consumer falls, since the market price of grain has fallen from $100 per tonne to $25 per tonne as a result of the subsidy price program. (g) The subsidy price program is more expensive for the government by $3 million ($5.625 million - $2.625 million). No, the subsidy price support program could become less expensive than the direct price support program if the demand for grain became more price elastic.

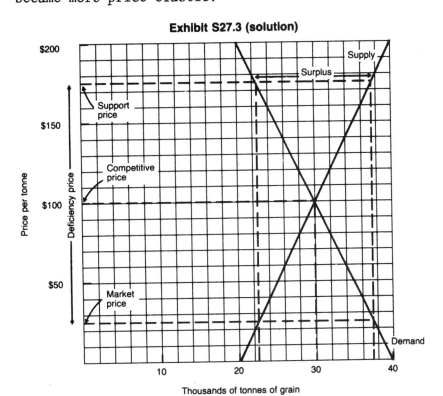

Exhibit S27.3 (solution)

CHAPTER 28

Self Test

1-c; 2-a; 3-a; 4-b; 5-b; 6-d; 7-c; 8-d; 9-a; 10-d.

CHAPTER 29

Self Test

1-d; 2-a; 3-a; 4-a; 5-d; 6-d; 7-d; 8-c; 9-b; 10-b.

Hands On

Problem 1. (a) Foreigners would be willing to pay more for Canadian assets than would Canadians if they earned a higher return for their investment because of more advanced technology, greater management expertise, access to larger markets, and so on. Since income levels in some foreign nations are higher and tax laws are different than in Canada, foreigners may have more wealth to invest than Canadians and may be willing to take different rates of return on their investments as a result. (b) The Canadian government could influence the reasons given in part (a) through agencies such as the Foreign Investment Review Agency (FIRA), that limit takeovers and encourage greater use of Canadian resources and management skills. Government subsidies could also be given only to Canadian-owned firms, taxes could be levied only on foreign-owned firms, and "buy Canadian" restrictions could be placed on all government contracts. All of these suggestions could reduce the return foreigners earn on Canadian assets. (c) The National Energy Program (NEP) instituted in the fall of 1980 gave tremendous incentives to Canadian-owned firms, which reduced the competitiveness of foreign-owned firms operating in Canada. Since foreign investment in Canada became less lucrative as a result of the NEP, direct foreign investment in Canada dropped dramatically in 1981.

CHAPTER 30

Self Test

1-a; 2-b; 3-d; 4-a; 5-d; 6-d; 7-b; 8-d; 9-b; 10-b.

Hands On

Problem 1. (a) Under perfect competition, the equilibrium wage rate would be $10 per hour and the equilibrium quantity of labor employed would be 100 labor hours per day. (b) See solution exhibit. The equilibrium quantity under monopsony is 80 labor hours per day. The equilibrium wage rate is $9 per hour. (Not $13 per hour! See "Don't Make This Common Mistake!") (c) The shortcut relies on the fact that the marginal labor

Exhibit S30.1 (solution)

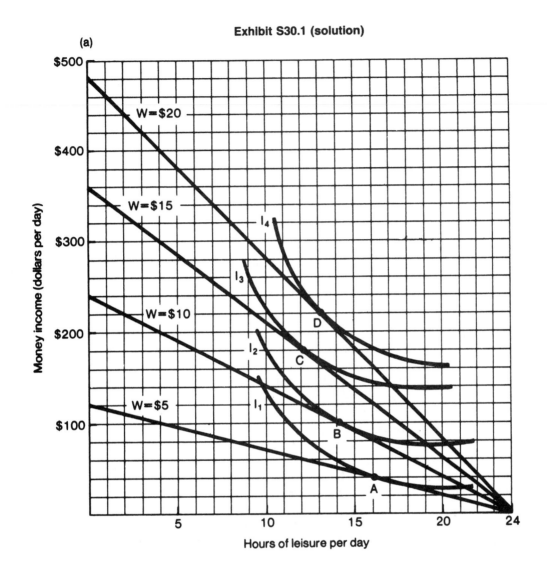

(a)

Money income (dollars per day)

$500
$400
$300
$200
$100

W=$20
W=$15
W=$10
W=$5

I₄
I₃
I₂
I₁

D
C
B
A

5   10   15   20   24

Hours of leisure per day

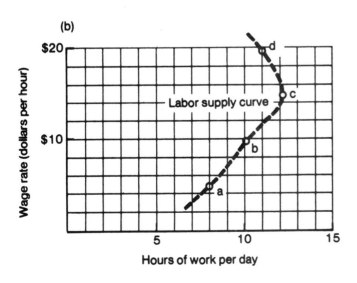

(b)

Wage rate (dollars per hour)

$20
$10

Labor supply curve

d
c
b
a

5   10   15

Hours of work per day

(a)

(b)

Labor Hours Per Day	Wage Rate	Total Labor Cost	Marginal Labor Cost
49	$ 7.45	$ 365.05	
			$ 9.95
50	7.50	375.00	
			10.05
51	7.55	385.05	
⋮			
⋮			
99	9.95	985.05	
			14.95
100	10.00	1,000.00	
			15.05
101	10.05	1,015.05	

cost curve passes halfway between the supply curve and the vertical axis at all wage levels. If you know elementary calculus, here is a simple proof. (If you don't know calculus, don't worry about it - just take the shortcut method on faith.) Let the supply curve be represented by the equation $W = a + bL$, where W is the wage rate, L is the quantity of labor supplied, and a and b are constants. Total labor cost equals the wage rate times the quantity of labor at any point on the supply curve. To obtain a total labor cost function, multiply the supply curve equation by L, getting the equation $T = aL + bL^2$. The marginal labor cost curve is the first derivative of this total labor cost equation. Thus, using T' to represent marginal labor cost, we obtain $T' = a + 2bL$. Comparing the equations for the supply curve and marginal labor cost curve reveals that both have the same vertical intercept, but the slope of the marginal labor cost curve is twice that of the supply curve. QED.

Problem 2. (a) Begin with the budget curve for a wage of $2.50 per hour. If the worker takes 24 hours per day of leisure, money income will be zero. Thus, the point (24,0) on the horizontal axis is one end of the budget line. If the worker were to work 24 hours per day, leisure time would be zero and total money income would be $60. Thus, the point (0,60) on the vertical axis is the other end of this budget line. Construct other budget lines in the same manner, as shown in the solution exhibit.
(b) At $2.50 per hour, the worker would maximize utility by taking 14 hours of leisure per day, that is, by working 10 hours per day. This is shown as the tangency of the $2.50 budget line to an indifference curve at Point A. The remaining points are shown in the solution exhibit.
(c) At $2.50 per hour, quantity supplied is 10 hours per day (Point a in the solution graph for Exhibit S30.4(b)). Fill in the other points and connect them as shown. (d) Leisure is a normal good. An increase in the wage rate is also an increase in the price (that is, the opportunity cost) of leisure, and also increases the worker's real income. The substitution

Exhibit S30.4 (solution)

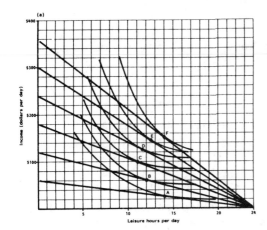

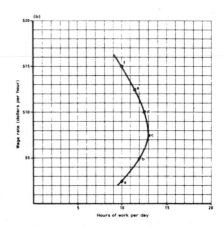

effect of an increase in the price of leisure will always be in the direction of reducing leisure. If leisure were an inferior good, the income effect of an increase in the wage rate would also cause a reduction in leisure. Thus, if leisure were an inferior good, both effects would work in the same direction, and the supply curve would never bend backward. The fact that this supply curve does bend backward at wages above $7.50 per hour indicates that leisure is a normal good, and that the income effect begins to outweigh the substitution effect at wages higher than $7.50 per hour.

Problem 3. The market price of the land is $66,666.67=($2,000/.03) with a 3 percent real interest rate and $100,000 with a 2 percent real interest rate. The difference in value with the two rates is $33,333.33.

Problem 4. The interest rate is 2¼ percent with a $50 payment, 7½ percent with a $150 payment, and 12½ percent with a $250 payment.

Problem 5. The answers are the same as in Problem 4. The questions use the term "interest" in two different ways. The rate is 2¼ percent for $50, 7½ percent for $150, and 12½ percent for $250.

Problem 6. The profit rate is calculated as net income divided by the value of funds or assets of a firm. For this firm, the profit rate is 6¼ percent. Yes, if the firm's assets could be sold for $1,600,000 and the funds used to purchase bonds paying 8 percent, the firm should sell the assets and buy the bonds. The bonds would raise net earnings to $128,000, rather than keep them at $100,000.

CHAPTER 31

Self Test

1-c; 2-d; 3-c; 4-a; 5-d; 6-c; 7-d: must also know elasticity of demand; 8-d: depends on relative bargaining power; 9-b; 10-b.

Hands On

<u>Problem</u>. (a) The competitive equilibrium would be $14 per hour and 200 workers employed. (b) The wage rate that maximizes the total wage bill is $17 per hour. At that wage, 170 workers would be employed. Find this by drawing a marginal revenue curve corresponding to the demand curve shown, i.e., a straight line from $34 on the vertical axis to 170 workers on the horizontal. (c) The supply curve measures the opportunity cost to the marginal worker of taking the job. For example, the reason you can't obtain more than 100 workers in this market if you pay $9 an hour is that all but 100 workers have something else to do that is worth more than $9 to them. For some workers, the best alternative activity on which the opportunity cost calculation is based may be another job. For others, the most favorable alternative opportunity may be that of searching for a still better job. For still other workers, the best alternative may be staying out of the labor force in order to engage in leisure, child care, or "underground" economic activities. The opportunity cost to the 120th worker is $10 per hour. To the 140th worker, it is $11 per hour. Beyond 120 workers (a wage of $22 per hour), the increase in total labor income (measured by the height of the marginal revenue curve) is less than the opportunity cost to the added worker of taking the job. A union might bargain for such a wage on the grounds that the benefit to all workers of lowering the wage is less, beyond 120 workers, than the opportunity cost the added worker bears. (d) The 100 workers would bargain for a wage of $24 per hour. That is as high as they could bargain and all keep their jobs, as this figure is drawn.

CHAPTER 32

Self Test

1-a; 2-c; 3-d; 4-d; 5-c; 6-d; 7-c; 8-d; 9-d; 10-a.

CHAPTER 33

Self Test

1-a; 2-d; 3-d; 4-d: the net reproduction rate is related to long-term trends, not to the growth rate at any given moment; 5-b; 6-d; 7-b; 8-a; 9-c; 10-d.

CHAPTER 34

Self Test

1-d; 2-b; 3-b; 4-a; 5-b; 6-c; 7-c; 8-d; 9-d; 10-a.

TO THE OWNER OF THIS BOOK:

We are interested in your reaction to the Study Guide for <u>Basic Economics</u>, <u>Second Canadian Edition</u>. Through feedback from you we can help improve this learning aid in future editions.

1. What is your major course of study?

___ Economics   ___ Engineering   ___ Humanities

___ Business/Commerce   ___ Social Sciences   ___ Other/specify

2. What was the best feature of this study guide?

___ Walking Tour   ___ Applications

___ Multiple Choice questions   ___ other (please specify)

___ Hands On questions

3. What suggestions do you have for improvement?

4. Will you be taking further courses in economics? ___ yes   ___ no

FOLD HERE

TAPE HERE

**Business
Reply Mail**
No Postage Stamp
Necessary if mailed
in Canada

POSTAGE WILL BE PAID BY

MICHAEL ROCHE
Acquisitions Editor
College Editorial Department
HOLT, RINEHART AND WINSTON
OF CANADA, LIMITED
55 HORNER AVENUE
TORONTO, ONTARIO
M8Z 9Z9